I0109907

The Death and Life of Chinese Civil Society

China Understandings Today

Series Editors: Mary Gallagher and Emily Wilcox

China Understandings Today is dedicated to the study of contemporary China and seeks to present the latest and most innovative scholarship in social sciences and the humanities to the academic community as well as the general public. The series is sponsored by the Lieberthal-Rogel Center for Chinese Studies at the University of Michigan.

A complete list of titles in the series can be found at www.press.umich.edu

The Death and Life of Chinese Civil Society

Mujun Zhou

University of Michigan Press
Ann Arbor

Copyright © 2026 by Mujun Zhou
Some rights reserved

(cc) BY-NC

This work is licensed under a Creative Commons Attribution-NonCommercial 4.0 International License. *Note to users*: A Creative Commons license is only valid when it is applied by the person or entity that holds rights to the licensed work. Works may contain components (e.g., photographs, illustrations, or quotations) to which the rightsholder in the work cannot apply the license. It is ultimately your responsibility to independently evaluate the copyright status of any work or component part of a work you use, in light of your intended use. To view a copy of this license, visit http://creativecommons.org/licenses/by-nc/4.0/

For questions or permissions, please contact um.press.perms@umich.edu

Published in the United States of America by the
University of Michigan Press
First published February 2026

A CIP catalog record for this book is available from the British Library.

Library of Congress Cataloging-in-Publication data has been applied for.

ISBN 978-0-472-07785-4 (hardcover : alk. paper)
ISBN 978-0-472-05785-6 (paper : alk. paper)
ISBN 978-0-472-90546-1 (open access ebook)

DOI: https://doi.org/10.3998/mpub.14408227

Open access version made available with the support of The Lieberthal-Rogel Center for Chinese Studies (LRCCS).

The University of Michigan Press's open access publishing program is made possible thanks to additional funding from the University of Michigan Office of the Provost and the generous support of contributing libraries.

Cover image credit: ajijchan / Shutterstock.com

The authorized representative in the EU for product safety and compliance is Easy Access System Europe, Mustamäe tee 50, 10621 Tallinn, Estonia, gpsr.requests@easproject.com

CONTENTS

Digital materials related to this title can be found on the Fulcrum platform via the following citable URL: https://doi.org/10.3998/mpub.14408227

FIGURES

TABLES

ACKNOWLEDGMENTS

The completion of this book has been benefited from many different people. First, I want to thank all my interviewees. When I started this project, I was in my early twenties and lacked social experience. In my interviews with liberal intellectuals, human rights lawyers, and NGO practitioners, I often asked stupid questions. After laughing at my questions, many of the interviewees still patiently explained their work to me, sharing their experience and offering insightful thinking about China's politics and culture. Without their generosity, this documentation would be impossible. During my fieldwork, I also relied on resources provided by several research institutes. In the department of sociology at Tsinghua University, Shen Yuan and Guo Yuhua introduced me to activists in the homeowners' movement and labor movement. In the school of philanthropy at Sun Yat-sen University, Zhu Jiangang, Hu Xiaojun, Chen Yuepeng, and Yan Guowei familiarized me with NGOs in various fields. In addition, Chang Tianle, Zhou Anan, Su Chunyan, and Liang Yaqian helped me establish networks and offered companionship in my intellectual exploration. I would also like to express my gratitude to these people.

This work has been born out of my dissertation. In the department of sociology at Brown University, where I got my PhD degree, Michael D. Kennedy, Patrick Heller, and Gianpaolo Baiocchi kindled my interest in the idea of civil society and the public sphere. My academic advisor, Michael D. Kennedy, was always encouraging to me. He was also tolerant of my slow and zigzag progress in completing all the requirements of the degree. I also want to say thank you to the other two professors in my dissertation committee, Patrick Heller and José Itzigsohn, for their guidance during my doctoral studies. Patrick Heller later read a draft of this book and provided helpful suggestions. During my stay as a postdoctoral research fellow at the center for Chinese studies at the University of California, Berkeley, I benefited a great deal from having conversations with Hsing You-tien, Thomas Gold, Kevin J. O'Brien, and Peter Lorentzen. Finally, at Zhejiang University, where I now work as a sociology teacher, my mentor, Zhao Dingxin, has been a great support. He has read several drafts of the book and offered sharp criticisms. Through responding to these criticisms, I have gradually commanded the art of writing convincingly.

During my stay in the United States of America, I received financial support from the dissertation fellowship at Brown University, the Chiang Ching-kuo dissertation fellowship, and the postdoctoral fellowship for Chinese studies at the University of California, Berkeley. Here in China, thanks to Zhejiang University's generous welfare housing policy, I have become economically comfortable. Through teaching sociology classes and advising students, I eventually feel that I can perform as a functioning member in society.

I thank three anonymous readers for reviewing my book manuscript and offering insightful criticisms, comments, and suggestions. To a large extent, their reading reports have reshaped the argument in this book. My acquiring editors at the University of Michigan Press, Sara Cohen and Marcella Landri, have spent much effort organizing the review. They have also kindly informed me of how to properly respond to readers' reports and helped me structure my revision. Delilah McCrea has been of great help during my preparation for submitting the final manuscript. My gratitude also goes to the editors. Of course, all mistakes in the book are mine.

PREFACE

Before starting the formal discussion of my research subject, I would like to talk about the tortuous intellectual journey that has brought me to the writing of this book. What has kindled my interest in China's public sphere is the intellectual debate between the liberals and the new left, which started in the late 1990s and continued until the early 2000s. The liberals and the new left were two intellectual groups formed in China in the late 1990s. When I was a college student (2004–2008), many of my intellectual friends were keen on discussing some of the controversial topics in the debate, such as "whether authoritarianism or neoliberalism constitutes a greater obstacle to China's modernization." For me, these discussions were rather abstract and confusing. I had no idea what they could mean to people's real political life. What had made me particularly confused were the liberals and their political agenda of building civil society. As early as the 1990s, the liberals began to advocate that China needed a civil society, that is, an independent space for participation, to constrain the state power and promote democratization. In the 2000s, some of the liberals added that a vibrant civil society could also solve the many problems brought by the market economic reform, such as inequality. I saw the liberals' interpretation of civil society as presenting a political ideal. But I wondered whether and how this ideal could be realized.

Between 2011 and 2014, I did fieldwork in Beijing, Shanghai, and the Pearl River Delta to collect data for my doctoral dissertation. My original plan was to figure out the role of the liberals in the formation of critical discourses and the translation of the idea of civil society across academic studies and social movements. Immediately after I started my fieldwork, I discovered that China's public sphere had a rather contentious ideological environment. Multiple, intersecting networks were formed, in which people debated on whether the political ideal advocated by the liberals was appropriate for promoting democratization in China, what kind of strategies could be employed to apply the ideal into practice, and whether social movements still needed the guidance of an abstract, comprehensive ideological thought. To catch up with these debates, I tried to follow as many types of activists as possible. I interviewed not only activists who were driven by the liberal ideology, but also those who started with more specific concerns.

My communication with activists from various fields led me to the conclusion that two widely held views at that time were flawed. The first widely held view was that the liberals' advocacy of civil society had achieved great success in the public sphere; as more Chinese people began to proactively defend their own rights, an independent space for participation and checking the state power was in the making. As far as I had observed, in the 2000s and early 2010s, the liberals did occupy an advantageous position in the production of critical public opinions; through offering legal aid and helping people establish NGOs, the liberals also did build some connections with various social movements that raised social and economic demands. However, the gap between the liberals, as a group of intellectual activists who advocated an abstract political ideal, and those social movement activists who were driven by more concrete concerns was huge. The allies built by the liberals were thus fragile and full of contentions.

Another view, which was contrastingly different from the first view yet also widely spread, was that the time for ideological debate had been passed in China—because of the increasingly complex techniques the state had employed for controlling social movement activism, in public discussions, people avoided talking about grand political ideals and mainly focused on short-term, economic interests. Yet what I had observed in my fieldwork was that many activists, especially the youth activists, still took the ideological debate seriously. In their daily activities, they discussed extensively the meaning of different intellectual discourses proposed by the liberals and the new left and deliberated with each other about how these intellectual discourses could be related to the issues they engaged in.

I used my ethnographic data as cross-sectional data and reported some of my findings in my dissertation, which was submitted in 2015. During the days I tried to turn the dissertation into a book, the Chinese state's attitude toward critical public discussions became more suppressive. About one fourth of my interviewees were detained. More than half of the organizations I visited were disbanded. As the state's control over the production of critical news was intensified, the liberals and their political project of building civil society gradually became marginalized and stigmatized. It was not until then that I began to recognize that many phenomena I had observed in the field, such as the contentious ideological debate, were based upon a very specific historical context. On the other hand, I also recognized that the quick disintegration of the project of building civil society corroborated some of my findings in my doctoral dissertation—fissures between different groups of activists in the social movement community had long existed.

Nevertheless, the dramatic transformation of the political environment in the mid-2010s put me in a depression. For a long time, I was not able to gather courage and strength to continue my book project. I could not convince myself that it was still meaningful to write about the liberals, a group of people who had begun to lose influence in the public sphere. Additionally, my attitude toward the liberals' project of building civil society had always been a critical one. I not only disagreed with the liberals on their interpretation of state-society relations, but also doubted the effectiveness of the strategies they had employed to apply their political ideals onto reality. Yet in an increasingly suppressive environment, I began to be skeptical about my own political stance. I was not sure whether it was moral and ethical to present my story in such a critical way.

Since 2017, I began to serve as a sociology teacher at Zhejiang University. While largely enjoying communicating with my students in class, I sadly discovered that the new generation of university students, who were just about ten years younger than I was, had already become strange to the situation in which people could openly and seriously talk about social issues and push the state to change its policies and laws. Many students had not even heard of the Sun Zhigang Incident, the historical event that had terminated the "custody and repatriation" law in 2003—for most intellectual activists of our generation, this was a milestone in the development of human rights advocacy campaigns in China. Even students who were keen on the idea of social movements had very limited knowledge of activism and activists in the past. In 2018, to support the collective action organized by workers at Jasic, a plant for producing welding machines, student activists from all over the country gathered at Shenzhen, where they launched a series of demonstrations and publicly expressed their belief in Marxism. In a discussion of the event during my office hours, a student of mine who was interested in labor rights issues said that this was the first time youth activists in China attended labor activism. When I told her that university students' participation in labor rights issues had long existed in Beijing and the Pearl River Delta since the 2000s, she was surprised as well as confused.

My students' attitude made me realize that the social movement community in China was a community that lacked collective memories. Despite authoritarian repression, resistance activisms of various kinds continuously emerged in the interstices of state control. However, because the formation of formal organizations was strictly limited, knowledge and experience of social movements could hardly be passed on between different generations of activists. Experiencing these new conditions, I began to see the value of documenting the liberals. I also began to see the value of historical studies. Although many actors in the liberal camp, notably human rights lawyers, investigative journalists, and internet-based public intellectuals, were no longer able to insert influence in the public sphere, we could at least look into the past, understanding under what condition they had emerged, what achievements they had made, and how their influence had declined.

These feelings and thoughts have eventually been crystallized into the theme of this book—a comprehensive description of the rise and fall of the liberals and their project of building civil society over the past thirty years.

Students on Chinese politics used to debate whether China has a civil society. Some of these students argue that the concept of civil society has originated from the West and is not applicable to China. Others use the concept to refer to a variety of organizations and networks that are outside the state system. For the second group of students, the relationship between civil society and the state is an empirical question that can be investigated. This book intends to sidestep the debate and see the dissemination of the idea of civil society as an ideational movement.

By saying that civil society in China was an ideational movement, I mainly want to convey three layers of meanings. First, I want to emphasize that an independent space for political participation had not actually existed in China. When the liberals advocated the idea of civil society, their public expressions were based upon their imagination of a desirable politics, rather than on reality. Second, I would like to point out that the imagination of politics can be consequential. Although the solidarity promoted by the liberals had been fragile, in the name of building civil society, Chinese people established working alliances, through which they managed to expose many problems arising during the market economic reform. Third, I suggest that it was not the liberals who had determined the influence of the idea of civil society in China's public sphere; rather, the influence of the idea had been contingent upon a series of complex political, social, and technological conditions that were out of the liberals' control.

To demonstrate the changing influence of the project of building civil society in China, I select five social movements and trace their development in the past three decades. These five movements were the environmental movement, the homeowners' movement, the labor movement, the feminist movement, and the New Rural Reconstruction Movement (which later evolved into the food movement). I select these five movements, because they had varied greatly from each other in their ideological expressions and their relations with the liberals. Specifically, the environmental movement was from the very beginning closely connected with the liberals. The homeowners' movement used to be regarded as the pioneer of the project of building civil society. But in the late 2000s, homeowners' organizations in different regions began to develop their own agenda. The labor movement and the feminist movement had also been regarded as part of the project of building civil society. But the issues these two movements addressed had largely been treated as of secondary importance in the 2000s. Hence both movements, especially the feminist movement, offered sharp criticism of the liberals since the late 2000s. Lastly, the New Rural Reconstruction Movement was from the beginning close to the new left and inimical to the liberals.

Analyses in this book mainly rely on data I have collected in five research projects. The first project was my dissertation. As I have mentioned above, between 2011 and 2014, I did fieldwork in Beijing, Shanghai, and the Pearl River Delta. During the fieldwork, I conducted over 150 interviews with 106 activists. My informants included intellectual elites who had advocated the idea of civil society in China since the late 1990s as well as those activists who had joined social movements in later years and engaged in activism that addressed more concrete issues. The social movement activism these people had organized involved a wide range of themes, including environmental protection, homeowners' rights, labor rights, women's rights, LGBT rights, HIV/AIDS prevention, poverty alleviation in rural areas, and cultural heritage preservation.

The second project was a study on homeowners' associations in Shanghai, which was conducted between 2006 and 2012. In this project, I interviewed 41 homeowner activists, from whom I became familiar with homeowners' associations' daily activities, their interactions with local government agencies and developers, and various conflicts happening in commercial housing communities. I also interviewed nine government officials whose work was related to the governance of homeowners' associations.

The third was a project on the historical transformation of labor NGO activism. Between 2012 and 2018, I visited 38 labor NGOs in six cities—Beijing,

Guangzhou, Shenzhen, Foshan, Dongguan, and Zhuhai—and conducted 60 interviews with labor activists. During my fieldwork, I attended labor NGOs' meetings, participated in activists' training programs, worked as an interpreter when English-speaking activists and scholars came to visit, and helped these organizations raise funds. Based on various sources, I also assembled an archive that contained information on the history of 78 labor NGOs.

The fourth project was a study on China's food movement. In this project, I worked with Xu Yi, a sociologist at Sun Yat-sen University. Our goal was to map various kinds of alternative food networks in China. Between 2011 and 2017, we visited 25 organizations in Beijing, Guangzhou, Shanghai, Shenzhen, Huizhou, and Chengdu and interviewed 50 activists. Our interviewees were mostly activists in consumers' cooperatives, activists in farmers' markets, and organic farmers.

The last project was a study on youth activists. In 2017 and 2018, I worked with a research team, which consisted of a group of social science students and NGO activists in Guangzhou. We investigated how youth activists had adapted to the changing political and social environment in China since 2013. In this project, we interviewed 26 youth activists, most of whom had worked in fields like environmental protection, labor rights, and women's rights.

During all the above-mentioned interviews, I often liked to discuss controversial issues with my interviewees. I often told them that I had talked (or planned to) with someone whose position was contrastingly different from theirs. In a few times, this irritated my interviewees and disrupted our conversations. But on many other occasions, this strategy brought my study to a deeper level. A case in point is my investigation over the "ethical dilemma" of human rights activism. When I was in the field in 2012 and 2013, many human rights activists were debating whether it was necessary to establish connections between "rights-defending" activism that mainly raised social and economic demands, and political activism that criticized China's authoritarian system and advocated constitutional democracy. While many activists supported that kind of connection, opponents pointed out that radicalizing "rights-defending" activism could further endanger participants of the activism and asked intellectual elites to understand the condition of socioeconomically disadvantaged participants and respect these people's feelings. In my fieldwork, I found that the divergence between different activists was huge. When I discussed this issue with the activists, they often flung out harsh words at others.

To explore how the "ethical dilemma" had come into being, I interviewed human rights lawyers, NGO leaders, and liberal intellectuals from both sides. To achieve a more comprehensive understanding of the issue, I also followed a few "rights-defending" cases and interviewed dozens of activists from socioeconomically disadvantaged groups. Being immersed in information obtained from people holding different positions, I began to see the subtleties of the issue. On the one hand, the concern that radicalizing "rights-defending" activism could endanger participants was real. The situation of many participants did become worse, due to suppression of the state, after they worked with human rights lawyers and NGO activists. On some occasions, these participants did blame the lawyers and activists for making use of the "rights-defending" activism for achieving their own political goals. But on the other hand, the courage and selflessness embodied in human rights lawyers and NGO activists had not been faked. For the sake of criticizing injustice in society and promoting democratization, many of these lawyers and activists did sacrifice a lot. Misunderstanding and mistrust had emerged among these two groups of people because they usually had very different backgrounds and their perception of the meaning of resistance and risk was divergent. This finding pushed me to go beyond choosing sides and reflect upon the liberal interpretation of civil society that dichotomized the state-society relations and view participants of civil society as homogeneous.

Apart from the interviews, my analyses have also heavily relied upon various archives (e.g., media reports, open letters, activists' blogs, and activists' underground publications) and existing research reports on NGO activism, social movements, online protests, and the production of critical news in China. I usually refer to data from multiple sources to cross validate my arguments.

This book involves public discussions on multiple sites. I write about the ideological debate among intellectual elites, as well as the critical news reports on mass media, NGO activism, and collective actions initiated by grassroots, socioeconomically disadvantaged activists. For readers who are familiar with some elements of China's public sphere, such as NGOs, online protests, and public intellectuals, my description of any of the elements may appear to be not sufficiently "thick." But I hope to convince my readers that this kind of sacrifice is necessary. What I want to present in this book is not the dynamics of any single form of public participation; rather, what I want to present is the formation of a common mentality behind different forms of public participation within a specific historical period and how this mentality has later disintegrated.

During the days I wrote the first draft of this book, protests were rising in several cities in China. University students and ordinary urban residents took to the streets, expressing their discontent with the government's COVID policies. Commentaries rose again that a vibrant civil society was emerging in China and that the younger generation was becoming more courageous to defend their own rights. Honestly, I cannot predict where these activisms will lead us to and whether they could have any long-term impact on China's politics and culture. All I can present is a careful documentation of things that have happened in the past. This book is dedicated to anyone who believes in or questions the possibility of promoting democracy through building civil society, both in China and in the international community. I hope readers, through learning my case, know more about the potential and constraint in the application of this idea.

Introduction

On April 24, 2013, sitting in a small but cozy meeting room at the Institute for Civil Society at Sun Yat-sen University, I had a long conversation with Jing,[1] a youth activist, on the ideological question in labor activism. This was the first year that China entered Xi Jinping's presidency. In southern cities like Guangzhou and Shenzhen, the state's attitude toward social movement activism was still tolerant. Since the passage of the Labor Contract Law (2007), labor protests demanding higher wages and better working conditions had been rising. Being attracted by workers' uprisings, scholars, lawyers, journalists, and students intervened in labor issues and advocated agendas with different ideological concerns. The liberals applauded the workers' practice of self-organization. The social democrats pushed the state to provide better protection of workers' social rights. The Marxists discussed the necessity of creating a new working-class culture. As these interventions proceeded, controversies among different groups arose. Jing happened to have connections with people in different camps. Tentatively, I asked about her ideological position and her opinion on the debate.[2]

Pausing for a moment, Jing offered me a tortuous answer. She started with her experience of becoming an activist in the environmental movement. Being influenced by senior activists in the field, she recognized the many problems caused by the unconstrained state power and began to identify with the liberals. In those years, she scorned all leftist social thoughts and firmly believed that "only those who were brainwashed by the government would believe in Marxism." But later, as she became interested in the issue of rural migrant workers in China, her position gradually changed. First, she quickly found that workers as individuals were powerless vis-à-vis employers in a so-called free market. Second, she realized that major participants in those organizations that the liberals had supported, such as NGOs, often had a middle-class background, while workers tended to be marginalized or even silenced. These observations led her to the conclusion that the liberty advocated by the liberals was "too abstract" for socioeconomically disadvantaged groups.

In her senior year, she attended a reading group organized by Workers' Friendly Society (Gongyou zhi Jia), a Beijing-based organization promoting new working-class culture, and was introduced to the Marxist theory of alienation. In the group, youth activists and activists from rural migrant workers' communities enthusiastically discussed the possibility of building solidarity and resisting the neoliberal economic order. The Marxist discourse presented in the lively discussions was so different from that in the monotonous state propaganda. Jing felt excited and began to acknowledge that "there might be something reasonable in Marxism."

On hearing the mention of Workers' Friendly Society, I interrupted Jing and asked, "So does that mean now you are on the left?" I expected a positive answer. Yet she took on a puzzled look and suggested that she was not sure. To elaborate her understanding, she said, "Historically, many regimes claiming to follow Marxism eventually turned to totalitarianism. I think China was one of them. I don't know whether there is a necessary linkage between the two." She asked about my opinion. I responded that this was a sophisticated question to which I had no definitive answer either. Then she continued to say, "I cannot wholeheartedly support Workers' Friendly Society's ideological position, though I really like the way it mobilizes workers. For me, the major problem is that they [activists at Workers' Friendly Society] have never articulated their attitude toward the state. If they can't articulate that, chances are that one day they go so far as to defend or cooperate with the authoritarian regime."

With respect to this kind of ambivalence toward ideological questions, Jing was not alone. In 2012 and 2013, I interviewed twenty-two youth activists attending labor activism. Many of them were flooded with different sorts of ideological discourses. They discussed extensively the meaning of these discourses and how these discourses could be related to the organization of workers. While very often feeling confused, they tended to refuse to be associated with any specific ideological position.

Bearing these conversations in my mind, I was a bit more shocked than many common watchers when I saw university students attend the Jasic labor protest in 2018. I was shocked because the ambivalent attitude, which used to be so prevalent among youth activists, seemed to be gone overnight. To support workers' collective action at Jasic, a plant producing welding machines in Shenzhen, students from a couple of Marxist reading groups all over China came together. In the summer and autumn of 2018, they organized a series of demonstrations and public speeches, in which they proudly expressed their belief in Marxism. When their parents and professors came, coaxing them to withdraw from the agitational activities, they shouted, "Marxism is my religion."[3]

What else surprised me in the Jasic incident was the absence of the liberal discourse in the students' activism. Not long ago, the liberal discourse that criticized the authoritarian state was quite influential among the youths who were interested in social movement activism. It was because of the popularity of the liberal discourse that many youth activists like Jing had taken a more cautious attitude toward various leftist discourses, such as Marxism. When these youth activists employed the Marxist discourse to discuss issues like inequality, they usually felt the need to dialogue with the liberals and draw on some of the discourses the liberals commonly used, such as "civil society," to legitimize their ideological position. For example, when Jing talked with me about her participation in the leftists' agenda of promoting a new working-class culture, she emphasized that this was mainly to "help the disadvantaged speak so that they could also enter civil society." But in the activism in 2018, the dialogue between different ideological orientations disappeared. The students advocated Marxism as if the linkage between the discourse and the issue they were concerned with, that is, migrant workers' rights, was beyond dispute.

A few years later, the students' enthusiasm in labor protests eventually subsided as the Chinese state intensified its supervision over political participation in universities. Recovering from a series of emotional turbulence, I found two points worth being articulated. First, despite the state's continuous efforts in suppressing independent political activities, social movement activism of different kinds had persisted in China during the past few decades. Second, while many of the people's focuses and concerns, such as labor rights, had remained, the ideological structure of the activism had changed.

The Questions

Since the 1990s, due to the advancement of the market economic reform and the development of new communication technologies, alternative channels for public discussion have emerged in China. In the newly rising channels, such as NGOs, the internet, and the commercially-oriented newspapers, people have proposed various projects that aim to criticize China's politics and society. Among these projects, the one having the greatest and the most lasting impact is the project of building civil society. Being raised in the late 1990s by a group of intellectual elites who were often referred to in China as the liberals (*ziyou pai*), the civil society project advocated to build an independent space for constraining the state power, increasing political participation, and promoting China's democratization.

I systematically examine the history of the project of building civil society in the past three decades and discover that what I have observed in labor activism represents a microcosm of the changing relationship between the project and social movements in China. In the early to mid-2000s, the idea of civil society was quite influential among various social movements. Activists in many movements that engaged in specific social issues, such as the environmental movement and the AIDS movement, identified with the liberals and regarded their activisms as part of the project of building civil society. Since the late 2000s, however, the influence of the liberals gradually began to decline. Prominent social movements in the 2010s, such as the labor movement and the feminist movement, also paid attention to the power dynamics between state and society. Yet apart from criticizing the state, activists in these movements criticized power inequalities within society as well. Instead of identifying with the liberals, these activists now and then openly criticized the liberals. As is shown in my above description of the political attitude of Jing and the students in the Jasic Incident, movement activists in the 2010s first contested the liberal interpretation of civil society, and then regarded the liberals' agenda of building civil society as irrelevant.

These transformations beg the following questions: What has accounted for the rise and fall of the liberals in China's public sphere? Why could the discourse of civil society serve as a "master frame" in the '00s, but not in the '10s? How was the connection between the liberals and those social movement activists maintained before the late '00s, and why did it begin to disintegrate thereafter? How has an intellectual project that claims to provide a package plan for China's political reform gradually lose prominence in the public sphere? What are the political implications of the transformations?

Several macro-level explanations can be offered here, such as the waning of the hegemony of liberalism in the international community, China's rapid economic growth, the rise of nationalist sentiment among the youths, and state's systematic repression of the expressions of alternative ideological discourses.

Larger Environment		Organizational Structure of Interstitial Publics		Dynamics of Civil Society as an Ideational Movement
- Political/social atmosphere - Economic condition - Development of communicative technologies	⇨	- Major participants - Power balance among major participants	⇨	- Associating the idea of civil society with political reality - Contestations aroused on the association

Figure 1. Analytical Framework

While these factors have certainly played a role in this case, the macro-level explanations are too general and fail to capture the texture of history.

This book provides an explanation that takes into account the interaction between the macro and the micro (Figure 1). I argue that the liberals and their project of building civil society had emerged from interstitial spaces formed during China's transition from socialism to a market economy. Later, as the power of the state and the market gradually institutionalized activities in the spaces, the organizational structure of the public sphere was changed. This transformed the way people combined political ideals and specific issues in public discussions and caused the eventual decline of the civil society project.

Specifically, I argue that, before the late 2000s, the liberals occupied a dominant position in the interstitial spaces. This situation had enabled them to project their imagination of politics onto people in wider society and discursively unify various resistance activisms. The prominence of the civil society project had also pushed the Chinese state to deal with some of the most egregious social conflicts rising during the economic reform. Since the late 2000s, however, the increasing intervention of the state and the transformation of the technological environment had partially institutionalized public discussions in the interstitial spaces. This had on the one hand destabilized the power of the liberals and on the other hand brought in a new generation of participants. The engagement between different types of participants aroused contestations and nurtured new forms of public expressions in which the combination of ideological frames and social issues became more exploratory and open-ended. As a result, the project of building civil society was challenged, and critical public discussions became fragmented. But the transformation had also incurred new forms of resistance activism whose public expressions were more fluid and unpredictable.

While this book is primarily about China, it intends to talk to a wider audience in three ways. First, this book joins the debate of the public sphere.

In discussing the location of the public sphere, I employ the concept of interstitial space. Interstitial space can be understood as the space where the exercise of power has not been fully institutionalized.[4] I argue that vibrant public discussions leading to the formation of critical public opinions often emerge from such a space. Moreover, I emphasize that these discussions can be ephemeral, as the autonomy of activities in an interstitial space is by no means guaranteed. Over time, the dominant power structure in a society can institutionalize public discussions in an interstitial space. Conventionally, scholars locate the public sphere in a space that is independent of state and market.[5] I contend that this concept is too fossilized. In contrast, the idea of interstitial space lends us a more flexible framework for thinking about the changing dynamics of the public sphere.

Second, I want to use China as a case to reflect upon the multiple, contradicting consequences of the global dissemination of the idea of civil society. Since the 1980s, with the end of the Cold War and the rise of neoliberalism in major capitalist economies, the discussion of the idea of civil society, both in academic and political circles, has revived.[6] Controversies have long existed on the political consequence of the revival of the idea of civil society, especially in non-Western contexts. While advocates of civil society suggest that the growth of an independent space for participation could increase the accountability of government and enhance democracy, critics argue that the discourse of civil society simply represents the hegemony of the West.[7] After scrutinizing the rise and fall of the idea of civil society in China in a span of almost thirty years, I reach a moderate conclusion. I suggest that, through advocating for the idea of civil society, the liberals had managed to mobilize resources, build allies, and thematize many social problems rising during a critical period in China's economic reform; however, the liberals' activism had also produced new forms of power inequalities and the solidarity formed between their allies had been rather fragile.

Third, at a more general level, this book also contributes to the discussion of dynamics in an ideational movement. It has long been discovered that the association of ideas and issues in public discussions is contingent; thus, incorporating a wide variety of political and social activism into a unified ideological camp always involves a power struggle.[8] Extant studies more often pay attention to how the association between an idea and specific political and social issues is constructed, or the "building of blocs."[9] In demonstrating how the idea of civil society had become influential among social movement activists, I too analyze the various strategies the liberals had employed in constructing the association. However, apart from that, I also highlight the multiple processes through which the association built by the liberals was contested. I show that, while bringing uncertainties, the contestations could be beneficial to the maintenance of the vitality of an ideational movement. These analyses shed light on some of the dilemmas people encounter when forging a political camp that is based on an abstract idea.

The rest of the introduction chapter is arranged in the following way. First, I critically review the literature on China's public sphere. Then I lay out my analytical framework and introduce how my study talks to various extant studies. In this part, I review scholarly discussions on three subjects, which are the theoretical relations between the public sphere and the concept of interstitial space, the political implication of the global dissemination of the idea of civil society, and the dynamics in an ideational movement. After that, I offer a general sketch of the rise and fall of the project of building civil society in China. The last section is an overview of the content of each book chapter.

Understanding the Public Sphere in China

Since the 1990s, there has risen a growing body of literature discussing the nature of China's public sphere. The literature involves a wide range of research subjects, including the NGO activism, online discussions and protests, the production of critical news reports, and social movements.[10] Early studies mostly focus on the conditions in which alternative public discussions occur. Factors like commercialization, the development of internet technology, the intervention of transnational organizations, and the withdrawal of state power are highlighted.[11] In recent years, the research interest in the field has turned to the increasing interventions of state power. Scholars analyze the measures the state has adopted to infiltrate, distinguish, and regulate public discussions.[12] There are also studies reflecting upon the limitations of the public sphere, pointing out the various power inequalities among participants.[13] The extant literature provides rich information on the interactions between the state, market, and public sphere. The analysis of this book will also draw on some of the data the literature has presented.

However, two important aspects have been understudied. First, there lacks a comprehensive review of the changing structure of China's public sphere in the past three decades. Most analyses in the extant literature have been generalized from cross-sectional data. Although, in recent years, there has emerged some longitudinal studies, these studies usually focus on single elements in the public sphere, such as social movement organizations in a specific thematic field.[14] In this project, I want to emphasize that what matters are not only the rise or fall of any single elements in the public sphere, but also how the way these elements are related to each other has changed over time.[15]

Let me use the changing position of NGOs to illustrate this point. In the 1990s and 2000s, when state control over NGOs was still porous, many NGOs, especially those in the fields of environmental protection and labor rights, established connections with agitational activities like protest. While creating more disturbances, the association between NGOs and protest activities had also helped to thematize social problems and translate fragmented discontents into articulated policy suggestions. But since the late 2000s, as the state began to employ more meticulous strategies to regulate NGOs, most of these organizations turned to service provision activism. Based on these facts, some scholars argue that, through inventing new techniques for governance, the authoritarian state in China is now able to peacefully coexist with a civil society that enjoys a certain degree of autonomy.[16] What these scholars ignore is the fact that, as these NGOs have become more cooperative with the government, their capacity to absorb resistance activism has also dropped. Discontents have since then been conveyed through other channels, such as youth activists' event-based concern groups. This implies that, rather than bringing "peace" to the public sphere, the state has simply pushed conflicts into a new terrain. Only by reviewing the internal structure of the public sphere can we recognize changing dynamics like this.

Second, the literature underestimates the sophistication of ideological debates. There is no lack of concern in the extant literature on the ideological expressions in China's public sphere. Studies on the intellectual sphere analyze the divergence between the liberals and the new left.[17] Studies on popular protests highlight the diverse ideological discourses people employ when proposing demands.[18] Recent studies on online platforms like Weibo explore the multiple meanings of the ideological discourses in public discussions.[19] But what has been changed during the past three decades are not only the ideological discourses people use but also the way abstract ideological expressions are inserted into the discussion of concrete issues. For example, public discussions on politics in the 1990s used to be flooded with debates on abstract ideas, such as "whether authoritarianism or neoliberalism constitutes a greater obstacle to China's modernization."[20] Nowadays, while these abstract debates still exist, they have become limited to activists' small circles. When abstract ideas like neoliberalism are mentioned in wider public discussion, they are often associated with or subordinated to the articulation of more specific interests. Recent studies on the "grassroots intellectuals" have recognized this trend.[21] But how this transformation has taken place is still unknown and needs to be historicized.

To examine these understudied aspects, I turn to new analytical approaches. To unpack the historical transformation of the structure of the public sphere, I turn to the theoretical discussion of interstitial emergence. To analyze the complexity of the ideological debates, I see the dissemination of the idea of civil society as an ideational movement and investigate the multiple political processes involved in the movement.

Interstitial Space and the Public Sphere

The Idea of Interstitial Publics

The idea of the public sphere has come to the study of politics as a normative theory.[22] It portrays an ideal situation in which the wills and opinions guiding political actions are formed on the basis of rational-critical discourse.[23] Social and political theorists have long been debating in what location a public sphere can rise.[24] The Habermasian tradition, as a prominent tradition, points to an "independent lifeworld" that is outside bureaucratic state and capitalist market economy. It is argued that both the state and the market are "systems" whose integration is based on instrumental actions in pursuit of power and money; hence, it is only in a space that is independent of the two institutions can the social integrative power of communication get to thrive.[25] In some theoretical discussions, this independent space is also referred to as a civil society being comprised of citizens' voluntary associations, networks, and social movements.[26]

While being morally compelling, the Habermasian tradition brings difficulties for empirical research. First, because both the state power and the market power can be pervasive, a space that is fully independent of the two institutions is hard to find. The applicability of the theory becomes even more questionable in non-Western societies, where the differentiation of major institutions is limited, and the boundaries of these institutions are often unclear. Second, the Habermasian approach tends to idealize civil society actors. Empirical research has repeatedly shown that, instead of engaging in communicative actions and forming solidarity, actors in the so-called civil society or "independent lifeworld" can also initiate conflicts and create hatred and violence.[27]

This study calls attention to the concept of interstitial space. In his analysis of the history of social power, Michael Mann describes interstitial space as being constituted of power networks that are poorly incorporated into the dominant power structure of a society. He argues that it is often in an interstitial space that new forms of interactions are invented and coins the term interstitial emergence to refer to the situation in which these new interactions induce a reorganization of social life.[28] According to Mann, interstitial space almost always exists in human society, because the institutionalization of social life cannot be total.[29]

In fact, the idea of interstitial space is not alien to the studies of the public sphere.[30] To some extent, the bourgeois public sphere investigated by Jürgen Habermas in his early work, *The Structural Transformation of the Public Sphere*, can also be seen as an interstitial emergence. The salons, coffee houses, and table societies where the bourgeoisie enthusiastically engaged in public discussions flourished in a time when feudalism had begun to decline, and the power of the modern bureaucratic state had not yet been fully developed. It was in this seemingly peripheral space that those norms that would have substantive influence over democratic deliberations, such as inclusivity and equity, were nurtured. Later, as the power of the bureaucratic state penetrated society, the bourgeois public sphere began to decline.[31]

In this study, I contextualize the analysis of the interstitial space in China's transition from socialism to a market economy. Since the 1980s, as the state's controlling power was destabilized, interstitial spaces where there lacked established rules emerged out of many different locations. Some of these spaces were within the state, or highly embedded in the state. Notable examples include marginalized or disadvantaged state organs like the All-China Women's Federation (ACWF). Some of the interstitial spaces were outside the state, or in places where the influence of state power was rather thin. A notable example was the internet space in the 1990s.

I emphasize that these interstitial spaces had not always been fragmented. Under certain historical circumstances, practices in different interstitial spaces could coalesce into new social spheres in which major participants had similar ideas or shared identities and behavioral patterns. A typical example was the formation of an NGO sphere in China. If we scrutinize the history of the development of NGOs in China, we may discover that founders of these organizations had been rather heterogeneous. Some of the founders were intellectual elites working for marginalized and disadvantaged state organs like the ACWF. To realize goals that had been denied or ignored within the bureaucratic state, these intellectual elites established NGOs and built allies with societal actors. Some founders were grassroots actors who sought to establish self-help networks to solve problems in their community. A notable instance was rural migrant workers who established organizations to provide affordable legal service in workers' communities. In early years, many of these organizations were not even non-profit organizations. Thanks to the intervention of universities, research institutes, and international foundations, people with different backgrounds constituted an NGO community. While the specific issues these people engaged in were diverse, in the 1990s and early 2000s, they had more or less held an "NGO identity," which claimed that NGOs, as "civil society organizations," were closer to common people, and were thus more sensitive to various problems in people's social life.

Alongside the NGO sphere, this book also highlights the "thought sphere" (*sixiang jie*) and the media sphere. The "thought sphere" is a sphere in which humanity and social science scholars openly discuss political and social theories to express their opinions on fundamental political questions that are pertinent to China's reform. The media sphere is a sphere in which journalists and editors advocate that news media serve as a "public institution" (*gongqi*) and criticize state's monopoly of information. As I will show in detail in later chapters, while the formation of both spheres had benefited from commercialization and a bourgeoning market economy, major actors in the spheres had also mobilized resources from within the state. I contend that it was in these spaces that were "in-between" state and society, rather than an "independent lifeworld," that critical public opinions were formed and China's development pattern since the 1980s was challenged. I thus call activisms in these spheres as constituting interstitial publics.

Some sociological studies on the public sphere argue that robust public discussions having the capacity to sustain democracy must be supported by strong regulative and communicative institutions.[32] My focus on the interstitial space does not contradict with this view. First, I am not arguing that interstitial publics are sufficient for promoting or sustaining democracy. On the contrary, I emphasize that critical public discussions emerging from interstitial spaces often tend to be temporal and ephemeral. I will elaborate the implications of this character in the next section. Second, the employment of the concept of interstitial space is to inquire into a different question, which is a genetic question: How is it possible that discourses and practices diverging from the logic of state and market, the two highly resourceful and powerful institutions, come into being? The idea of interstitial space implies that people do not need to have an intact civil society with a clear boundary against the state and the market to initiate meaningful public discussions. Instead, these discussions could emerge interstitially—between the pores of state and market institutions or around their edges. The idea thus widens the scope for the search of the locations of the public sphere.

The Changing Dynamics of Interstitial Publics

Recent organizational studies on interstitial space focus on the roles of the interstitial space in promoting institutional change.[33] These studies argue that actors in interstitial space usually enjoy much autonomy to establish overlapping networks, draw resources from different spheres, develop hybrid intellectual products, or even invent new identities and communication styles.[34] This study endorses this view. However, I still want to emphasize the other side of the shield: Although interstitially emergent actors sometimes do enjoy a certain degree of autonomy due to the lack of established rules, the autonomy is not institutionally guaranteed. Over time, it is possible that practices in an interstitial space are institutionalized by the dominant power structure in society and thus lose critical edge. By institutionalization, I refer to the development of rules, norms, or procedures that have the capacity to constrain social actions. This can result from the fact that dominant institutions like the state and corporations in the market command the power to regulate the space, or that practices in the space become so routinized that they no longer constitute challenges to any established institutions.

The institutionalization of the interstitial publics this book examines has happened almost immediately after the emergence of the interstitial spaces. I suggest that the forces of institutionalization have come from multiple sources. On the one hand, confronting the rise of various alternative public discussions, the Chinese state has sought to establish new rules. The centralization of state power, which has accelerated since the late 2000s, has also facilitated the enforcement of these rules. On the other hand, since the 2010s, the role played by the market has gradually changed. As I have mentioned above, in the 1990s and 2000s, a bourgeoning market economy and commercialization played a crucial role in supporting the interstitial publics, as the market provided many resources with which actors in the interstitial publics could deviate from those discourses and practices advocated by the state. However, since the 2010s, the logic of maximizing profit has begun to prevail in several spaces that had been penetrated by the commercial power of the market, such as the commercialized newspapers and the social media space. Resultantly, the commercial power has become more homologous with the power of the state. As these systemic powers have become more pervasive, the condition of interstitial publics has transformed.

In elaborating the institutionalization process of China's interstitial publics, I highlight the following three points. First, I propose that we recognize that institutionalization is a lasting process. The development of rules and procedures—even if it is promoted by powerful institutions like the state—takes time.[35] In other words, there would usually be a time interval between the interstitial emergence of some activities and the situation in which these activities are finally institutionalized. I suggest that this seemingly transitory period constitutes a period of uncertainty. Chances are that the practices and discourses formulated during the period simply vanish with the institutionalization. But it can also be that these practices and discourses become so widespread that they produce long-term impact over the interaction between the interstitial space and the dominant power structure. As I will elaborate, such a phenomenon has repeatedly occurred in China's interstitial publics since the 2000s.

Second, I suggest that the institutionalization of interstitial space tends to be uneven when different actors are involved. In my case, due to its dependence on the state, the "thought" sphere began to be institutionalized as early as the first half of the 2000s. As the professional regulations on the publication of academic works and the promotion of scholars became increasingly well-defined, humanity and social science scholars became less incentivized to communicate with the public on sophisticated, abstract political ideals. But during that period, the media sphere and the NGO sphere were still expanding. An implication of this character is that the internal structure of an interstitial public could be changed during its institutionalization.

Third, I contend that, when the institutionalization is carried out in a top-down fashion, without sufficient negotiation with interstitially emergent actors, unintended consequences are likely to occur. A common unintended consequence is that interstitially emergent actors begin to skirt around the intervention of external powerful institutions and search for new interstitial space. As these actors move to other social domains, they may merge with new networks and initiate new forms of action. This proposition is of particular importance for us to understand the new trend of the development of the interstitial publics in China after the mid-2010s.

Because institutionalization is a lasting, uneven process that may incur unintended consequences, the transformation of interstitial publics is often non-linear, containing contradicting tendencies. This implies that it is hard to use a single index to describe the attributes of an interstitial public. Instead of saying that an interstitial public has become more "radical," "conservative," "proactive," or "inactive," I unpack the structure of public discussions throughout my historical analysis.

Studying Civil Society as an Ideational Movement

The Civil Society Debate in Non-Western Context

Since the 1980s, the rise of neoliberalism in major economies and the fall of communism in central and eastern Europe arouse passion among scholars for "rediscovering" civil society. In discussing the possibility of democracy and political change, some scholars use the concept of civil society to signify the realm of market economy and private interests, while others view civil society rather as the activity of social forces distinct from both state and market.[36] In general terms, civil society has been regarded as a good thing. It is argued that a strong civil society is able to constrain the over expansion of authoritarian state power and protect the integrity of private life.[37] The associational practices in civil society can also school citizens in the skills for communication and nurture a public culture that encourages mutual understanding;[38] moreover, civil society increases, alongside formal institutions, channels for political participation and thus "deepens" democracy.[39] The influence of the discussion has gone beyond the academic community. Since the end of the Cold War, civil society has become the language of political dissidents, social movement activists, and international foundations.[40] Many governments and corporations have also used the concept to express their agenda.[41] Numerous resources have been invested in civil society institutions like NGOs and voluntary associations.

Nevertheless, the frequent employment of the concept of civil society incurs wide criticism. Scholars have been particularly critical of the applicability of the concept in non-Western societies. For example, anthropologist

James Ferguson contends that the civil society thesis and the state/society dichotomy inherent to the thesis are Eurocentric. According to Ferguson, the civil society thesis ignores that power in Africa has long been exercised by entities other than the state, such as colonialists' private corporations; it also tends to be blind to the fact that the so-called civil society in Africa, which is comprised of internationally funded NGOs, is often anti-democratic.[42]

Similar debates have also happened among students of China. Since the 1980s, being influenced by the global revival of the idea of civil society, historians, political scientists, and sociologists began to employ the concept to explain history and politics in China. Some of these scholars see the eruption of the Tiananmen Protest in 1989 as a sign of a rising civil society and argue that the incipient civil society has been brought forth by the market economic reform.[43] Some draw on historical studies on commercial cities in the Qing Dynasty and argue that civil society emerged in China as early as the 19th century.[44] Criticism, on the other hand, points out that these views are empirically not grounded. Social movement scholar Zhao Dingxin contends that civil society organizations played marginal roles in the mobilization of the student movement in 1989; the rapid mobilization of the movement had rather to do with the particular ecology of the urban space in Beijing, which was in fact a legacy of China's socialist practices.[45] East Asian historian Frederic Wakeman suggests that most capitalist organizations and institutions in commercial cities in the Qing Dynasty, which have been regarded as evidence of the existence of civil society in premodern China, enjoyed very limited autonomy from the state.[46]

I have mixed concerns over these debates. On the one hand, I am sympathetic to the criticism of the applicability of the concept of civil society. Since the 1990s, the Chinese liberals claimed that they were trying to build a civil society. But as I will elaborate in detail in this book, neither the liberals nor the organizations they had established were fully independent of the state. The contrary is true, many of them were to different degrees embedded in the state. Therefore, instead of presuming that these organizations are independent forces that can promote democratization, we need to be attentive to the changing context and investigate their condition on the ground. From this perspective, I agree with the advocacy of African studies scholar Mahmood Mamdani, who is also a critic of the civil society thesis, that we need to study the "really existing civil society."[47]

Yet on the other hand, I also want to emphasize that the talk of ideas, even when they are not well grounded in reality, can be consequential. This is because it is not just what history and reality actually are that may influence political change; how we think about history and reality, and how we think about our capacity to promote changes, also matter. In this aspect, the influence of the discussion of civil society in China provides an illustrative example. Because the liberals firmly believed that civil society was crucial for political reform and that an incipient civil society was already in the making in China, they established NGOs to engage in social issues, encouraged the production of critical news, and built allies with leaders in various grassroots protests. The imagination of politics eventually created new facts—although the organizations and networks formed in the liberals' activism had not evolved into any grand resistance movement like the Solidarity Movement in Poland, they had nonetheless, in a critical period in China's economic reform, thematized many social problems in the public sphere and profoundly changed the culture of public discussion.

Based on these concerns, I suggest that we see the dissemination of the idea of civil society in non-Western context as an ideational movement. By ideational movement, I refer to a movement that seeks to project a certain imagination of reality onto people in wider society, despite the existence of an interpretation of the reality supported by some forms of dominant power structure. In this book, instead of joining the debate on whether China has a civil society, I regard the Chinese liberals' practices of advocating civil society as a solid fact. Of course, I will still examine how the liberals talk about China's civil society and whether their description of various social movement activism has diverged from the "really existing civil society." But I will spare more efforts in explaining how the idea of civil society, as a concept that has mainly originated from Western society, has become associated with many political facts and concerns in China and how this association has galvanized people into action.

Multiple Processes Involved in an Ideational Movement

It has long been discovered that the association of ideological discourse and social issues in public expression is not axiomatic. Rather, the association process often tends to be temporal and contextual.[48] The post-structuralist approach for studying political culture emphasizes that incorporating social activism that addresses a variety of issues and concerns into a unified ideological camp involves a power struggle.[49] My analysis of civil society as an ideational movement in China builds on and extends these discussions. Specifically, in documenting the liberals' expressions and various debates they had aroused in the public, I highlight three points.

First, I highlight that the intension of the concept of civil society significantly changed when it traveled across the boundary between academic studies and social movements. As I will elaborate, to make the concept appear to be more compelling, throughout the 1990s and the 2000s, the liberals adjusted their presentation of the civil society thesis by altering in their public expression the major participants of civil society, the organizational basis of civil society, and the goal of civil society activism. Nevertheless, the strategy of altering the intension of an idea still had its limits. To incorporate more issues into their political agenda, the liberals had also promoted many simplified or reductionist interpretations of sophisticated social facts. For example, to illustrate that the idea of civil society was indeed relevant to China's political transition, in the early and mid-2000s, the liberals argued that the various resistance activisms organized by different social groups at that time, such as peasants, workers, and homeowners, were all evidence of the existence of a vibrant civil society. While these activisms had emerged out of rather different conditions and proposed diverse demands, the liberals tended to ignore the variations and unitarily interpret the activisms as a rising countermovement seeking to constrain the authoritarian state.

Second, I argue that the liberals' efforts in associating the idea of civil society and China's political reality had constantly encountered challengers. The authoritarian state was a major challenger. But it was not the only challenger. Many non-state actors had also attended the contestations over the civil society thesis. In this book, I analyze contentions between the liberals and three groups of actors—the new left, socioeconomically disadvantaged activists in human rights activism, and activists in movements that claimed to represent subaltern interests. I show that, at different stages, these three groups of actors had debated with the liberals about the intension of the concept of civil society and the applicability of the concept in the discussion on specific issues. They had also pointed out the problems brought by the liberals' simplified readings of many social facts.

Third, I contend that the consequence of the contestations over the idea of civil society is open-ended. Challengers' questions over the meaning of the idea of civil society and the applicability of the idea in the Chinese context could undermine the constructed association between the idea and reality and thus ruin the liberals' efforts in launching an ideational movement. As I will show in this book, this happened during the various debates centering on civil society. But I also want to emphasize that, on some occasions, the contestations aroused by challengers could also have a positive impact. This is what had happened in public debates on labor rights and feminist rights in the late 2000s and early 2010s—by bringing more facts or more perspectives for understanding these facts back to public discussion, the contestations had urged some of the liberals to reflect upon their position and make their political project more inclusive. From my point of view, the contestations played a crucial role in sustaining the vitality of the project of building civil society in a time when the power of the state had already become pervasive in critical and alternative public discussions.

The Rise and Fall of Civil Society as an Ideational Movement

To unpack the processes in which the project of building civil society was formed, enlarged, concretized, and later disintegrated, I divide the historical transformation of China's public sphere in the past three decades into four stages (see Table 1). Each stage features distinctive interstitial publics emerging out of distinctive social, political, and technological environments. Accordingly, major participants in public discussions and the way they are organized are also changing, which leads to the transformation of the dynamics of the civil society debate. The first two stages are the periods in which the liberals and their project of building civil society interstitially emerged, whereas the latter two stages are the periods in which the project incrementally declined and disintegrated. The content and the form of public discussions in each stage will be examined in detail in the following chapters. In this chapter, I will only provide a general sketch of the whole historical process.

The Interstitial Emergence of the Civil Society Project

As the country moved away from a planned economy in the 1980s, the Chinese state began to withdraw its power from society. In urban regions, independent academic publishing, reading groups, salons, and public lectures flourished. In these newly rising venues, humanity and social science scholars working in state sponsored universities and research institutes reflected upon the Cultural Revolution, discussed the possibility of a humanitarian Marxism, and openly criticized government's policies. Their activisms promoted the formation of a "thought sphere," in which intellectual elites engaged in public debates on political and social theories to express their concerns about China's reform. Being influenced by the modernization theory, many scholars believed that, whereas the West, featuring market economy, democratic politics, and the protection of individual liberty, represented a more "advanced" society, China, lacking these things, was "backward;" the only way for China to achieve prosperity and return to the international community was, therefore, to embrace the West. These scholars advocated their idea through translating Western theoretical works and making documentary films. These activisms were later referred to as the New Enlightenment Movement (*Xin Qimeng Yundong*). It served as the progenitor of the 1989 student movement.

Although the student movement was suppressed, the relatively open political environment had largely remained in the 1990s. Because of the influence of the neoliberal ideology and the pressure from the international community, the Chinese state loosened its control over society again after Deng Xiaoping's Southern Tour (1992). With the interstitial emergence of dozens of magazines dedicated to theoretical and ideological debates, activities in the "thought sphere" returned around the mid-1990s. As the intellectual debates on China's reform were deepened, the New Enlightenment Movement was disintegrated into two opposing camps—the liberals and the new left. The liberals largely inherited the spirit of the New Enlightenment Movement and insisted that the authoritarian state was the root of all problems in Chinese society. On the other side, the new left held a more critical attitude toward the New Enlightenment Movement and highlighted social conflicts caused by the capitalist market and neoliberal globalization. With the rise of these debates, public life gradually revived from the shadow of the failure of the student movement. I hence call the first stage (1992–2002) the stage of revival.

It was during this stage that the idea of civil society was introduced. Being influenced by the writings of dissident intellectuals in eastern Europe, social science scholars began to talk about the possibility of building a civil society in China. In their early discussions, civil society was described as a space consisting of market economy and citizens' autonomous associations. It was emphasized that such a space could constrain the arbitrary state power and empower citizens to participate in politics. The advocates of civil society in the '90s shared with the intellectuals in the '80s a dichotomous thinking of politics and history. Yet the dichotomy proposed in the '90s was new. Whereas major antitheses accentuated in the '80s were between the conservatives and the reformers, China and the West, and the planned economy and the market economy, in the '90s, the emphasis went to the antithesis between state and

Table 1. Stages of the Transformation of the Public Sphere

	1992–2002 Revival	2003–2007 Counter Hegemony	2008–2013 Internal Contestation	2014–2019 Fragmentation
Political Environment	Advocacy of "small government, big society"; decentralization of state power	Advocacy of a "harmonious society" (fairness and justice); decentralization of state power	Increasing vigilance toward non-governmental forces; advocacy of the "administration of society"	Rise of nationalist sentiments; recentralization of state power
Social and Technological Environment	Restart of the economic reform; incipient internet space with very limited participants	Emergence of urban middle class as beneficiaries of the reform; increasing social conflicts	Expansion of internet users brought by the development of mobile and social media technology	Slowdown of economic growth
Interstitial Space for Alternative Public Discussion	The "thought" sphere	The media sphere, the NGO sphere	The media sphere, the NGO sphere	Newly emerging interstitial spaces
The Institutionalization of Alternative Public Discussion	Very few	Decline of the "thought" sphere due to the institutionalization of academic studies	Partial institutionalization of the NGO sphere and the media sphere	Suppression of the media sphere and the NGO sphere
Major Actors for Producing Critical Opinions	Humanity and social science scholars in state-run institutes	Activist journalists, the "rights-defending" lawyers, NGO activists, internet-based public intellectuals	Activist journalists, the "rights-defending" lawyers, NGO activists, internet-based public intellectuals, activists from subaltern groups	Youth activists, internet-based public intellectuals

Liberals' Networks and Their Position	Return of the liberals; limited engagement with issue-oriented public discussions	Expansion of the liberals; close engagement with less powerful, issue-oriented participants	Destabilization of the liberals; close engagement with empowered, issue-oriented participants	Marginalization of the liberals; largely segregated from issue-oriented public discussions
Discussions on the Idea of Civil Society	Introduction of the idea of civil society; limited influence in public discussions	Incorporation of various resistance activism into the civil society project	Deliberation on whether the civil society project benefits disadvantaged groups	Marginalization of the idea of civil society
Prominent Social Movements	AIDS movement, environmental movement	Weiquan Movement, environmental movement, homeowners' movement	Labor movement, feminist movement, environmental movement, food movement	Labor movement, feminist movement
Major Demands Thematized in the Interstitial Publics	• Independent space for associations • Autonomous public participation	• Containment of state power • Independent space for associations • Autonomous public participation • Government transparency • Protection of private property	• Containment of state power • Independent space for associations • Autonomous public participation • Government transparency • De-commodification • Solidarity among disadvantaged groups • Protection of social rights	• De-commodification • Solidarity among disadvantaged groups • Protection of social rights • Anti-discrimination

society. During the debate between the liberals and the new left, the idea of civil society was gradually associated with the liberals and became the liberals' political project. In the 1990s, many activists who had experienced the student movement embraced the idea of civil society, because they believed that the idea provided an alternative framework for thinking about the possibility of a peaceful transition to democracy. Nevertheless, the influence of the idea at this stage was still limited. Except for a couple of intellectual elites, very few people talked about it in wider society.

Changes took place in the early 2000s. Since the beginning of the Hu-Wen regime (2003), the Chinese state began to emphasize that its development goal had shifted to building a "harmonious society" (*hexie shehui*), rather than simply boosting economic growth. This generated a political atmosphere that was more tolerant of the discussion of social problems. Meanwhile, the economic reform since the 1990s, which heavily relied upon international trade and business, created an urban middle class in coastal regions. As the beneficiaries of the reform, these middle-class residents were less interested in a radical political agenda like regime change. Yet these people usually held a rather progressivist attitude toward social reform issues. Thanks to the development of the internet, they became the new participants in public discussions.

During this stage, the "thought" sphere featuring abstract ideological discussions declined due to state intervention and the institutionalization of academic studies. But the rapid development of the internet technology, the intervention of international foundations, the burgeoning market economy, and discrepancies between different state sectors brought in new interstitial spaces. Around the early 2000s, activities in these spaces coalesced into two new spheres for alternative public discussion. These two new spheres were the media sphere, in which journalists and editors produced critical news reports and criticized the state's monopoly of information, and the NGO sphere, in which activists of different kinds established independent organizations to expand the space for participation. With the structural transformation of the interstitial publics, the condition of the ideological debate between the liberals and the new left also changed. Whereas the new left turned to the international academic community and found an audience abroad, the liberals turned to the media sphere and the NGO sphere and found allies among activist journalists, media-based public intellectuals, NGO activists, and human rights lawyers. While actors in the new liberal camp were rather heterogeneous with respect to their ideological stance, what had brought these actors together was exactly the idea of civil society, or an imagination of politics that rested upon the antithesis between state and society. In the early to mid-2000s, these actors built multiple, intersecting networks.

The expansion of the project of building civil society had largely to do with the popularization of the discourse of *weiquan*, which literally meant defending rights. The discourse of *weiquan* was originally a state discourse, being employed to highlight the state's efforts in making laws to protect citizens' rights. Yet the liberals and their allies turned the discourse upside down and used it to criticize the state. In China, the 2000s was a period in which contentious collective actions were rampant. Locally based protests and demonstrations spontaneously emerged, expressing concerns on issues like environmental pollution, the corruption of local government officials, and the problems in land appropriation and the privatization of state-owned enterprises. In the interstitial publics, the liberals and their allies argued that all these diverse activisms belonged to one single movement, which was the Weiquan Movement. They also suggested that the movement signified a rising civil society trying to constrain the authoritarian state. To render their interpretation of the Weiquan Movement more plausible, the liberals adjusted their discussion of civil society. In this process, many questions people used to debate in the "thought sphere" in the 1990s, such as the institutional foundation of civil society and its major participants, were largely obfuscated. Because the liberals, to a large extent, discursively unified various resistance activisms, I call this stage (2003–2007) the stage of counter hegemony.

The burgeoning Weiquan Movement successfully exposed many social problems arising during the economic reform and pushed the state to deal with some of the most egregious conflicts in society. However, the liberals' dichotomous thinking of state society relations had also caused a series of problems. First, because the state was simply regarded as a threat to liberty and human rights, the liberals mainly considered the possibility to constrain the state power. This framework systematically excluded many rights issues in which the state needed to play positive roles, such as the construction of social safety networks. Second, the liberals' understanding of civil society also tended to ignore concrete institutions. Many advocacy campaigns they launched thus lacked detailed policy suggestions. This severely harmed the sustainability of many resistance activisms. Lastly, the dichotomous thinking also ignored differences within civil society. This created new forms of power inequality between intellectual elites and socioeconomically disadvantaged participants in social movements. Based on these facts, I contend that the Weiquan Movement, as a counter-hegemonic movement, was hastily formed. The problems inherent to the movement foreshadowed the future decline of the project of building civil society.

The Contradicting Disintegration of the Civil Society Project

The first factor that had triggered the transformation of the interstitial publics in the second half of the Hu-Wen regime was the development of the communication technology. With the rapid development of the internet infrastructure and the social media technology, getting online became much cheaper and easier in the late 2000s. On newly emerging social media like Weibo, which came into being in 2009, many people who previously had no channels for participation began to voice their concerns. Some of them openly criticized the liberals for their oversimplified understandings of politics and history. The popularization of social media severely impacted the traditional paper media, where most activist journalists were based. Since 2012, the circulation and advertisement income of several prominent newspapers began to plummet.

During this stage, the Chinese state's capacity to regulate public discussions also increased. After the Sichuan Earthquake (2008), the state sought to incorporate NGOs. The threshold for registration was lowered. Funds were offered to those more cooperative organizations through "purchasing service" programs. After the rise of the Arab Spring (2010), censorship in the news media was strengthened. The state also detained a couple of human rights lawyers who had relatively radical agendas like regime change. Several NGOs that had been involved in agitational activities were also disbanded. It was during this stage that civil society became a politically sensitive term.

The transformations in the technological and political environment generated subtle and intricate influences on the structure of the interstitial publics. On the one hand, as prominent NGOs, human rights lawyers, and activist journalists were suppressed, the domination of the liberals was largely destabilized. On the other hand, the expansion of the space for public communication and the increase of resources had brought in new actors. In the second half of the Hu-Wen regime, some socioeconomically less advantaged actors, such as rural migrant workers and university students, successfully formulated influential organizations and networks. Unlike many liberals, these actors' participation was often driven by very specific concerns. Nevertheless, the state's intervention in the interstitial publics was still porous and fragmented in this stage. This left space for the liberals to adapt to the changes. By adjusting their discourses and practices, some liberals were able to maintain their networks in the interstitial publics. China's public sphere thus entered a stage in which old and new actors coexisted and frequently encountered each other.

In such a circumstance, several organizations and networks representing disadvantaged groups, such as peasants, workers, and women, began to contest the liberals' interpretation of civil society. It was not until this stage that some of the new leftists' criticism was reified. In public discussions on issues like food safety, rural migrant workers' social rights, and China's family planning policies, activists representing the subaltern groups debated with the liberals on questions like whether the discourse of class should be empha- sized when talking about civil society, whether the rising market economy in China had promoted or inhibited the development of civil society, and whether the state could play any positive roles in protecting the rights of the disadvantaged. Many of the activists eventually reached the conclusion that the civil society project proposed by the liberals was parochial. The contes- tations between old and new actors brought in alternative critical discourses as well as new perspectives for thinking about social problems. But the popu- larization of the alternative discourses had also incurred divisiveness, both in the interstitial publics as a whole and within some social movements. I hence call this stage (2008–2013) the stage of internal contestation.

During the last few years of the Hu-Wen regime, the frictions between China and the West became more frequent as China achieved greater eco- nomic influence in the international community. Domestically, nationalist sentiments arose, both among state leaders and ordinary people. The state's propaganda turned to the discourse that the idea of civil society was a West- ern ideology, whose dissemination in society could undermine China's polit- ical stability. After the Umbrella Movement in Hong Kong (2014), the state's intervention in the interstitial publics became more coherent and unified. Censorship of news reports was further strengthened. Many NGOs that had been tolerated or even got registered in the previous stage were disbanded after the passage of the philanthropy law and the law on regulating over- seas NGOs. Meanwhile, the market power had also become more perva- sive. Corporation-led foundations became a major donor for NGOs. These foundations, together with the government sectors running "purchasing service" programs, introduced the mechanism of market competition to the NGO sphere. For the sake of survival, newly emerging NGOs usually packaged themselves as cooperative, professional organizations that were able to provide solutions to social problems, rather than agitational organizations actively engaging in social conflicts. Experiencing these transformations, the liberals' networks, as well as some of the networks representing disadvantaged groups, began to disaggregate.

However, in a situation in which the economic growth had slowed down, the authoritarian state was far from capable of resolving all social conflicts. Nor was it able to eliminate the formation of critical public opinions in a society where much of the population had already gained a considerable amount of autonomy in the market economic reform. Therefore, although the organizations and networks that had articulated an agenda were suppressed, the public expression of discontent had not ceased. On the internet, collective criticisms over issues like labor rights and women's rights now and then occurred. During these processes, new actors once again emerged. Illustratively embodying the ethos of the stage were the youth activists. Through formulating voluntary networks, intervening in hotspot events, and establishing social media on the internet, the youth activists sustained the space for alternative voices. In contrast to their predecessors, the youth activists did not show much interest in establishing formal organizations. Seeing NGOs as too conservative and insensitive to injustice, the youth activists usually only formed loosely organized, event-based concern groups. With the rise of these new actors, the interstitial publics became more decentered.

I call this new stage (2014–2019) the stage of fragmentation, because the formation of critical public opinions had been deprived of any relatively stable organizing structure. Lacking any long-term agenda, the employment of ideological discourses in social movement activism became highly fluid and contingent upon immediate situations. For example, by criticizing the state's failure in protecting women's rights, online feminist activism sometimes held a seemingly liberal stance. But on many other occasions, participants of the activism might also draw on Marxist or nationalist discourses. In newly emerging public discussions, the liberals as a group were marginalized or even stigmatized. Instead of trying to incorporate various kinds of social movement activism, as they had done in the 2000s, they became more defensive and inclined to fall back upon their own community. As most participants of public discussions no longer felt necessary to debate with the liberals on the idea of civil society, the project of building civil society was disintegrated and the spirit of the New Enlightenment Movement, which had not been eradicated by the failure of the 1989 student movement, eventually faded away.

The Organization of the Book

My writings on the historical transformation of China's public sphere follow a chronological order. The six empirical chapters are divided into two parts. Whereas the first three chapters discuss the interstitial emergence of the project of building civil society, the latter three discuss the project's contradicting institutionalization. Chapter one covers the revival stage (1992–2002). It describes how public life had gradually revived from the shadow of the repression of the 1989 student movement and how the idea of civil society had been introduced. Chapter two and chapter three cover the stage of counter hegemony (2003–2007). Chapter two discusses the expansion of the liberals' networks during the first few years of the Hu-Wen regime. Chapter three demonstrates how the liberals had projected their imagination of politics onto people in wider society and discusses the multiple, contradicting consequences of the Weiquan Movement.

Chapter four and chapter five cover the stage of internal contestation (2008–2013). Chapter four discusses the emergence of new actors and the structural transformation of the interstitial publics during the second half of the Hu-Wen regime. Chapter five documents the contestations between the liberals and three social movements representing subaltern interests, namely the New Rural Reconstruction Movement, the labor activism, and the feminist activism. It compares the three movements in terms of their relations formed with the liberals during the contestations. Chapter six covers the stage of fragmentation (2014–2019). It describes the marginalization of the liberals and the rise of new forms of activism.

In the concluding chapter, I summarize my empirical findings and discuss the implications of the book. With respect to the studies on the public sphere, I suggest that the concept of interstitial space provides a more flexible tool for exploring how alternative and critical public opinions could emerge. With respect to the future of the project of building civil society, I point out that, as the state power vastly expands in the COVID pandemic, the liberal interpretation of civil society is still relevant to critical public discussions in China today—if not more relevant. Nevertheless, the liberals nowadays must recognize that their criticism over politics is only one of the many criticisms available in the public sphere and that they must communicate with actors in other resistance activisms from scratch to forge new alliances. Finally, I talk about the implication of my study for understanding dynamics in an ideational movement. I contend that launching an idea-based solidarity movement involves unavoidable paradox; to transcend the paradox and construct an emancipatory political project at a more substantive level, such a movement needs to be open to various public debates that question and challenge any stabilized association between idea and interest.

PART ONE

The Interstitial Emergence of Civil Society as an Ideational Movement

CHAPTER 1

The Gradual Revival of Public Life, 1992–2002

With the death of Mao Zedong in 1976, discontent with China's socialist practices and the communist rule began to rise. In the late 1970s, drawing on Marxist concepts like alienation, ideologists and officials working within the communist party criticized the dehumanizing political practices during the Cultural Revolution and advocated to build a more humanitarian socialism.[1] Writers published realistic novels that portrayed the sufferings of intellectuals during the rule of the Gang of Four.[2] At the popular level, people posted "big character posters" (*dazi bao*) on a brick wall on Xidan Street in Beijing and demanded democracy.[3]

During the 1980s, as the market economic reform was deepened, fissures between high-level state leaders began to emerge. To legitimize their political stance, many state leaders chose to ally with actors outside the state. With a series of political reforms that aimed to separate the communist party from administrative authorities, leaders in many state-run institutes, such as universities, newspapers, and publishing companies, obtained a considerable degree of autonomy. The incipient market economy in urban regions also provided people with alternative resources. These conditions facilitated the rise of various cultural and intellectual activisms. In newly emerging channels, such as salons and independent publishing, scholars, journalists, poets, and novelists exposed social problems, criticized China's traditional culture, and advocated for further political and economic reform.[4] These activisms were later referred to as the New Enlightenment Movement. They eventually led to the rise of the 1989 Student Movement. However, with the state's military crackdown, the student movement ended up in catastrophe. Within the first few years after the failure of the movement, all the cultural and intellectual activisms rising in the '80s went into abeyance.

This chapter documents how, after the tragic ending of the student movement, public life in China revived in the 1990s. My documentation has two major themes. First, I want to discuss how the idea of civil society had been introduced to Chinese audiences in the 1990s. To describe this process, I introduce a specific sphere that played a crucial role in promoting critical public discussions in China's history—the "thought sphere." The "thought sphere" was a sphere in which intellectuals of different kinds openly discussed theoretical and ideological questions to express their criticism over China's reform. I suggest that, while emerging in the 1980s, the "thought sphere" had been able to survive the suppressive environment after the student movement and thrive in the 1990s. Second, I want to explain how the idea of civil society had been closely associated with the liberals. Around the turn of the century, there rose two opposing intellectual camps in China's "thought sphere," which were the liberals and the new left. I contend that, the association between the liberals and the idea of civil society was not inevitable. Rather, it was through a series of debates between the two camps that building civil society gradually became the liberals' political project.

The content of this chapter is arranged in the following way. In the first section, I discuss the social and political background after 1992. Then I introduce the condition of the "thought sphere" in the 1990s. Because the "thought sphere" had been formed during the 1980s, I have to go backward a little bit in this section and introduce some forms of intellectual activism that took place in the '80s. Then in discussing the "thought sphere" in the '90s, I emphasize the emergence of various independent journals run by scholars. I also review the intellectual debate happening at the turn of the century that had divided China's "thought sphere" into two opposing camps—the liberals and the new left. Next, I offer a detailed analysis of how the idea of civil society was introduced. After that, I discuss how, during a series of intellectual debates, the idea gradually became associated with the liberals. Before the concluding section, I briefly discuss the circulation of the idea of civil society among NGO activists in China in the 1990s.

The Social and Political Background after 1992

As the student movement ended in catastrophe on June 4, 1989, intellectuals who had been proactive in the 1980s went into a panic. These intellectuals, together with many ordinary Chinese people, feared that the failure of the student movement would bring China back to Mao's time. Within the first few months after the military crackdown at the Tiananmen Square, intellectual friends in Beijing did not even visit each other. Most of the intellectual activisms in the 1980s thus went into abeyance.

The public doubts were not dispelled until 1992, when China's retired paramount leader, Deng Xiaoping, took a southern tour and reaffirmed that the market economic reform would continue. After 1992, the privatization of the economy began to accelerate. During the term of Jiang Zemin (1993–2003) and Zhu Rongji (1998–2003), tariffs and trade barriers were reduced, state monopolies in many industries were removed, the banking system was reformed, and much of the social welfare system established during the socialist era was dismantled. These policies yielded robust economic growth and the prosperity of urban coastal regions. In big cities, consumerist culture became prominent. With the development of the entertainment industry, more people began to turn to films and popular music to learn Western culture. In response to these transformations, many intellectuals in China redirected their energy and enthusiasm to commercial or business activities.[5]

In contrast to the economic reform, the political reform was halted. To legitimize the economic reform, Deng Xiaoping said, "I don't care if the cat is black or white so long as it catches rat."[6] While this pragmatic attitude had saved the reform from the lengthy ideological debate on whether a market economy was essentially capitalist, it had nonetheless also suppressed the space for public discussions on some fundamental political issues of the regime. In the 1990s, political activism like the organization of the Democracy Party of China was suppressed.[7] To control social movement activism, the Chinese state also began to adopt more refined strategies. Criticism on specific social problems was tolerated. More repressive measures like detainment were employed only when critics challenged the leadership of the communist party.[8] On the other hand, as the state power became decentralized in the reform, most social movement activisms that proposed concrete social and economic demands began to target local state agencies.[9] As a result, it became increasingly difficult for intellectuals to build high public profiles and initiate social movement with national influence.

However, despite the stagnation of the political reform, in the 1990s, the Chinese state's control over the press, news reports, and the citizens' associational life was still rather porous, compared with the situation today. Several factors had played a role here. The first factor was the pressure from the international community.[10] In the early 1990s, while China was eager to participate in global trade to boost its economy, the reputation of its government in the international community had dropped to the lowest point due to the crackdown on the student movement. To redeem its reputation, the state released quite a few political dissidents. To show its openness toward political and cultural activism, Beijing even held the 4th World Women Conference, in which thousands of feminist movement activists from all over the world were invited.[11]

Second, during the Jiang-Zhu regime, the Chinese state was influenced by the neoliberal idea that excessive government intervention was problematic. Some government departments, such as the Ministry of Civil Affairs, even proactively advocated that it was good to have "small government and big society" (*xiao zhengfu da shehui*).[12] Although it was mainly government intervention in the market that the neoliberal idea opposed, the idea had nonetheless legitimized the growth of some non-market forces, such as charity organizations and community organizations.[13] Practically, because of the welfare spending cut, some government departments, especially those at the local level, did begin to look to non-governmental forces for delivering services to the people. I will elaborate this point in chapter two, when I discuss the formation of the NGO sphere.

Finally, with respect to the understanding of China's reform, divergencies still widely existed among different state sectors. Under the pressure of the uprising of the student movement, state leaders in China largely reached consensus on some principal issues, such as the necessity to defend the rule of the communist party.[14] However, when it came to some more detailed concerns, such as "how privatization of state-owned enterprises should proceed," or even "what kind of role the state-sponsored institutes should perform in protecting rights," state actors in different sectors usually had rather diverse thinking. This left opportunities for actors outside the state system. Together, these factors created the condition in which various forms of public life could revive.

The Revival of the "Thought Sphere" in the 1990s

The Origin of a "Thought Sphere"

In the 1990s, cultural and political activism promoting the formation of critical public opinions were many and various. Many studies on this era have analyzed activities like the production of critical news.[15] I will talk about these activities in the following chapters. But in this chapter, I leave these activities aside and focus on intellectual activism in the "thought sphere." This is because the "thought sphere" was rather important to civil society as an ideational movement in China—it was where the idea of civil society was introduced to a Chinese audience.

The term "thought sphere" has come from students of intellectual history in China, such as Xu Jilin and Wang Hui.[16] These students have sometimes also called the sphere a "public thought sphere" (*gonggong sixiang jie*). I adopt their terms, instead of using some more general terms like the public intellectual sphere, because I believe that the terms better capture the essence of the specific intellectual activism in China before 2000. In Chinese, the word "thought" (*sixiang*) is often used to denote abstract, comprehensive, and sophisticated thinking, or the product of such thinking. In many contexts, it is also regarded as the antithesis of specialized and technical knowledge. In the "thought sphere," participants talked about social, political, or even philosophical theories to express critical opinions. Many of their discussions appeared to be scholarly debates at first sight, as they were flooded with abstract concepts and jargon. But these discussions did face the public and involve strong real-world concerns.

The formation of China's "thought sphere" dates to the 1980s.[17] Major participants of the "thought sphere" were various kinds of intellectuals, or more precisely, scholars, writers, editors, and journalists working at state-run institutes. As the political atmosphere became relatively open after the end of the Cultural Revolution, these intellectuals began to introduce theories from the West and criticized China's politics and culture. In the '80s, these intellectuals made public interventions mainly through translating and openly discussing Western scholarly works, organizing public lectures and salons, and issuing documentary films. The activisms of the "thought sphere" were a major constituent of the New Enlightenment Movement.

Back in the '80s, the intellectuals' understanding of China's problems and the solutions they proposed were both holistic. It was widely believed that, whereas the West, featuring market economy, democratic politics, and the protection of individual liberty, represented a more "advanced" society, China, lacking these things, was "backward."[18] These intellectuals also attributed China's failure in modernization to its traditional culture and advocated that the only way for China to return to the international community and achieve prosperity was to embrace the West.[19] Many debates on Western theories had been subordinated to this mentality. The discussion of Jean-Paul Sartre and Friedrich Nietzsche was a case in point. Sartre and Nietzsche were the two most frequently cited Western philosophers in China in the '80s. In introducing their theories, the intellectuals in the "thought sphere" had often described them as advocates of individualism and opponents of autocracy. They emphasized that Sartre's and Nietzsche's theories embodied the spirit of Western modernity, while these two figures' criticism over Western societies were simply ignored.[20]

Many studies on the intellectual activism in the 1980s criticized intellectuals' superficial understandings of both Western theories and China's political reality.[21] It was argued that these superficial understandings had to do with the Chinese state's long-term ideological control. In Chinese universities, since 1952, disciplines that were highly relevant to the understanding of politics and society, such as political science and sociology, were labeled "pseudo-sciences" of the bourgeoisie and abolished by the state. In other social science disciplines like economics, scholars were only allowed to study and teach Marxist theories.[22] Although the state's ideological control had been destabilized in the 1980s, the whole intellectual community at that time was ill-equipped for analyzing both the West and China's social and economic problems.

Nevertheless, for most audiences of public discussion in China at that time, the articulation of the intellectuals in the "thought sphere" was inspiring. Before the 1980s, Chinese society had been cut off from the West and suffered intellectual starvation for decades. As the opening-up started, Chinese people were enthusiastic about any cultural and intellectual products that could familiarize them with things happening in the West. Therefore, the activism of the "thought sphere" achieved wide, national influence, especially among the youth. The success of the *Toward the Future* (Zouxiang Weilai) series served as an illustrative example here. The *Toward the Future* series was produced by a group of scholars who then served at the Chinese Academy of Sciences. Before it was banned by the government in 1989, the series in all published 76 books. Most of these books were translations of social science works from the West. Between 1984 and 1988, the series sold more than eighteen million copies. Its readers included even high school students and workers in factories.[23] At the height of their splendor, intellectuals in the "thought sphere" regarded themselves as the "enlighteners" (*qimeng-zhe*). Influential figures among them, such as Jin Guantao, Fang Lizhi, and Li Zehou, were entitled the "mentors of the youth" (*qingnian daoshi*).[24]

The Transformation and Continuity of the "Thought Sphere" in the 1990s

Because of the failure of the student movement, most intellectuals became more low profile in making public interventions during the first few years after 1989. Nobody dared to call himself or herself an "enlightener." A common practice in the 1990s was to run academic journals. Before the 1990s, there were very few professional academic journals in China, especially in humanities and social sciences. Major outlets for scholars' articles were comprehensive journals, newspapers, and magazines, which were usually under direct control of the state's propagandist departments. The practice of peer review barely existed. Through establishing professional academic journals run by scholars, the intellectuals hoped that they could carve out a space for independent voice.

The rise of the scholar-run journals was a typical interstitial emergence. While a bourgeoning publishing market in the 1990s and the intervention of international foundations had provided these journals with financial resources,[25] many of these journals had also been to different degrees embedded in the state. With respect to their origins, these journals can roughly be categorized into four groups. The first group were journals published outside China's censorship system. Typical examples in this group were *The Twenty-first Century* (Ershiyi Shiji), the *China Social Sciences Quarterly* (Zhongguo Shehui Kexue Jikan), and the *China Book Review* (Zhongguo Shuping). All three were produced in Hong Kong.

The second group of journals were those that were produced by organs within the political system of the state. Typical examples were the *Orient* (Dongfang) and *Strategy and Management* (Zhanlue yu Guanli). These two journals were produced by the China Association of Oriental Cultural Studies and the China Institute of Strategy and Management, respectively. Both organizations were founded by high-level state leaders in the 1980s.[26] The state organs involved in the production of the journals were usually associated with the political factions in the communist party that advocated further reform. Yet they tended to grant the editorial board a large degree of autonomy in the selection of topic and editing. Because of their high embeddedness in the state, these journals usually had publishing licenses. On some occasions, journals in this group received financial support from international donors. For example, the *Orient* had received financial support from the Henry Fok Ying-tung Foundation in Hong Kong.[27]

The third group of journals were produced by scholars whose connection with the state was relatively loose. Because of these scholars' low embeddedness in the state, it was difficult for them to obtain the publishing license. They hence employed a strategy called "publishing journals as books" (*yishu daikan*). This strategy had worked well in the 1990s, because at that time the censorship of books was much more lenient than that of journals.[28] Instances in this category included the *Scholars* (Xueren) and *Res Publica* (Gonggong Luncong). Both were published at state-endorsed publishing companies. Some of the journals in this group had also received financial support from international donors. For example, the *Scholars* had received funds from a Japanese organization called the Foundation for International Friendship and Academic Studies.[29]

Lastly, there were "old" magazines being transformed by "new" editors. Typical examples were the *Reading* (Dushu) and the *Skyline* (Tianya). Both journals were established in the late 1970s, focusing on literary criticism. Under the editorship of Wang Hui and Han Shaogong, respectively, both had been converted into journals for debating political theories in the mid-1990s.

On these academic journals, intellectuals reflected upon the activism in the 1980s. In the first few years after 1989, scholars like Wang Hui and Chen Pingyuan began to criticize the New Enlightenment Movement. They suggested that the interpretation of both Chinese tradition and Western theories by the "enlighteners" was oversimplified.[30] The critics also pointed out that, because the "enlighteners" had often been too hasty to make use of academic studies to substantiate their political views, their arguments tended to be "frivolous," "empty," and "of poor quality."[31] Based on these criticisms, some intellectuals began to advocate "academia for academia's sake." Around the mid-1990s, a campaign for promoting the "professional standards" (*xueshu guifan*) of academic study in China was launched. Humanity and social science scholars began to discuss issues like how to properly cite other people's work and whether the introduction of a peer review system would promote the quality of academic study.[32]

Nevertheless, it would be wrong to assume that the intellectual activism in the 1990s had been cut off from that in the 1980s and that intellectuals in China had thereupon become professional academics focusing on specialized research subjects. The contrary was true—continuities widely existed between the '90s and '80s. First, many founders and editors of the abovementioned journals had been involved in the cultural and intellectual activism in the 1980s. For example, the founders of *The Twenty-first Century*, Jin Guantao and Liu Qingfeng, were also the chief editors of the *Toward the Future* book series. Deng Zhenglai, the founder of the *China Social Sciences Quarterly* and the *China Book Review*, had participated in editing *The Twentieth Century Library* (Ershi Shiji Wenku), a book series produced by "Culture: China and the World," a prominent intellectual group in the 1980s. Zhong Peizhang, the chief editor of the *Orient*, had played important roles in connecting the editors of *Toward the Future* and some reformist state leaders before 1989.[33] One of the executive editors of the *Orient*, Liang Xiaoyan, was also an executive editor of *Toward the Future*.

Second, the boundary between the academic journals and the wider public was still rather ambiguous. As I will elaborate in the following sections, while most authors of the journals were scholars holding positions in state-sponsored universities and research institutes, there were still some authors who were independent scholars and some of these independent scholars even played leading roles in organizing various intellectual debates. The major audience of these journals had not been limited to professional scholars either. For example, in the 1990s, many high school students who were interested in politics were keen readers of the *Reading* and the *Skyline*.[34] Considering these factors, it is not difficult to understand that, around the mid-1990s, when many social problems caused by the economic reform emerged, these academic journals were quickly involved in various political debates.

The Disintegration of the New Enlightenment Movement

As I have mentioned above, under the influence of the modernization theory, intellectuals in the "thought sphere" in the 1980s believed that China should embrace culture and political institutions of the West. In the 1990s, the Chinese intellectuals' communication with the international academic community increased. Scholars who had received training in Western countries or had lived abroad began to join the intellectual debate. Compared to their predecessors, these scholars tended to have more complex understandings of the so-called Western society. Moreover, with the deepening of the economic reform, new social problems, such as unemployment brought by the privatization of state-owned enterprises, began to emerge around the mid-1990s. Suspicions over the teleological narrative of the modernization theory thus arose. Through a couple of debates, intellectuals as participants of the "thought sphere" were divided into two camps, the liberals and the new left (for a summary of representative figures and political views of the two camps, see Table 2).[35]

Table 2. The Debate between the Liberals and the New Left

	The Liberals	The New Left
Representative figures	Zhang Shuguang, Fan Gang, Li Shenzhi, Zhu Xueqin, Xu Youyu, Liu Junning, Xu Jilin, Ji Weidong, Qin Hui	Wang Shaoguang, Cui Zhiyuan, Gan Yang, Wang Hui, Han Yuhai, Chen Yangu, Kuang Xinnian, Wang Binbin
Views on the fundamental problems	Authoritarian state and its monopoly of market and society	China's participation in neoliberal globalization and capitalist market economy
Views on the economic reform	Privatization and the market economy are the foundation for liberty; state monopoly should be further reduced	Privatization and the market economy exploit the disadvantaged; state capacity should be strengthened to reduce inequality
Views on the goal for a political reform	Constitutional democracy that protects people's civil and political rights; rule of law	A strong nation-state that can protect people's social rights in neoliberal globalization; popular democracy
Views on China's socialist past	China's socialist practices were a total failure	China's socialist practices built the foundation for the later economic take-off
Views on modernity and modernization	Modernity is singular; the western approach of modernization is universal	Modernity has plural forms; the western approach of modernization contains contradictions and can be transcended
Theoretical origins	Classical liberalism, social liberalism	Marxism, Maoism, post-colonialism

Putting sophisticated political views into boxes risks oversimplification. This is also true for a summary of the political views of the liberals and the new left in China. But the bifurcation between the two camps was real and deep, as intellectuals in the two camps had completely different diagnoses of fundamental problems facing China at the turn of the millennium. The new leftist scholars contended that, as Chinese society became increasingly embedded in neoliberal globalization, the capitalist market economy had become a new source for producing alienation, injustice, and power inequality.[36] The liberals, on the other hand, disagreed with the new left on its judgement that a capitalist market economy had already taken root in Chinese society. In their opinion, the problem facing China in the 1990s was not quite different from that in the 1980s, which was the state monopoly of market and society.[37] With respect to the issue of injustice and inequality, some liberals pointed to the existence of oligopoly in privatization. They argued that it was the absence of bottom-up participation that had led to the maldistribution of wealth during privatization; because what had prevented people from participation was obviously the bureaucratic state, the greatest source for producing power inequality in China was still the state, rather than the market.[38]

Based on the different diagnoses of fundamental problems, the two camps elucidated contrasting opinions on China's transition from socialism to a market economy. The liberals saw China's socialist practices as a total failure. They criticized the planned economy as inefficient and political movements like the Cultural Revolution as terrifying and dehumanizing.[39] They were generally positive with the state's decision to implement a market economic reform, but nonetheless regarded the liberalization and privatization of the economy as being incomplete.[40] With regards to the goal for a political reform, they advocated the adoption of constitutional democracy and rule of law to counterbalance the overarching state power.[41] The new left, on the other hand, had a more complex feeling with China's socialist past. Some of them argued that it was during the socialist era that China laid a solid foundation for industrialization, without which the later economic takeoff was unlikely to happen.[42] Some praised socialism for delivering basic education and medical care programs in rural areas and lamented the decline of these programs during the market economic reform.[43] Accordingly, the new left advocated the strengthening of state capacity to reduce inequality and protect citizens' social rights.[44] With regards to the goal for a political reform, new leftist scholars saw constitutional democracy and rule of law as serving the bourgeois interest.[45] Drawing on some of Mao's political thinking, they advocated a popular democracy (*da minzhu*) that granted people substantive opportunities for participation.[46]

Behind these controversies were scholars' contrasting attitude toward the New Enlightenment Movement in the 1980s, or more precisely, their diverse understanding of the concepts of modernity and modernization. Whereas the new leftist scholars were suspicious of the agenda proposed by the "enlighteners," the liberals believed that the spirit of the New Enlightenment Movement was still valuable. Being influenced by various kinds of critical and post-modernist theories, the new left was highly critical of the Western approach of modernization. They associated the modernization process in the West with colonialist expansion and the exploitation of many disadvantaged groups and argued that the Western approach should be transcended.[47] Moreover, many of them hoped China would find an alternative approach.[48]

The liberals acknowledged the many contradictions inherent to the modernization process in the West. Nevertheless, they emphasized that, through the expansion of democracy and citizenship rights, many dehumanizing practices that used to be prevalent in Western societies had been mitigated; this illustrated that modernity in the West contained the possibility of self-correction.[49] Hence, the liberals suggested that China should not rashly deny the many Western institutions that had already been proved to be effective in advancing humanity, such as constitutional democracy and rule of law.[50]

The feud between the liberals and the new left lasted for several years. In the late 1990s, it extended to some commercially-oriented publications and achieved profound influence in the wider public. While many audiences of the debate might not be able to fully understand the details of all the theories the intellectuals had discussed, they became interested in the different labels of political and ideological stance. Please notice that, because of the practice of socialism in history, the coordinate of ideological stances in China were, overall, more "leftist" than that in many Western countries, such as the United States of America. In the United States, someone who supports the increase in welfare spending—even if he or she recognizes the value of market economy and identifies with the protection of private property—is likely to be labeled as being on the left. But in the ideological debate in China's "thought sphere" in the 1990s, such a person was more likely to be categorized as a liberal. Back then, those who supported classical liberalism and those who supported social liberalism were both categorized as the liberals, which was believed to be on the right.[51]

By bringing in more perspectives and information for thinking about China's reform, the debate between the liberals and the new left pluralized the public sphere. But looking back, we may discover that many of the discussions, such as the debate on whether the state or the market was the fundamental factor for producing inequality and alienation, lacked sophistication. Current research on late development countries has repeatedly informed us that the state/market debate is not an either-or issue, as in practice the state power and the market power often interplay.[52] Therefore, what truly matters here are how the two forms of power interplay and how the interaction between the two forms of power has led to diverse outcomes in different contexts. However, like their counterparts in the 1980s, intellectuals in the debate in the 1990s talked about the state and the market as if they were unitary institutions having holistic influence over social life. The ideological debate seldom went into empirical details.[53] This vividly illustrated that the "thought sphere" in the 1990s, though being flooded with new issues and theories, still bore the imprint of the 1980s.

The Introduction of the Idea of Civil Society

The Initial Discussion of the Idea of Civil Society

The discussion of the idea of civil society was initiated in the early 1990s.[54] The critical figure who had initiated the discussion was the late social science scholar, Deng Zhenglai. Deng was born in Shanghai in 1956 and moved to Sichuan with his parents in the 1960s during the Third Front Movement.[55] In the 1970s, he worked as an apprentice in a medical apparatus plant. It was after the Cultural Revolution that he went back to school and obtained his degrees, first a BA degree in English literature, and then an MA degree in international law. From Deng's career path as a scholar, we can see that the intellectual community in China in the 1990s was still relatively open and lacked established rules. In 1985, after graduating from China Foreign Affairs University, Deng made the decision to work as an independent scholar. He then earned a living by translating Western scholarly works. As I have mentioned in a previous section, Deng had been actively involved in the cultural and intellectual activism in the 1980s; after the 1989 Student Movement, he founded two journals, the *China Social Sciences Quarterly* and the *China Book Review*. Throughout the 1990s, although Deng had not been employed by any universities and research institutes, he had remained to be one of the scholars who had the highest citation rate in law and political science.[56] When he died in 2013, commentaries suggested that he was "the organizer of many important scholarly debates" in China.[57]

In 1992, Deng and his coauthor, Jing Yuejin, who was then a political scientist working at the Renmin University of China, published an article called "Constructing China's Civil Society" (*Jiangou Zhongguo de Shimin Shehui*) in the opening issue of the *China Social Sciences Quarterly*. The article associated the idea of civil society with modernization.[58] In the beginning of the article, Deng and Jing described the modernization process in China since the Opium War (1840) as having been repeatedly disrupted by two forms of "extreme condition." According to Deng and Jing, a legitimation crisis often occurred in China when a political reform was introduced, causing anomie, social disorder, or even the disintegration of the nation. To cope with the disorder and the legitimation crisis, the political structure then turned to traditional culture and military power, which resulted in the formation of a highly centralized, totalitarian state. The two authors hence argued that the most critical task in China's modernization was to construct a "beneficial" (*liangxing*) interactive relation between state and society.[59]

After setting up the problem, the idea of civil society was proposed as the solution. Deng and Jing defined civil society as an "independent," "self-organizing" space that was based on "contractual relations" among citizens. With respect to the balance of state-society relations, civil society had a two-way function. On the one hand, by practicing self-organization, civil society could defend citizens from the overexpansion of the state. On the other hand, because civil society was "apolitical" (*fei zhengzhihua*), it could also provide citizens with some basic order when a political reform aroused turbulence in the state.[60]

Deng and Jing shared with the intellectuals in the 1980s the concern about China's modernization. In this sense, the initiators of the discussion of civil society were children of the 1980s. However, the discussion also greatly diverged from many prominent social thoughts in the '80s. Although eventually evolving into a populist movement, cultural and intellectual activism in the '80s usually bore a layer of elitism. Intellectuals in the New Enlightenment Movement tended to see common people as being conservative and ignorant—that was why they had called themselves the "enlighteners." In 1989, right before the uprising of the Tiananmen protest, some of the "enlighteners" were still caught up by the discussion of "new authoritarianism," which advocated the return of a strong authoritarian state having the capacity to promote privatization and the economic reform.[61] In contrast, Deng and Jing's discussion of civil society gave much attention to the non-state, bottom-up, "grassroots," and "plebeian" forces, such as the peasants who had proactively promoted the land de-collectivization in Anhui Province and the spontaneously emerging small business owners in Zhejiang Province.[62] In my opinion, this conversion was critical to the vitality of the idea of civil society in the following two decades.

Back to the article published in 1992, the two authors' description of the process of building civil society in China was still quite broad-brush. It was argued that the process mainly had two steps.[63] The first step was the development of a market economy, which could eventually carve out an independent space in the private, or the economic sphere. In the second step, the independent space extended to the public sphere, providing citizens with channels for participating in politics and influencing state policies. Deng and Jing had not explained what kind of independent space could be carved out with the development of a market economy. Nor had they explained how it was possible to move from step one to step two. But the ideas in the article were fresh enough to arouse controversies.

The Controversies over the Idea of Civil Society

The first round of debate on civil society centered on whether it was possible to build a civil society in China. Critics argued that civil society was a Western concept, and that China lacked the tradition of self-organization.[64] In response, to illustrate that the penetration of state power in society had never been total, defenders of the concept published scholarly works that explored the survival of autonomous public life in China's history.[65] The second round of debate regarded civil society as a normative ideal. The focus of the debate was whether such an ideal was desirable for Chinese society. This round of debate was more intense. After this round of debate, the idea of civil society began to be associated with the liberals.

How the association between the liberals and the idea of civil society had been formed is worth being discussed here. A common narrative, which had been widely circulated among the liberals, was that new leftist scholars were agents of the authoritarian state—the new leftists did not support civil society, because they wanted to defend the authoritarian regime. In my opinion, this was not a solid explanation. First, both camps had many scholars working in state-run institutes. As I will elaborate in detail in the next chapter, the relations between the liberals and the state were also complex. Second, while it was true that several new leftist scholars later turned to statism, this happened in the late 2000s.[66] In the 1990s, many of them were still highly critical of the state's neoliberal policies. In the following paragraphs, I intend to offer a more balanced review of the debating process.

The first intellectual group enthusiastically applauding the idea of civil society in China were scholars who advocated further liberalization and privatization of the economy. Representative figures included Zhang Shuguang, Liu Junning and Wang Dingding. These scholars, most of whom were economists, equated civil society with the market, or more precisely, a sphere in which egoistic individuals engaged in entrepreneurial activities.[67] The theoretical foundation for their support of the idea of civil society was classical liberalism, which argued that market economies were a spontaneous order and that individuals acting in their own self-interests could unintendedly bring about public good and greater social benefits. On the left side, scholars retorted. Drawing on the theories of Polanyi and Marx, new leftist scholars like Wang Hui and Wang Shaoguang argued that the so-called spontaneously emerging market was formed by state interventions[68] and that the self-organization space supported by market economies only benefited the bourgeoisie.[69]

In the late 1990s, the liberals who leaned toward social liberalism, notably Xu Jilin, joined the debate. Xu and a few other scholars introduced civil society theories proposed by post-Marxist scholars, notably Jürgen Habermas, Jean L. Cohen, and Andrew Arato.[70] Unlike the economists, Xu Jilin emphasized that civil society could not be reduced to the economic sphere in which people engaged in profit-seeking activities; instead, it should be seen as a third realm being outside the state and the market, consisting of citizens' voluntary associations, social movements, and other institutions for public communication.[71] Had the new left taken these new interpretations seriously, the idea of civil society might have become a common ground for the two camps. But in fact, these new interpretations received almost no response. This was certainly not because new leftist scholars were unfamiliar with the theories discussed by the social liberals. The contrary was true. New leftist scholars like Wang Hui and Chen Yangu had also paid much attention to Habermas and his theory of the public sphere. However, in their discussion of Habermas, emphasis went to Habermas's criticism on how capitalist market economy had colonized people's public life, while Habermas's commentary on civil society of the public sphere was largely ignored.[72]

In my opinion, the major divergency between the social liberals and the new left lay in their interpretation of the various newly emerging channels for public communication in the 1990s. The channels included some of the TV programs that exposed social problems and internationally assisted NGOs. The social liberals were generally positive toward these new channels, since they believed that these channels had expanded the space for articulating alternative public opinions. The new leftist scholars, on the other hand, held a more critical attitude. For example, when talking about the TV programs that exposed social problems (e.g., corruption at the local level), Wang Hui emphasized that these programs had not emerged out of a space that was independent of the state; rather, they had been initiated by political forces within the state; the state had tolerated, or even encouraged, these programs, because they were in accord with the political interest of the state.[73] With respect to the NGO activism, Wang Hui suggested that NGOs were not independent either, because they were usually financially supported by international foundations.[74] Wang Shaoguang, on the other hand, highlighted that these new channels had not provided citizens with equal opportunities for participation.[75]

If we scrutinize the criticisms offered by the new left, we may discover that some of their arguments were actually well grounded. At the empirical level, many of the new leftist criticisms had not been quite different from those sociological studies on civil society in the English-speaking academic community that argued that the really existing civil society organizations often lack independence, reproduce inequalities, and cannot withstand neoliberalism.[76] But still, the approach for criticism adopted by the new leftist scholars had diverged from that of many empirical studies in the English-speaking academic community. On most occasions, sociologists' criticism over civil society is a kind of immanent critique.[77] By immanent critique, I refer to a way of criticism that sees the normative ideal inherent to certain concepts as intrinsically valuable. To be more specific, many sociological studies on civil society have taken the normative ideals inherent to the idea of civil society, such as solidarity, self-organization, and voluntariness, as intrinsically valuable. The content of the immanent critique is to point out how practices in the really existing civil society have diverged from the ideals. The underlying assumption of this kind of critique is that civil society activism is contingent and not unchangeable—through criticism and reflection, people can correct mistakes and build institutions and organizations that could one day push us closer to the ideal.

New leftist scholars' criticisms of civil society, on the other hand, were a kind of "unmasking" critique. By "unmasking" critique, I refer to a way of criticism that reduces the presentation of normative ideals to the manipulation of power and interest. In this case, the new left saw the idea of civil society as an ideology, whose formation and circulation in society should be reduced to the manipulation of the capitalist power. Hence, the content of their criticism was to point out how the manipulation had happened. For example, in his comment on those NGOs that provided legal aid service to rural migrant workers, Wang Hui said that these organizations had only paid attention to individual rights; because these organizations were not able to promote working class solidarity, workers' "subjectivity" (*zhutixing*) was still absent. According to Wang Hui, this illustrated that NGOs were "in the last instance" "neoliberal."[78] Wang Shaoguang went one step further. In an article that discussed the idea of civil society, he blatantly argued that "civil society is nothing but a myth fabricated by neoliberalism."[79] It was new leftist scholars' particular way of criticism that had determined that they could only fully negate the concept, rather than transform civil society activism from within.

However, in the end, the new leftist scholars were not able to articulate how people's "subjectivity" could be saved in an environment that, in their opinions, were penetrated by the neoliberal logic. In the article that criticized civil society as the "myth" of neoliberalism, Wang Shaoguang proposed that, Chinese people should build a "people's society" (renmin shehui), which was supposed to be more inclusive and equal.[80] But he had not explained how a "people's society" could be organized. With respect to the institutional basis of the "people's society," he mentioned institutions of China's authoritarian socialist system, such as the people's congress and the "mass organizations," without recognizing a simple fact—it was just because these institutions had often failed to provide citizens with channels for participation that people began to search for alternative channels. Commenting on new leftists' distaste of the idea of civil society, the social liberal scholar, Xu Jilin, argued that the new left had repudiated the idea of civil society, because they had turned to statism.[81] In my opinion, the reverse argument also works—because the new leftist scholars could not see hope in the incipient social movement activisms that were weak, flawed, but concrete, they eventually turned to a grander and more abstract political power, which was the authoritarian state.

All in all, in the early 2000s, at the end of the debate between the liberals and the new left, both camps agreed that civil society was a political project exclusively "owned" by the liberals.[82] It was not until the late 2000s that the association between the liberals and the idea of civil society was destabilized.

Civil Society as an Incipient Ideational Movement

From the above descriptions, readers may get the impression that the discussion of civil society in China in the 1990s was mainly theoretical and abstract. While this impression was largely true, I would like to emphasize that, even in the '90s, the influence of the idea of civil society went beyond the scholarly debate. Outside the "thought sphere," the idea had been well received among many activists who had been involved in the 1989 Student Movement.

For those who had experienced the protest at the Tiananmen Square, a question haunting them in the first few years after 1989 was, why had the movement, being attended by students who sincerely loved the country and hoped to bring democracy and prosperity to the country, ended up in bloodshed and violence? The idea of civil society offered them a soothing answer. After reading Deng and Jing's article that emphasized civil society's function in promoting "beneficial" state-society relations, many of these activists came to such a conclusion—the student movement had failed to bring democracy to China, because civil society was underdeveloped in the country in the 1980s. When talking about their experience in the 1980s, many of my interviewees mentioned that the student movement had been poorly organized. They also suggested that, had the movement been supported by strong organizations that knew how to unite people and negotiate with the state, the tragic ending might well have been avoided.[83]

The idea of civil society that activists liked had also been reinforced by a popular opinion at that time that attributed the democratic transition in eastern Europe to the existence of civil society.[84] For Chinese people who had experienced the 1989 Student Movement, the meaning of the transition of eastern Europe was not only that some countries that used to be under the communist rule became democracies, but also that the democratic transition in these countries was peaceful.[85] In the 1990s, the political writings of some dissident intellectuals in eastern Europe, notably Václav Havel, were translated into Chinese.[86] Havel, together with Adam Michnik, became the role models for those activists who still wanted to promote democratization in China. In private, these activists talked about the Solidarity Movement in Poland and the Velvet Revolution in Czechoslovakia and discussed how similar things could happen in China.

More importantly, the idea of civil society pointed to new directions for social action. When I did fieldwork in Guangzhou in 2013, I interviewed an activist who had participated in the student movement. The activist told me that, after seeing so much blood and sacrifice, he had been trapped in misery and desperation for a long time after 1989. During that period, he had no idea what he as an intellectual could do to promote political reforms in China. Eventually, it was Deng Zhenglai's article on civil society that had helped him resume the courage. When I asked him how that could be, he explained,

> I was attracted by Deng Zhenglai's argument on the "beneficial state-society interactions." In my opinion, what he tries to convey is that democratization does not necessarily start from confronting the state. Instead, it could start from building an independent space. In the space, you have people's self-

organization. You have voluntary associations and mutual-help networks. You have the public discussion that can teach people how to listen to others. . . . You have a lot of good things. These things may not necessarily lead China to democracy. But with these things, China would be better prepared for a democratic transition.[87]

For the children of 1989, especially those who were fluent in English and had connections with some government departments, one thing they could do to promote civil society in the 1990s was to work with international foundations and establish NGOs. To avoid confrontations, they usually chose those fields that were believed to be less politically sensitive at that time, such as environmental protection. Among the NGOs established in the 1990s, the most well-known one was the Friends of Nature (*Ziran zhi You*), an environmental NGO established in 1994. The founders of the organization were Liang Congjie, a professor of history and a member of the national committee of the People's Political Consultative Conference;[88] Liang Xiaoyan, a professor of world history; Yang Dongping, a professor of education; and Wang Lixiong, a novelist. Liang Xiaoyan and Wang Lixiong had both actively participated in the cultural and political activism in the 1980s.

Around 2000, activists' efforts achieved initial success. In the field of the environment, environmental NGOs like the Friends of Nature launched campaigns to fight unlawful hunting.[89] In the field of public health, the campaign for preventing AIDS mobilized participants from the wider society. With the help of local doctors and youth activists from universities, NGOs like Aizhi Action Project (*Aizhixing*) spotlighted the outbreak of HIV caused by a blood plasma factory in Henan Province and official attempts to cover up the story.[90] These achievements gave activists confidence. An activist who had attended the AIDS prevention campaign told me in an interview,

> Before the campaign, everybody was talking about civil society. But no one knew exactly what civil society looked like. Then, through independent research, voluntary activities organized by students, and hot online discussions on BBS, the scandal in Henan eventually came out and the government began to pay attention to these issues. For many of us, this was the process in which an abstract idea came down to the earth.[91]

Nevertheless, at this stage, the influence of the activists who believed in the idea of civil society was still weak. Social conflicts of different kinds were already rising at the turn of the millennium due to the implementation of economic reform policies. In China's northeastern regions, or the "rustbelt," state-owned enterprise workers protested the privatization that deprived them of their social compacts. In rural areas, corruption was rampant. Yet NGOs had seldom touched upon these issues. Even in the field of environmental protection, where NGOs were believed to play an important role in "exploring the boundaries of advocacy,"[92] the major focus of NGOs appeared to be on wild animals like antelopes and snub-nosed monkeys. In the 1980s and the 1990s, the rapid development of township and village enterprises caused hundreds and thousands of environmental pollution accidents every year. In rural areas, victims of these pollution accidents petitioned local governments. But only in rare instances did environmental NGOs intervene in these environmental justice movements.[93] It was not until the early 2000s that this situation began to change.

Conclusion

This chapter documents the revival of public life in China after the 1989 Student Movement, with a particular focus on the introduction of the idea of civil society and the controversies the idea aroused. I first introduce the cultural and intellectual activism in the 1980s. Next, I describe the political and social environment in the 1990s and argue that, despite the stagnation of political reform, state's control over society was still rather porous; this had created the condition in which certain forms of intellectual activism could revive. Then I discuss the condition of the "thought sphere" in the 1990s. I analyze the ideological debate between the liberals and the new left and contend that the major divergence between the two camps was in the intellectuals' diagnosis of the fundamental problem facing China in modernization. After that, I discuss how the idea of civil society had been introduced to the Chinese audience and how the idea had become the liberals' political project. By focusing on the specific approach the new leftist scholars employed in criticism, I also provide a detailed analysis on why the new left had withdrawn from the project of building civil society. At the end of this chapter, I describe some initial attempts at advocating the ideal of civil society in the wider public.

Many extant studies on the public sphere in the 1990s highlight how activisms in the 1990s had diverged from their counterparts in the 1980s. It is suggested that, since the Chinese state adopted more refined strategies for implementing control, activisms proposing radical agendas like regime change were gradually marginalized. The bourgeoning market economy and the rapid development of communication technologies provided citizens with new channels for participation. As a result, public discussion on more concrete issues arose and the space for articulating critical opinions became more pluralized.[94] I partially agree with these views. But in this chapter, I have mainly emphasized the continuity between the '80s and the '90s. First, by focusing on the "thought sphere," I highlight the commonalities between the intellectuals in the '80s and the '90s in their mode of public intervention—talking about political and social theories and offering comprehensive explanations of society. I also emphasize that it was in such public interventions that the idea of civil society was introduced to the Chinese audience. Second, I highlight that many advocates of civil society in China in the '90s had been involved in the activisms in the '80s and that these people's choice of the political ideal of civil society had to do with their reflection upon the '80s.

Hence, in my opinion, although the Chinese state's suppression of the 1989 uprising had halted the cultural and intellectual activisms of the New Enlightenment Movement in the 1980s, the movement had produced lasting influence. The specter of the movement had haunted China's public sphere throughout the 1990s and the 2000s, mainly through the activisms organized by the liberals. In the 2000s, alternative spheres for producing critical public opinions, notably the media sphere and the NGO sphere, became mature. In these new spheres, the liberals' influence continued to expand. This is what I am going to discuss in the following chapters.

CHAPTER 2

The Expansion of the Interstitial Publics, 2003–2007

As Hu Jintao and Wen Jiabao took over as China's president and premier in March 2003, the political environment in China changed. On the one hand, the new leaders proposed that the Chinese state's development goal had now shifted to building a "harmonious society," rather than simply boosting economic growth. This opened a space for discussing various social problems. On the other hand, the economic reform since 1992 had brought many social conflicts. In both urban and rural areas, popular protests triggered by issues like environmental pollution and corruption were rising. Thanks to the rapid development of internet technology, these contentious activities became more visible to the public. Because of these transformations, critical public discussions became increasingly vibrant. It was during this period that the liberals and their political agenda of building civil society achieved the widest influence in the public sphere. The dominance of the liberals would not be destabilized until the late 2000s.

In this chapter (chapter two) and the next chapter (chapter three), I will discuss the spread of the idea of civil society in the public sphere and its consequences. I suggest that, in the early 2000s, the "thought sphere" featuring open debates on political and social theories gradually declined due to state interventions in social science academic studies. Yet at the same time, other spaces for alternative public discussions, namely the media sphere and the NGO sphere, emerged interstitially from both within and outside the state. The development of these new spaces largely benefited the liberals. Among journalists making critical news reports, NGO practitioners, media-based public intellectuals, law scholars, and human rights lawyers, the liberals found new allies. I contend that what had brought these different actors together was exactly the idea of civil society, or an imagination of politics that was based upon the antithesis between state and society.

To advocate the political ideal of civil society, the liberals turned to various resistance activisms, such as environmental protests and homeowners' protests, and argued that these activisms signified the rise of a civil society in which citizens defended their individual rights vis-à-vis the authoritarian state. I argue that the liberals' intervention in the resistance activisms incurred multiple, contradicting consequences. On the one hand, the liberals' valorization of the fragmented resistance activisms had inspired many people to take actions to defend their own rights. In the name of building civil society, people formed working alliances, in which they thematized a variety of social issues and alarmed the state of the many problems arising during the economic reform. On the other hand, I point out that the liberals' interpretation of civil society had largely ignored power and subordinate institutions. As a result, the working alliances formed by the liberals often marginalized the concerns of disadvantaged groups and reproduced inequality. These alliances also tended to be fragile and lacked the capacity to withstand state intervention.

In this chapter, I focus on the structural transformation of the interstitial publics and the formation of a new liberal camp. In the next chapter, I turn to social movements and analyze how the liberals had incorporated various resistance activisms into their political agenda of building civil society. The rest of this chapter is arranged in the following way. In the next section, I introduce the political and social background in the mid-2000s. Then I discuss how the "thought sphere" had become marginalized. This is followed by a section that documents the rise of the media sphere and the NGO sphere. At the end of the chapter, I discuss how the structural transformation of the interstitial publics had influenced the ideological debate between the liberals and the new left and describe the formation of a new liberal camp.

The Political and Social Background Since 2003

For many Chinese people, it was through two critical events happening in the spring and summer of 2003 that they recognized that China's political atmosphere had been changed. The first event was the outbreak of severe acute respiratory syndrome, which was also known as SARS.[1] Cases of SARS began to rise in southern China as early as November 2002. However, due to obstructions to information flow within the government hierarchy and the fragmentation of China's public health system, no effective measures had been taken during the first few months of the epidemic. In the beginning, the Chinese government tried hard to downplay the threat of the disease. On the state-controlled media, very little information was given with respect to the contagiousness of the disease and the situation of the epidemic. The information blackout heightened anxieties, fear, and speculation. Eventually, it was the pressure from outspoken physicians within the country, the World Health Organization, and the Western media that had pushed the Chinese state to change its coping strategies. In April 2003, the Hu-Wen administration ousted government officials who had mismanaged the public health crisis, invested financial resources in medical care, and launched mass-based campaigns for preventing the spread of the disease. Besides these measures, the government also began to publicize and update the number of SARS cases in each province on a daily basis. These measures were widely praised among the public. With concerted efforts, the epidemic was finally under control in June.

The second event, which was even more dramatic, was the Sun Zhigang Incident.[2] The incident was closely related to an institution in China called "custody and repatriation" (*shourong qiansong*). The law of "custody and repatriation" required people who migrated across regions to obtain a "temporary living permit" (*zanzhu zheng*) from local police and authorized the police to detain those who failed to show the permit in inspections. Established during the socialist era, the institution was originally used to regulate vagabonds in cities. But as a large number of peasants moved to cities after the economic reform, it became an instrument for managing and controlling urban populations. Because of the lack of supervision, the enforcement of the law often involved corruption and human rights abuse.[3] In the early 2000s, discontent with the institution was already high among rural migrant workers and various kinds of scholars.

In the Sun Zhigang Incident in 2003, public anger toward the institution was finally ignited. Sun Zhigang was a clothing designer from Hubei Province, employed by a garment company in Guangzhou. On March 17, he was detained for not being able to show the "temporary living permit." Three days later, he died after being sent to hospital by the police. The *Southern Metropolis Daily* (Nanfang Dushi Bao), a newspaper based in Guangzhou, reported Sun's death and suggested that he had been ill-treated.[4] The tragic news evoked widespread compassion and anger. On the internet, people participated in the discussion of the incident and expressed criticism toward the laws that restricted individual freedom. On May 14, three law scholars,

Xu Zhiyong, Teng Biao, and Yu Jiang proposed a petition to the state council, in which they argued that the practice of "custody and repatriation" was
unconstitutional and called for the abolishment of the institution.[5] While
applauding the petition, the public doubted the possibility of the abolishment, as many government departments had a vested interest in maintaining
the institution. Then, to many people's surprise, on June 20, the state council
announced that the "custody and repatriation" law was abolished.

The real motivation behind the government's quick response is still
unknown.[6] It could be that the high-level state leaders simply wanted to pac-
ify the public anger. It could be that the leaders in the newly elected Hu-Wen
administration wanted to show to the public that they were different from
their predecessors. It could also be that these leaders had long recognized
that the "custody and repatriation" law had hindered the free movement of
labor power, which was bad for the formation of a market economy, and
that they had also planned to remove the law.[7] Nevertheless, the incident
had symbolic significance. For many, it showed that the government listened
to the people's voice and that a bottom-up approach for reform was possible. The abolishment of the "custody and repatriation" institution as well
as the resolution of the SARS crisis brought hope to those Chinese people
who yearned for democratization. During the first few years of the Hu-Wen
administration, the commentary was prominent that China had entered a
"Hu-Wen New Deal" (*Hu-Wen Xinzheng*).[8]

These people's optimistic view had been reinforced by the political program raised by the new administration. In July 2003, President Hu Jintao proposed the concept of a "scientific outlook on development" (*kexue fazhan
guan*), through which he advocated to alter the previous development pattern that focused solely on economic growth and adopt a more balanced
pattern that took environment, social justice, and the protection of human
rights into consideration. This new development goal was later generalized as
building a "harmonious society." Policy-wise, the new administration elimi-
nated agricultural taxes for peasants, enforced minimum wage in cities, and
expanded the social insurance coverage for low-income residents.[9] Although
the issuance of these policies involved complex politics and they eventually
had only limited effects on reducing inequality, the government's positive
attitude toward establishing social security and safety nets had nonetheless
opened a space for criticizing social problems.

In the larger society, two transformations are worth being mentioned
here. The first one was the rise of popular protests triggered by issues like

environmental pollution, corruption in land appropriation, and wage arrears. In fact, many of these protests had already existed in China in the 1990s. But because these actions were mostly rather fragmented, rarely were they known to the wider public. In the 2000s, with the help of the internet, NGOs, human rights lawyers, and some bold news media, they became more visible. More details of this process will be elaborated on in the next chapter.

The second one was the rise of the so-called middle class. China's economic reform that prioritized international trade and the development of cities since 1992 had created many white-collar jobs in coastal urban regions. People who had taken these opportunities were usually college graduates or those who had professional skills. What had reinforced their class identity was the commercialization of housing since 1998, through which many of them had become property owners.[10] As the beneficiaries of the reform, the middle-class residents tended to be less interested in a radical political agenda like regime change. But they were rather concerned with social reform issues, such as the improvement of public health, environmental protection, and the promotion of government transparency. Moreover, these people were generally less tolerant when their own rights were violated. The development of the internet in the 2000s had also provided this group with many opportunities to participate in public discussions.

With the abovementioned political, social, and technological transformations, China's public sphere took on a new look.

The Waning of the "Thought Sphere"

In a time when the larger environment seemed to become more open to critical public discussions, the "thought sphere" in which intellectuals engaged in debates on social and political theories began to disintegrate. This was because major participants of the sphere, the social science scholars, had begun to work in a more regulated system for producing knowledge. As I have mentioned in the previous chapter, reflecting upon their experience in the 1980s, in the early 1990s, leading scholars in the "thought sphere" launched a campaign for promoting the professional standards of academic studies. The purpose of the campaign was to establish a set of rules for judging what could be counted as legitimate knowledge so that academic studies in China could become more independent of the state.

But since the mid-1990s, the state had become the major rule maker in the field. Different from the campaign initiated by the intellectuals, which had focused on raising the quality of academic research, the state's intervention aimed to transform scholars and their intellectual products into quantifiable and measurable subjects.[11] To achieve this goal, the state's education departments and universities set up "core journals" (*hexin qikan*), allocated research grants, and detailed the rules for scholars' promotion. In the 1990s, the impact of the state's intervention on the activities of the "thought sphere" was still inconspicuous, because most intellectuals participating in public debates at that time had received their training in the 1980s; before the state increased its intervention, these intellectuals had already become well-established. But for those who started their career path in the 1990s, obtaining recognition in specialized academic fields became a more urgent task and participating in public discussions in the "thought sphere" became a distraction.[12] As a result, by the mid-2000s, the "thought sphere" was already short of newcomers.

Recognizing that the intellectuals' bottom-up efforts in establishing professional rules had been counteracted by the state's top-down interventions, many intellectuals protested. For example, Deng Zhenglai, the scholar introducing the idea of civil society to a Chinese audience, organized a series of discussions in the early 2000s. In these discussions, he pointed to the lack of autonomy of China's social science studies, criticized those intellectuals who had cooperated with the state, and advocated to reflect upon the "machine for producing knowledge" (*zhishi shengchan jiqi*).[13] However, compared with the state, these intellectuals were far less resourceful. In the name of building "world-class universities" (*shijie yiliu daxue*), the Chinese state had invested a great amount of money in universities and research institutes since the late 1990s.[14] While improving the research facilities and the Chinese intellectuals' living conditions, the state's investment had also cultivated a large group of academic knowledge producers who, willy-nilly, attended the game of publication and the application of research grants. In the 2000s, most of the journals organized by intellectual groups in the 1990s were gone. Among professional scholars, the new influential journals now were those "core journals" endorsed by the state, which were usually based in state-run universities and research institutes.

A disclaimer before I continue my analysis. By suggesting that the "thought sphere" had declined, I am not suggesting that intellectuals of different kinds in China had no longer participated in public discussion since the mid-2000s. The contrary was true. With the involvement of commercial power, intellectual elites quickly found alternative channels, such as the commercially-oriented newspapers and the internet, for making public interventions. This is what I am going to elaborate in the rest of the chapter. Even within the state system, many intellectuals managed to utilize the resources granted by the state to achieve their own goals. But the form of the intellectuals' public intervention had changed. To appeal to the wider public, many intellectuals began to avoid theoretical discussions that were too sophisticated and employ a language that was more comprehensible to ordinary people. With different intellectuals adopting diverse channels for articulating their ideas, the intellectuals' public intervention had also become more segmentalized.[15] The sphere in which many intellectuals engaged in public debates on social and political theories, trying to raise holistic approaches for promoting China's modernization, had thus gone.

The Rise of New Spaces for Public Discussions

Activities emerging from other spheres, namely the media sphere and the NGO sphere, quickly filled the lacuna left by the disintegration of the "thought sphere." The media sphere was a sphere in which news professionals and other actors formulated and circulated critical public opinions that were based on the reportage of and the commentary on news and current affairs, while the NGO sphere was a sphere in which people formed autonomous organizations and associations to address social issues and establish common concerns. Both spheres had emerged in the 1990s. But they had become mature and developed in the 2000s. In the following sections, I will elaborate how the new spaces for critical public discussion had interstitially emerged.

The Formation of a Media Sphere

The Interstitial Emergence of Critical News Report in the 1990s
In principle, there was no independent media in China. All newspapers, magazines, and television stations were supposed to be managed and supervised by certain organs of the state or the Communist Party. The state regulated the media through a licensing system, while the terms of the license restricted the content of publications. Censorship also widely existed. But arguably, news writing had long been playing crucial roles in the formation of critical public opinion in contemporary Chinese society. In the 1980s, writers and journalists combined news reports and literature and created a new form of

writing called the "reportage literature" (*baogao wenxue*), through which they described social problems in literary language and criticized China's politics and culture. These writers and journalists also took an active part in the New Enlightenment Movement.[16]

After the 1989 Student Movement, the activism of the "reportage literature" was terminated. But since 1992, the making of critical news reports gradually reemerged. Two forces had driven the expansion of the space for critical news reporting—the intention of the central government to check and supervise local-level government and the commercialization of news media. In the economic reform since 1992, the power of the state was decentralized and central government's capacity to control regional and local government had decreased.[17] In many places in China, corruption was rampant and people's discontent with local government officials was high. To constrain the misconduct of local government officials and enhance the legitimacy of the center, around the mid-1990s, news media backed up by the center began to make critical news reports that exposed social problems at the local level.[18] Typical examples in this aspect were a series of TV programs released by the Central China Television (CCTV), notably the *Focus Report* (Jiaodian Fang-tan) and the *News Probe* (Xinwen Diaocha). These programs offered coverage on issues like the embezzlement of public funds in the building of infrastructure and the mine disasters caused by government wrongdoings.[19] Because of their sharp style of criticism, they had constantly received high ratings.

Commercialization was another force. The transformation of newspapers was a case in point. Throughout the 1990s, since the central government had continuously withdrawn subsidies for regional and local newspapers, under-funded regional and local newspapers were pushed to seek survival opportunities in the marketplace.[20] A common practice among these newspapers was to use an existing publishing license to launch a spin-off newspaper that was more commercially oriented. Initially, to attract readers and increase advertisement income, these spin-off newspapers downplayed the propaganda content assigned by the state and offered more coverage on sports, entertainment and other local issues that were more relevant to ordinary people's social and economic life. Later, as the competition in the newspaper market became more intense, some of the commercially-oriented newspapers began to publish muckraking reports that revealed social problems arising during China's economic reform.

Extant studies on Chinese newspapers offer different opinions on the impact of commercialization. Some critics point out that the commercialization of newspapers had reinforced the inequalities brought by China's participation in neoliberal globalization. For example, Zhao Yuezhi argues that, with the withdrawal of state funds, many newspapers that used to serve disadvantaged groups like women, peasants, and industrial workers had experienced a sharp decline in circulation.[21] Zhao also criticizes the penetration of commercial power in public discussion.[22] Other scholars, notably Daniela Stockmann, emphasize that the freedom enjoyed by the commercially-oriented newspapers had remained limited. While journalists could criticize specific social problems at the local level, they were not able to touch upon some more fundamental issues in China's political system. According to Stockmann, by skillfully managing a social space in which people could articulate their concerns, the Chinese state had actually found a new way to facilitate its authoritarian rule.[23]

While I am sympathetic to these views, my point is a straightforward one—the commercialization of media in the 1990s had largely pluralized the actors involved in the making of news; with the rise of some locally-based newspapers, a lot of social issues that would otherwise be unnoticed were now exposed, magnified, and thematized for public discussion. In this aspect, the most illustrative example was the success of the *Southern Weekly* (Nanfang Zhoumo).[24] The *Southern Weekly* was a spin-off newspaper of the *Nanfang Daily* (Nanfang Ribao), which was managed by the Guangdong Committee of the Communist Party. Established in 1984, the *Southern Weekly* used to be a rather localized newspaper focusing on entertainment news. But since the late 1990s, it began to report on political and social scandals nationwide, such as the collusion between local government and criminal gangs, the contamination of food, and the spread of AIDS in rural areas. These reports attracted many urban middle-class readers who were interested in social reform issues and won the newspaper great influence. By the turn of the century, with a circulation of over 1.6 million, *Southern Weekly* had become the newspaper having the largest readership in the country.[25] In various public discussions at the turn of the century, the newspapers were often praised as the "conscience of the media sphere" (*meiti jie de liangxin*).[26]

What is worth mentioning here is that the two factors—discrepancies between different levels of government and commercialization—had not worked independently. Those media that were backed up by high-level government authorities like CCTV had also been influenced by the commercial logic. To increase the audience ratings, many producers and directors at CCTV had proactively learned from the Western media to improve their skills of news gathering and editing.[27] On the other hand, the commercially-oriented news media had also often been supported by various political forces from within the state. The success of the *Southern Weekly* again served as an illustrative example here. Because of its geographical location and its various experiments in attracting foreign investments, Guangdong Province had long been regarded as the pioneer in Deng's economic reform. In the 1990s, the Guangdong Committee of the Communist Party had offered political asylum to the *Southern Weekly*, because it regarded the newspaper as a social force advocating further reform. According to the memoir of a senior editor at the *Southern Weekly*, in the late 1990s, whenever higher government authorities threatened to shut down the newspaper, the Guangdong Committee saw it as political struggles between the conservatives and the reformers within the party. Before the Sun Zhigang Incident, to bolster their position within the party, leaders in the committee often tried hard to defend journalists and editors who had produced critical news reports.[28]

The Development of the Media Sphere in the Early to Mid-2000s

During the 2000s, the confrontation between the newspapers that produced critical news reports and the state had become more frequent. In 2003, Cheng Yizhong, the editor at the *Southern Metropolis Daily* (another spin-off news-paper of the *Nanfang Daily*), was detained for corruption and bribery. In the public, it was widely believed that the detainment had to do with the newspaper's previous reportage on the SARS crisis and the Sun Zhigang Incident.[29]

Another event had even wider influence. In 2006, the *Freezing Point Weekly* (Bingdian Zhoukan), which was managed by the *China Youth Daily* (Zhongguo Qingnian Bao), reprinted an essay that criticized the interpreta-tion of the Boxer Rebellion in the official history textbook. The Boxer Rebel-lion, also known as the Yihetuan Movement, was a peasant uprising against Christians and foreigners, which took place in northern China around 1900. Various official history textbooks in China usually described the rebellion in positive terms, praising it as a bottom-up fight against Western colonialists and invaders. The essay published by the *Freezing Point Weekly* questioned this view, arguing that participants of the rebellion were "ignorant," "savagely cruel," and "uncivilized." It also blamed the official textbooks for misguiding the youth.[30] Looking back, we may discover that the essay's description of the Boxer Rebellion was lop-sided, as it failed to take the larger historical context—Westerners' colonialist expansion in late Qing China—into consid-eration. Had a social space been allowed in which historians holding different positions could debate with each other on the historical details, the public would be better informed of the problem of all one-sided interpretations of history. However, instead of allowing such debate to happen, the Chinese government simply compelled the *Freezing Point Weekly* to suspend publication. The suspension of the newspaper alarmed many journalists and editors who had believed that the freedom of press in China was making progress.

Because of such events, in the 2000s, many scholars had argued that the Chinese state's control over news media had become tightened.[31] However, from today's perspective, the formation of critical public opinions based on news reports was still vibrant in the early to mid-2000s. I suggest that this was because the state's efforts in controlling the making of critical news reports had been counteracted by two factors, the pluralization of commercially-oriented news media and the aggressive development of the internet in China in the 2000s.

First, around 2000, inspired by the commercial and social success of the *Southern Weekly*, "metropolis newspapers" (*dushi bao*) based in different places, such as the *Huashang Daily* (Huashang Bao) and the *Beijing News* (Xinjing Bao), began to engage in investigative journalism. Newspapers and magazines offering in-depth reports in specialized fields like economics and finance also emerged. Notable examples included the *Caijing Magazine* (Caijing Zazhi) and the *Economic Observer* (Jingji Guancha Bao). The critical issue here was that these newspapers and magazines had been managed and backed up by different state sectors. The discrepancies between different state sectors had created the interstitial space that journalists and editors could exploit. In the 2000s, these journalists and editors had often engaged in a practice of what they called the "cross-regional supervision" (*yidi jiandu*): when the publication of a news report in a newspaper was obstructed due to its criticism over issues that involved the interest of some local political power, journalists and editors could refer the report to a second newspaper and publish the report in a different place.[32]

The development of the internet was another factor. Chinese people had expressed their opinions on public issues on the internet as early as the 1990s. But at that time, the major platform for public discussion was the BBS (Bulletin Board System). Since most BBSes in the 1990s were university based— notable examples included the SMTH (based in Tsinghua University) and the YTHT (based in Peking University)—major participants of online discussions were university staff, students, and alumni. In the 2000s, with the rapid expansion of the internet infrastructure led by the state, the number of internet users grew exponentially. With the involvement of commercial power, new platforms for online discussion, such as commercially-oriented online forums and blogs, emerged. Compared to that of the BBSes, these new platforms were much easier to access. Active participants of online discussion now included the educated class living in big cities.[33]

Before the late 2000s, the expansion of the participants of online discussion had facilitated the making of critical news in at least two ways. On the one hand, the internet accelerated the spread of information, which increased the difficulties of censorship. The Sun Zhigang Incident was a case that illustrated this point. Before publishing the report on Sun's death, editors at the *Southern Metropolis Daily* shared the report with Sina and Sohu, two major portal websites in China. Only one day after the publication of the report in the newspaper, government authorities commanded that the reportage on the issue terminate. But by that time, many people had already read the report on the internet and the problems of the "custody and repatriation" law were already being heatedly discussed among internet users.[34] Because of the internet's function of circumventing censorship, most journalists working for commercially-oriented newspapers in the early to mid-2000s had a rather positive attitude toward the development of the new communication technologies.

On the other hand, as the internet had a more decentralized communication structure, more people could participate in the production of news. This helped to bring in topics that conventionally could not appear in Chinese newspapers, such as protests.[35] A typical case here was the anti-PX protest in the city of Xiamen. In 2007, to protest the construction of a PX chemical plant, thousands of residents in Xiamen went into the streets. While the newspaper media was not able to report the issue in the beginning, participants of the protest used the internet to record their activism and keep the public updated. On blog websites like *Bullog* (Niubo Wang), they posted photos of people gathering and published entries to express their concerns. With these efforts, the protest eventually achieved national influence.[36] As the anti-PX protests became "de-sensitized," newspapers like the *Southern Weekly* stepped in and initiated public discussions on issues like citizens' participation in environmental impact assessments. The existence of such practices indicates that the media sphere featuring the production and discussion of critical news was still vibrant in the early to mid-2000s, despite increasing state intervention.

The Formation of an NGO Sphere

A Brief History of NGOs in China, 1992–2007

As I have introduced in the previous chapter, Chinese people began to establish NGOs as early as the 1990s. International foundations were an important
promoter in the development of NGOs in China in early years. Being influenced by the idea that civil society was good for democracy and development, which had become prominent in the international community after the
end of the Cold War,[37] international foundations started to invest in NGOs
in China since 1992. Before 2000, major granters of Chinese NGOs were the
Ford Foundation and the World Wildlife Fund. These two foundations had
been working closely with the Chinese government since the 1980s. In the
1990s, they supported NGOs in fields like rural community development,
the protection of women's rights, and the environment. Most of these NGOs
were in Beijing and southwestern China (Yunnan, Guizhou, and Sichuan).[38]
The first wave of NGO activists were mainly intellectual elites who were fluent in English and worked in state-run institutes.[39]

In the 2000s, more international funds were poured into China. These
included money from foundations that sought to promote changes in specialized fields, such as the Bill & Melinda Gates Foundation, and those foundations that supported more general resistance movements for democracy,
such as the National Endowment for Democracy and the Open Society
Institute. Rather than working with the Chinese government, foundations in
the latter group often directly supported groups arising from the bottom up.
Donors falling into this category also included embassies and consulates of
several Western countries.

Another important promoter for NGOs in China were the universities
and research institutes. Around 2000, research centers for studying NGOs
and civil society interstitially emerged. These centers were usually attached to
state-run universities and received financial supports from both the Chinese
state and international foundations. Notable examples included the Institute
for NGOs at Tsinghua University, the Institute for Civil Society at Peking
University, and the Institute for Civil Society at the Sun Yat-sen University
(also known as the ICS). Apart from supporting academic studies of NGOs,
these centers had launched training programs for NGO activists and served
as the mediators between international foundations and localized NGOs.
Among these centers, the most influential one was the ICS.[40] Since 2003,

the ICS had periodically held the "Huangpu Camp for NGO Leadership,"[41] a capacity building program for training NGO activists. Many prominent NGO activists who later played important roles in fields like labor and women's rights had been trainees of the program.

Due to the incoming of new international funds and the intervention of research centers for studying civil society, the NGO sphere entered a period of expansion in the 2000s.[42] The number of NGOs rapidly increased. Their locations now included big cities in all coastal provinces. Founders of NGOs began to include people who were socioeconomically disadvantaged, such as rural migrant workers and victims of environmental pollution in rural areas, though these people were still the minority during this period. Among scholars and practitioners, these organizations were often called the "grassroots organizations" (*caogen zuzhi*).[43] The thematic fields in which NGOs worked had also become more pluralized. With financial support from foundations like the National Endowment for Democracy, NGOs engaging in human rights activism had emerged. Although these NGOs were few and most of them were Beijing-based, they played leading roles in many advocacy campaigns. Moreover, the various training programs and conferences held by the research centers enhanced the communication among NGOs from different regions and thematic fields. Around the mid-2000s, many NGOs, including both the "grassroots" ones and the ones established by intellectual elites, began to recognize each other through a common identity as members of an NGO community.[44]

Explaining the Interstitial Emergence of NGOs

In explaining the rise of NGOs in China, scholars point to China's economic reform that has cut welfare spending at the local level. It is argued that the state has tolerated NGOs because these organizations could deliver services to disadvantaged groups.[45] Some scholars highlight the measures the Chinese state has taken to shape NGO activities. It is argued that the Chinese state has introduced NGOs to service provision activities by offering funds and penalizing those organizations that engage in confrontational activities like human rights advocacy.[46] In my opinion, these views capture a general logic of the Chinese state in its governance of NGOs; they are helpful for understanding the development of the relations between NGOs and the state in the long run. However, if we closely examine the condition of NGOs before the late 2000s, we may find that these views overlook the complex interactions between the state and NGOs and the various political concerns involved.

First, in the 1990s and early 2000s, actors from within the state's bureaucratic system were important promoters of NGOs in several fields.[47] The purpose of these actors to establish NGOs was to seek allies in wider society and accomplish goals that they were not able to accomplish within the political system. An illustrative example here was the role of the All-China Women's Federation (ACWF) in the development of NGOs. The ACWF was a "mass organization" (*qunzhong zuzhi*) established by the Communist Party.[48] Although the organization was supposed to represent the interests of women, it had almost no power to set up gender-related agendas in the making of policies. For instance, in the 1980s, the ACWF had been excluded in the making of China's family planning policy, which was so closely related to women's reproductive health.[49] In the early 1990s, as the state's spending on the organization had continuously been cut, many people working at the ACWF began to seriously discuss whether it was possible for the organization to become more autonomous from the state and play a more proactive role in the women's movement.[50] These people were also among the first wave of Chinese people who were exposed to international funds and the idea of NGOs. After the 4th World Women's Conference held in Beijing, they established dozens of NGOs for advocating women's rights, mainly with the help of the Ford Foundation.[51]

Among these NGOs, three had produced lasting influence. The first one was Rural Women Knowing All (*Nongjia Nü*), an NGO established in 1996 for providing services to women rural migrant workers. This organization later turned out many labor activists. The second one was the Media Monitor Network for Women (*Funü Chuanmei Jiance Wangluo*), which was also established in 1996. This organization was a precursor of the media advocate of feminism. It became widely known in 2009 as the Feminist Voices (*Nüquan zhi Sheng*). The last one was the Network for Anti Domestic Violence (*Fan Jiabao Wangluo*), which was started in 1998. Working with lawyers, scholars, and volunteers from communities, the organization had proactively advocated the legislation against domestic violence in China throughout the 2000s. Its efforts eventually midwifed the passage of the Anti-Domestic Violence Law in 2015.

Second, while some NGOs had been initiated by people who were outside China's bureaucratic system, they had later formed coalitions with government sectors that were relatively marginalized in the state. Their cooperation with these government sectors had emboldened, rather than tamed, their activities. A case in point were the environmental NGOs. Early founders of environmental NGOs in China were mostly humanity scholars, journalists, and writers. Notable examples included the Friends of Nature, the Global Village (*Diqiu Cun*), and the Green Homeland (*Lü Jiayuan*). In the 1990s, these organizations mainly engaged in environmental education projects. As I have introduced in chapter one, the few campaigns these organizations had launched were on the protection of wild animals, such as antelopes and snub-nosed monkeys.[52]

In the early 2000s, the ministry of environmental protection in China threw the environmental NGOs an olive branch. Although the Chinese state had long acknowledged the importance of environmental protection, back then, the ministry of environmental protection was a government sector that was short of resources and staff. At the local level, provincial and municipal government usually prioritized economic growth, while the administration for environmental protection lacked the capacity to enforce environment-related laws. To strengthen its coalition with environmental NGOs, the ministry openly praised these organizations, shared information with them, and provided them with venues for participation.[53] Being backed up by the ministry, the environmental NGOs launched a series of environmental campaigns in the 2000s that touched upon the issues of environmental justice and public participation. Among these campaigns, two had achieved wide influence—the campaign against dam construction on the Nu River and the campaign against the anti-seepage project at Yuanmingyuan Park.[54] While both campaigns had aroused huge controversies and achieved only partial success, they had problematized the lack of public participation in environmental protection.

Lastly, before the late 2000s, there was not a unified system for regulating NGOs in China. To manage NGOs as newly rising organizations, the state council issued a law in 1998, which categorized NGOs as "private non-enterprises" (*minban fei-qiye*). All "private non-enterprises" were required to register at the administration for civil affairs. But before registration, an organization needed to obtain a permit from a "supervisory institute" (*zhu-guan danwei*), which had to be a state organ whose function was relevant to the supposed activities of the organization. For example, a labor NGO may request the All-China Federation of Trade Unions to serve as its "supervisory institute." The rationale was to create a "double management" (*shuangchong guanli*) system that put NGOs under the control of both the administration of civil affairs and relevant state organs. However, the law had not specified the procedure through which a permit could be obtained. Nor had it detailed the responsibilities of the "supervisory institute." Hence, most state organs simply declined an NGOs' request to avoid trouble. This implied that, in practice, very few NGOs were able to find a "supervisory institute."[55] As a makeshift option, most NGOs turned to the administration for commerce and were registered as corporations.[56]

This situation had benefited NGOs that engaged in agitational activities, since, back in the early 2000s, the two government sectors these NGOs regularly came into contact with—the administration for commerce and the administration for state security—did not quite often share information with each other. Even if the state security department closed an NGO at one point, the organization could get registered under a different name sometime later. In fact, quite a few NGOs engaging in human rights activism in the early years had such an experience. A typical example here was a Beijing-based NGO called Sunny Constitutional Democracy (*Yangguang Xianzheng*), which was established in 2003 by the lawyers and law scholars who had attended the Sun Zhigang Incident. The organization's registration at the administration for commerce was revoked in September 2004, after it organized a campaign for protesting the closedown of the YTHT BBS and advocating freedom of speech. A few months later, the organization changed its name to the Coalition of Citizens (*Gongmeng*, also known as the Open Constitution Initiative) and got registered again. From the mid- to late 2000s, *Gongmeng* attended activisms that involved issues like land rights, property rights, and ethnic minorities' rights. In 2009, Xu Zhiyong, the leader of the organization, was shortly detained. But after he was released, the organization changed its name to Citizens (*Gongmin*) and began to engage in human rights activism again. It was not until 2014 that the organization was finally disbanded.

In a word, in the 1990s and early 2000s, the opportunities for establishing NGOs were many and varied. Because of the fragmentation in the regulation system and the complex political interests involved, NGO activities were far from being stabilized.

The Transformation of the Ideological Debate

The Further Divergence Between the Liberals and the New Left

With the decline of the "thought sphere" and the rise of the media sphere and the NGO sphere, the form and content of public discussions in the interstitial publics changed. While the open debate on political and social theories was still present, public expressions that were closer to people's everyday concerns became increasingly prominent. Confronting these changes, the liberals and the new left chose different strategies.[57]

As I have discussed in the previous chapter, the new left tended to see the new channels for public expression like the commercialized media and the NGOs as inherent to the rise of neoliberal globalization. Moreover, generally, compared to the liberals, new leftist scholars had better English language skills and were more informed of the trend in the international academic community. Hence, these new leftist scholars largely turned away from the newly emerging interstitial spaces in China and turned to the international academic community. Wang Hui was a case in point. Since the early 2000s, Wang Hui's scholarly works had been translated into English, Japanese, Italian, and Korean. In 2013, he was even awarded, conjointly with Jürgen Habermas, the Luca Pacioli Prize, a prestigious recognition to reward outstanding scholarship. With such expositions, new leftist scholars in China became known internationally and found an audience abroad.

In contrast, the liberals embraced the newly rising interstitial spaces. Some of the liberals, such as Qin Hui, Xu Youyu, and Zhu Xueqin, launched columns at prominent newspapers like the *Southern Weekly* and offered timely commentary on news and current affairs. During this process, the liberals found new allies. These allies included journalists and editors producing critical news on commercial media, the intellectuals working at the research centers for studying NGOs and civil society, and some NGO activists. I have introduced these actors in my above discussion on the media sphere and the NGO sphere. The liberals' new allies also included some media-based public intellectuals whose rise had been facilitated by the development of the internet technology. While some of these media-based public intellectuals had institutionalized cultural capital, that is, high degrees or positions in well-known universities and research institutes, others simply lacked the capital. A typical example in the latter group was Han Han, a racing driver from Shanghai who had dropped out of school at the age of seventeen. In 2007, Han Han launched a blog on the website of Sina to satirize various social and political problems. For a long time, this blog was the one having the largest readership in China. The liberals' new allies also included some human rights lawyers and law scholars. Together, these actors formed a new liberal camp.

The Rise of a New Liberal Camp

Compared to that in the "thought sphere" in the 1990s, the new liberal camp was even more heterogeneous. People in the camp disagreed with each other on many things. For example, these actors had not agreed with each other on whether it was acceptable to cooperate with the state when trying to criticize and solve social problems. Most NGO activists, especially those who worked in the organizations that engaged in specific social problems, saw cooperating with the state as a reasonable option. But for many radical human rights lawyers, the state was the root of all problems.

Another example was these people's divergent attitude toward populism. Many journalists working at the *Southern Weekly* were rather sympathetic to the sufferings of the lower-class people and regarded their practice of journalism as a way to speak for the poor. In writing the muckraking reports, they usually employed great amounts of literary, sensational language and bluntly expressed their indignation against social injustice, rather than keep a more balanced and detached attitude.[58] But the liberal law scholars had often criticized the tendency of populism in China's legal system. For instance, He Weifang, a professor of law at Peking University, used to proactively advocate to remove the word "people" from "people's court" (*renmin fayuan*), as he believed that a court "should be consisted of intellectual elites and those with professional knowledge," while the term "people's court" sounded "too plebeian."[59]

Yet I would argue that the new liberal camp was still a coalition based on common values. What brought these heterogeneous actors together was exactly the idea of civil society, or more precisely, an imagination of politics that was based upon the antithesis between state and society. In this imagination, the state power often tended to violate individual liberty and rights, whereas civil society, consisting of voluntary associations, independent media, and various resistance movements, constituted a basis on which people could defend rights and the integrity of their social and private life. I will talk more about this imagination in the following chapter. In this chapter, I will only give readers two examples of public discussions—one in the media sphere and the other in the NGO sphere—to illustrate how actors in the new liberal camp understood the antithesis.

In the media sphere, journalists and editors making critical news advocated that news media become a "public institution" (*shehui gongqi*) that served the public interest through promoting the disclosure of information.[60] These journalists' and editors' attitude was well demonstrated in the public discussion on the profession of journalism, which was initiated on the first Journalist's Day in China (November 8, 2000). On that day, the Chinese government held a series of public events, in which journalists' role was portrayed as the "news workers" (*xinwen gongzuozhe*) of the state and the party.

Meanwhile, the *Southern Weekly* produced a special issue to sing a different tune. The issue praised several muckraking reporters for their courage to break the political restrictions in the reportage of news and "speak truth to power."[61] It also spared much space for commemorating Chu Anping, a liberal journalist who had criticized the domination of the communist party in the 1950s and was later persecuted during the Anti-rightist Campaign.[62] The message conveyed in the issue was clear—because the state in an authoritarian regime often tended to cover up the reality, the practice of good journalism involved confrontations with the state.[63] These discussions had later evolved into the criticism of the state discourse that media was the party's "mouthpiece" (*houshe*).[64]

In the NGO sphere, the intellectuals studying NGOs and NGO activists highlighted the NGOs' function of expanding the space for participation. In advocating this idea, an underground magazine called *Minjian*, which literally meant folks or a non-governmental sphere, played a crucial role (Figure 2).[65] Being financially supported by the Oxfam Hong Kong, the editorial board of the *Minjian* magazine consisted of activists from the ICS, journalists from the *Southern Weekly*, and several media-based public intellectuals. Between 2005 and 2010, the magazine documented the development of China's NGOs in general and reported the NGOs' interventions in various advocacy campaigns. Although its publication had never been licensed, the magazine had reached a wide audience. Before 2007, even some government officials were its regular readers.[66] In the magazine, it was often argued that organizations within the authoritarian system tended to be insensitive to newly rising social problems and were insufficient for channeling people's demands; it was only in those organizations outside the authoritarian system, such as NGOs, that social problems could be seriously discussed, and genuine political participation could be activated.[67]

Here I want to remind readers that, in theoretical terms, the interpretation of civil society shared by actors in the new liberal camp had already begun to diverge from the original discussion initiated by Deng Zhenglai and his colleagues in the 1990s. A crucial difference was this: When Deng Zhenglai and his colleagues talked about civil society, they regarded it as a political ideal. But for the critical journalists, the liberal public intellectuals, the NGO practitioners, and the human rights lawyers, civil society was not only a political ideal; it was already an emergent fact in China.

行动改变生存

民间报告
在合作中学会合作
胡杰：悲悯的凝视
特别专辑
为了行动的艺术
这时，想起了李扁头县长
背负期望的独行客
公民社会的美丽心灵

民間

Min Jian

> 2005年9月 秋火

Figure 2. Cover of the *Minjian* Magazine. Photo taken and permission granted by Zhai Minglei, the former chief editor of the *Minjian* magazine.

The Organizational Configuration of the New Liberal Camp

The new liberal camp did not have any de facto leaders. Many activists in the NGO sphere and journalists in the media sphere identified with the political agenda raised by the liberals in the "thought sphere." But the influence of the latter group on the former group was mostly spiritual. The new liberal camp did not have any unitary organizations either. Intellectuals and activists from different locations and thematic fields established their own organizations, and these different organizations were only loosely connected with each other. Hence, organizationally, the new liberal camp had been rather fragmented. But there were a few kinds of organizations whose influence went beyond their location and thematic field.

The first kind of these organizations were human rights lawyers' organizations, notably *Gongmeng*. As I have mentioned above, after the Sun Zhigang Incident, *Gongmeng* had attended a variety of human rights activisms. Before 2009, *Gongmeng* organized a monthly held salon called the "law journalists' club." Participants of the salon included not only "law journalists," but also law scholars, human rights lawyers, NGO activists and many university students who were interested in promoting democratization in China. A variety of political issues had been discussed in the salon, such as the promotion of government transparency and judicial independence, the reportage on criminal cases, and the cooperation between the human rights lawyers and investigative journalists.[68]

The second kind were leading organizations in particular thematic fields, notably the Rural Women Knowing All and the Green Homeland. Respectively, these two organizations used to focus on the issues of women rural migrant workers and environmental protection. But as these organizations accumulated knowledge and experience in advocacy, they began to hold training programs and salons that attracted activists from other fields. For example, since 2000, the Green Homeland started a project called the "environmental journalists' salon," which invited activists from environmental NGOs all over China and journalists making critical news reports to meet monthly. Activists from other fields, such as rural development, sometimes also attended the salon. In the salon, participants usually discussed issues like public participation and government transparency.[69]

The third kind were university-based research institutes. The most typical example here was the ICS. As I have just mentioned, the ICS was the organizer of the well-known training program, the "Huangpu Camp for NGO

Leadership"; working with editors and journalists from the *Southern Weekly*, the ICS also created the *Minjian* magazine. Apart from these activities, during the Hu-Wen regime, intellectuals from the ICS often attended various human rights activisms. Similar instances in this category included the Women Law Research and Service Center (*Funü Falü Yanjiu yu Fuwu Zhongxin*) at Peking University and the Helping Center for Victims of Pollution (*Wuran Shouhaizhe Yuanzhu Zhongxin*) at China University of Political Science and Law.[70] These organizations were usually well connected with actors from not only the academic community but also the NGO sphere and the media sphere.

Lastly, there were also research institutes that were outside China's public university system. Notable examples included the China Development Brief and the NGOCN. Created in 1996 by Nick Young, a British journalist, the China Development Brief published a series of research reports on NGOs in China.[71] In the 2000s, the organization had also served as an intermediary between grassroots NGOs in different fields and various international foundations. Being established by a group of youth activists based in Yunnan Province, the NGOCN sought to promote the integration of China's NGO community. The organization moved to Guangzhou in 2011, with many of its members joining the ICS.[72]

Through activities held by the abovementioned influential organizations, actors from different spheres in the new liberal camp formed multiple, intersecting networks, in which they exchanged information and resources. With the formation of these networks, a certain degree of coordination within the camp became possible.

If we examine the geographical location of the influential organizations that had the capacity to organize cross-sectional activities, we will discover that the density of the liberals' network had been highly uneven. Almost all the influential organizations had been gathered in two cities, Beijing and Guangzhou. The fact that Beijing had become a center for the new liberal camp was not very surprising to me. Beijing had long been China's political and cultural capital. The city was also a place where top universities and research institutes gathered.

The fact that Guangzhou, rather than other big cities in China like Shanghai, became another center for the liberals was a bit puzzling for me in the beginning. I discussed this issue with many of my informants, both in Beijing and Guangzhou. They generally provided me with two types of answers. The first type highlighted that Guangdong Province had been the pioneer in Deng Xiaoping's market-oriented economic reform and that local governments (including both the provincial government and the municipal government) had been tolerant of NGOs and the critical media. The other type of answers underscored Guangzhou's geographical proximity to the city of Hong Kong. When being asked about the life course through which they became activists, many activists in the Pearl River Delta who were born after the 1980s proudly talked about the influence of Hong Kong cultural products. One activist said,

> I had never watched any CCTV's Spring Festival Gala (Chunwan) before I went to college. It's too rustic for us. Young people who were raised up in Guangdong like me usually watched a lot of TVB programs in our childhood. I especially liked various kinds of legal dramas from Hong Kong. It was from these legal dramas that I learned the Miranda warning. "You have the right to remain silent. Anything you say can be used against you in court." This was where I got the first impression of rule of law and the protection of human rights.[73]

Because of many historical reasons, Hong Kong had long served as a "hub" through which China communicated with the West. Even after China decided to "open up" in the 1980s, it was via various organizations and institutions in Hong Kong that information and resources from the international community entered China.[74] The development of many well-known organizations in Guangzhou had also been under the influence of Hong Kong. For example, the Chinese University of Hong Kong had been one of the co-founders of the ICS. In any case, these informants all agreed that Guangzhou was very important for the liberal camp.[75] The central status of the city would stand until the mid-2010s.

Conclusion

This chapter offers an overview of the background against which civil society as an ideational movement expanded. In the beginning, I briefly introduce the transformation of the political and social environment in China during the first term of the Hu-Wen regime. Then I discuss the structural transformation of the interstitial publics. I argue that, while the "thought sphere" had declined due to state intervention in social science academic studies, other spaces for alternative public discussions had emerged interstitially from both within and outside the bureaucratic state system. In the early to mid-2000s, activisms in these spaces had coalesced into two spheres, the media sphere and the NGO sphere.

By employing the concept of interstitial emergence, I emphasize that the spaces in which critical public opinions were formed in the early to mid-2000s were polygenetic. Specifically, these spaces had emerged out of discrepancies between different state sectors, the marginalized state sectors that sought to obtain more political power, the rise of new communication technologies, the intervention of international foundations, and a bourgeoning market economy. In documenting the political and social activisms in the spaces, I intend to avoid a functionalist description, which tends to suggest that these activisms had emerged or been tolerated in China *because* they had in some way benefited the authoritarian system—the production of critical news reports on commercial media informed the state of the many social problems, whereas NGOs channeled demands from disadvantaged groups and provided these groups with social service programs. As I have illustrated, although many state actors—or more precisely, actors who were to different degrees embedded in the state—were involved, there was not a "master plan" behind the involvement of these actors; in fact, state actors' concerns during this stage had been rather different from one another.

Moreover, I highlight that, even in an authoritarian environment like China, the state's power to manage political and social activisms should not be assumed a priori. Of course, in a political regime where constitutional constraint on the exercise of state power arguably does not exist, the state lacks no despotic power in preempting the formation of critical public opinions. As I have shown above, the Chinese state now and then arbitrarily shut down newspapers or NGOs when these actors were identified as a threat to the stability of the regime. But the management of political and social activisms involves not just the exercise of despotic power. To deal with numerous societal actors whose practices and ideological positions are volatile and ambiguous, the state also needs certain forms of regulatory power, which must be based either on consistent policies and laws or on institutionalized negotiations with societal actors. I suggest that, with respect to the development of the latter form of power, the Chinese state had fallen behind, at least during the first term of the Hu-Wen regime. I illustrate this point by analyzing the various "loopholes" in China's NGO registration system. Because of these "loopholes," organizations with various goals got to survive during this stage. These included "moderate" organizations that had mainly engaged in service provision activism but had the potential to cooperate with advocacy organizations, as well as those organizations with relatively "radical" political agendas like *Gongmeng*.

At the end of the chapter, I argue that, with the transformation of the interstitial publics, the dynamics between the liberals and the new left had changed. Whereas the new left had moved closer to the international academic community, the liberals had turned to newly rising interstitial spaces. In this process, the liberals found new allies among actors like journalists, NGO activists, and human rights lawyers. I also emphasize that what had brought the heterogeneous actors into the new liberal camp together was these people's identification with the idea of civil society. With the new allies, the liberals came to a much better position from which they could project their imagination of politics onto people in wider society. This is what I am going to discuss in the next chapter.

CHAPTER 3

The Hasty Formation of a Counter-Hegemonic Movement, 2003–2007

As I mentioned at the end of chapter one, to advocate for the idea of civil society, activists who attended the 1989 Student Movement tried to establish NGOs. But in the 1990s, the capacity of NGOs to incorporate social issues had been rather limited. Around 2003, actors in the new liberal camp (hereafter, the liberals) gradually began to recognize that, instead of organizing activisms all by themselves, they could turn to activisms initiated by people in wider society. In the mid- to late 2000s, the liberals got involved in many spontaneously emerging resistance activisms, such as the environmental protests launched by victims of pollution accidents. The liberals openly applauded the rise of these activisms, valorized them, intervened in their mobilization, and offered their participants various kinds of aid. I suggest that it was during this process that the political project of building civil society became prominent.

While the participants of the resistance activisms were diverse and their demands were multifarious, the liberals tended to ignore the variations and called the activisms by a general name of the Weiquan Movement (*Weiquan Yundong*), which literally meant the "rights-defending movement." To demonstrate that the idea of civil society was indeed relevant to China's politics, in their public expressions, the liberals largely simplified the origins of the resistance activisms and interpreted people's resistance as a reaction against the control of the authoritarian state. This chapter demonstrates how the simplification process has been carried out and discusses its multiple, contradicting consequences.

I see the liberals' efforts in incorporating various resistance activisms as an attempt to build a counter-hegemonic movement. My analysis of hegemony and counter-hegemony borrows from Antonio Gramsci. In Gramsci's political writings, hegemony can be understood as a form of domination.[1] Rather than mere ruling by force, hegemony rests on people's internalized belief that currently existing economic and political institutions are the best, or only, way of organizing social relationships. During times of economic or political crisis, however, the flaws of the hegemonic order may become more visible. These are moments of opportunity for counter-hegemonic movements to advance their critiques of the system. The concept of counter-hegemony perfectly catches the liberals' practices of advocating civil society and the Weiquan Movement—calling into question the authoritarian rule and showing that alternatives to the status quo exist, are needed, and are achievable.

Nevertheless, I highlight a major difference between the Weiquan Movement advocated by the liberals and the counter-hegemonic movement in Gramsci's writings. Being developed in the context of the anti-capitalist struggles of the first half of the 20th century, Gramsci's idea of counter-hegemony is predominantly class-based. To win the "war of position" in the battle between hegemony and counter-hegemony, Gramsci argues that the proletariats need to cultivate their own organic intellectuals—intellectuals who are more directly related to the economic structure of a society and who can give their class homogeneity and awareness of its own function.[2] However, the supposed organic intellectuals, here the liberals, were more like the traditional intellectuals in Gramsci's theory—those intellectuals who conceive of themselves as having no basis in any social class and adhering to no particular class discourse. In fact, the liberals had often avoided talking about class issues in their public discussion of civil society. The presumption behind this avoidance was the imagination of universal interest—as long as civil society, or an independent space for participation, is created, all citizens, regardless of his or her socioeconomic status, would be benefited. I will elaborate on this point in my analysis of the Weiquan Movement and discuss its political implications.

The rest of the chapter will be arranged in the following way. In the next section, I examine the history of the discourse of *weiquan* in China since the 1990s and introduce how the discourse had transformed from a state discourse to a counter-hegemonic discourse being associated with the idea of civil society. Then I analyze how the liberals had projected their understanding of civil society, or an imagination of politics that placed the antithesis between state and society onto the various social movement activisms in wider society. Next, I demonstrate how, in the name of building civil society, the liberals had intervened in people's *weiquan* activism and what achievements these interventions had made. Before the concluding section, I discuss the various negative consequences incurred by the liberals' reductionist interpretation of the Weiquan Movement. In the concluding section, I summarize my analysis of the development of the interstitial publics in China between 2003–2007.

A Brief History of the Discourse of *Weiquan*

The discourse of the right (*quanli*) had entered China's public sphere as a state discourse. In the beginning, the right discourse was associated with the state's project of legal reform. After the Cultural Revolution, to restore social order, support the development of a market economy, attract foreign investment, and constrain corruption, the Chinese state carried out a series of legal reform programs. In the 1980s and the 1990s, hundreds of commercial and civil laws were enacted. These laws had stipulated many of the rights citizens were entitled to.[3] To demonstrate the state's determination in protecting rights, in 2004, the national people's congress even passed a resolution to add "protection of human rights" into China's constitution. In its political propaganda, the Chinese state employed the discourse of the right to highlight its efforts in protecting citizens' rights through legislation.

Since the 1990s, out of complex concerns, the Chinese state began to disseminate the knowledge of laws and encouraged citizens to take legal actions to defend rights. A most illustrative example here was the state's advocacy of consumer rights. As China moved away from a planned economy, a commodity economy began to revive. Because of the lack of supervision, the newly emerging commodity market was flooded with counterfeited goods, which severely harmed fair competition. To regulate the incipient commodity market, the state advocated consumers raise their "rights consciousness" (*quanli yishi*) and passed the Law on the Protection of Consumer Rights and Interests in 1993. To encourage consumers to defend their own rights when purchasing goods of poor quality, the state used its media to widely publicize the details of the law, set up hotlines for providing legal aid, and sponsored the formation of a consumers' association.[4] In similar ways, in the 1990s and early 2000s, the state had also familiarized citizens with other forms of rights, such as women's rights and children's rights. It was in these processes that the discourse of *weiquan*, literally meaning defending rights, was frequently mentioned. Back then, the term *weiquan* was often used to refer to those actions of defending one's legal rights through state-endorsed channels.[5]

Of course, the rights the Chinese state encouraged citizens to defend had been partial and limited. First, as many students of Chinese politics had pointed out, the state had been more proactive in advocating commerce-related rights and civil rights than in political rights.[6] Second, even in the field of commerce-related rights and civil rights, the state's advocacy of citizens' rights had been contingent upon its judgment of the conditions of social and economic development. For example, in the 1990s, when privatization was regarded as being crucial for the economic reform and the low price of labor power was regarded as China's comparative advantage in the global economy, the state's advocacy of labor rights had been relatively weak. Except for emphasizing that workers had the right to sign contracts with their employers and get paid for their work, the state had seldom mentioned that workers were also entitled to social rights or welfare rights. It was not until the Hu-Wen era, when the expansion of domestic demand was seen as the key to promoting further economic growth, that the state began to enact new labor laws that provided more detailed regulations on the protection of workers' social rights.[7]

As early as the 1990s, many liberals criticized the *weiquan* discourse proposed by the state. In the "thought sphere," liberal scholars like Zhang Shuguang (economist) and Liu Junning (political scientist) contended that an unchecked state power more often violated citizens' rights and liberty and that the institutions set up by the state for protecting rights often tended to fail; to defend rights, therefore, people needed to restrict the state power and hold the state power accountable. The liberal scholars also suggested that an independent civil society constituted the basis on which people could achieve these goals.[8]

Challenges of the state discourse also came from lawyers. In the 1990s, a market-oriented reform of the legal profession took place. In the reform, Chinese lawyers were disentangled from the role of "state's legal workers" (*guojia de falü gongzuozhe*) and granted a series of autonomy, including the autonomy to act in courts as agents for litigation, obtaining remuneration, and establishing private law firms.[9] This provided opportunities to human rights lawyers who had tried to promote social change through litigation. Among these human rights lawyers, some had become involved in politically sensitive issues, such as the freedom of speech and religion, the right of ethnic minorities, China's family planning policies, and land appropriation. In the public, these kinds of lawyers were often referred to as the "rights-defending lawyers" (*weiquan lüshi*).[10] The ideological stance of these "rights-defending lawyers" tended to be quite close to that of the liberals in the "thought sphere." They also regarded the lack of constitutional democracy as the greatest threat to human rights and advocated the necessity of a resistance movement.[11]

However, since these criticisms were rather abstract, they had very limited influence. It was not until the Sun Zhigang Incident in 2003 that the liberals found an appropriate case through which they could explain the rationale of the idea of civil society to the wider public. I have introduced the incident in the beginning of chapter two. In the incident, Sun Zhigang's tragic death aroused public anger toward the "custody and repatriation" law, a law that restricted citizens' freedom to move across regions. Facing the insurgent public anger, the state council quickly abolished the law. In the interpretation of the liberals, the advocacy of rights in the incident had been realized in the confrontation between state and society. First, what had deprived Sun Zhigang of his life and liberty were a detention center in Guangzhou and the "custody and repatriation" law, both of which embodied the power of the state. Moreover, when the state power violated citizens' rights, it was various "social forces," such as the critical reportage of the issue in newspapers, online discussions, and law scholars' petitions, that had created a strong public opinion and eventually forced the state to abolish an unjust law. According to the liberals, these "social forces" were nothing but civil society.[12]

With the liberals' interpretation of the Sun Zhigang Incident, the discourse of *weiquan* was endowed with a new meaning. It implied that citizens' rights were not benefits bestowed by the state. Rather, on many occasions, they were achieved through opposing the state. To commemorate the event and celebrate the success of civil society, many liberals called 2003 the "first year of rights-defending activism" (*weiquan yuannian*) in China.[13]

Since the Sun Zhigang Incident, the liberals tried to project their imagination of rights and civil society onto people in wider society. Coincidentally, the Chinese society in the 2000s was a place where resistance activisms frequently occurred. The economic reform since 1992 had caused vast social contentions (for major social contentions in the 2000s, see Table 3). In rural areas, peasants protested the environmental pollution caused by a new round of industrialization as well as local government officials' corruption in land appropriation.[14] In urban areas, veteran state-owned enterprise workers protested the privatization that had deprived them of their social compacts; rural migrant workers protested wage arrears, the poor working conditions, and the lack of worksite safety; while the middle-class homeowners protested real estate developers' encroachment of their property rights.[15] A report issued by

Table 3. Major Social Contention in Chinese Society in the 2000s

Origins of Social Contention	Major Participants	Major Demands
Environmental pollution	Victims of pollution, mainly peasants	Stop pollution, economic compensation
Environmental impact assessment in construction	Urban residents, mainly homeowners	Stop projects that potentially harm environment
Land appropriation	Peasants	Economic compensation, penalize corrupted local government officials
Privatization of state-owned enterprises	Veteran state-owned enterprise workers	Economic compensation, social security
Labor capital disputes	Mainly rural migrant workers	Pay raises, improve working conditions, social security
Housing relocation in urban renewal projects	Urban residents	Economic compensation
Disputes between developers and homeowners	Homeowners	Protection of private property, economic compensation
Resettlement of ex-service personnel	Veterans	Job opportunities, social security
Discrimination against Hepatitis B carriers	Hepatitis B carriers	Anti-discrimination
Spread of AIDS	AIDS patients	Economic compensation, social security
Food security scandal	Victims of adulterated food products	Economic compensation

China's Academy of Social Science estimated that each year the number of these resistance activisms had surpassed 100,000.[16]

The liberals argued that the abovementioned contentious activities had a commonality—they were all initiated by citizens who struggled to defend their own rights. Therefore, all these activities could be seen as belonging to a single movement. The liberals called this movement the Weiquan Movement. To avoid political risks, they sometimes also used terms like the Wei-quan Activism (*Weiquan Xingdong*), or the New Civil Rights Activism (*Xin Minquan Xingdong*). According to the liberals, the fact that many Chinese people were still proactively expressing their demands that had been denied in formal channels and defending their own rights through agitational activities illustrated well that the hegemonic control of the authoritarian state was limited and that a civil society was in the making.[17] With such a reformulation, the discourse of the right was associated with the liberals' political agenda of building civil society.

The Obfuscation of the Idea of Civil Society

Nevertheless, an inconvenient fact for the liberals emerged—the interpretation of civil society offered by the liberal scholars in the "thought sphere" was already inappropriate for understanding the Weiquan Movement. As I have introduced in chapter one, except for a handful of social liberalists, most liberal scholars in the 1990s had grounded their discussion of civil society in their analysis of the relationship between the rise of a market economy and democratization. These liberal scholars believed that the market was crucial for the formation of a civil society, because a developed market economy could nurture the growth of a propertied class that was relatively less reliant on the state. In the imagination of these liberal scholars, to practice self-organization and coordinate commercial relations, the propertied class would establish a variety of intermediate associations; these associations would then pave the road toward wider and more aggressive participation in politics.[18] Yet the development of the Weiquan Movement had largely diverged from this imagination. To render their interpretation of the Weiquan Movement more plausible, the liberals in the 2000s began to adjust their discussion of the idea of civil society.

First, the participants of civil society had been different from the liberals' assumption. While the propertied class, like homeowners, did proactively participate in some of the activities of the Weiquan Movement, a vast many of the participants of the movement came from socioeconomically disadvantaged groups like peasants and migrant workers. Based on the new situation, the liberals began to downplay their preference over the entrepreneurs and emphasize that all citizens, regardless of their socioeconomic status, were potential participants of civil society. Liberals' attitude had been illustrated in the transformation of the Chinese translation of the term civil society. In the 1990s, the Chinese translation of the term adopted by most scholars was *shimin shehui*, which literally meant "town people's society," or "urban residents' society." This translation had its origin in the German word, *bürgerliche*

Gesellschaft.[19] In the 2000s, with the advocacy of the ICS at Sun Yat-sen University and the *Minjian* magazine, *gongmin shehui* became a more popular translation. In Chinese, the term *gongmin* meant citizens. It did not have any class basis and in principle could be used to refer to all members of a political community. When talking about the choice of the translation, one of the editors of the *Minjian* magazine told me,

> We use gongmin instead of shimin, because we want to include the peasants. About a half of the Chinese people are still peasants. We don't want them to see the concept of civil society as being irrelevant to their life.[20]

Second, the rise of the Weiquan Movement in the 2000s had little to do with the commerce-related associations. As a matter of fact, emerging spontaneously, most of the contentious collective actions were not even initiated by any formal organizations. Some primary associations might be formed during mobilization. Yet these associations tended to quickly disband after state suppression or cooptation.[21] To make their political ideal more compatible with the reality, many liberals began to argue that the true organizational basis of civil society were multiple, intersecting "action networks" (*xingdong wangluo*).[22] The liberals' use of the term "action" (*xingdong*) here had approximated the sociological concept of agency, or the agential activities that had the potential to overcome constraints imposed by structure.[23] According to the liberals, in an ideal situation, an "action network" was grassroots based, formed by volunteers, and devoid of any hierarchical structure. It was also flexible, as it could hide itself in everyday life and show its strength only when participants decided to make a public intervention.[24] Many liberals believed that, in a political environment where the formation of independent organizations (e.g., independent unions) was most of the time strictly prohibited, the "action networks" offered the best chance for expanding the space for participation.[25]

What is worth mentioning here is that the threshold for attending "actions" had been continuously lowered throughout the 2000s. In the beginning, one needed to attend a protest to claim that he or she was involved in an "action." Later, participating in an online discussion of a protest was sufficient to be counted as an "action." In the late 2000s, even watching an online discussion of a protest became an "action." To argue that the "action" of watching was also consequential, Xiao Shu, the famous columnist at the *Southern Weekly*, even wrote an essay titled "China Could Be Changed by Onlookers" (*Weiguan Gaibian Zhongguo*).[26]

Lastly, the goal of many activities in the Weiquan Movement had also diverged from the early imagination of the liberals. Rather than advocating self-organization and further economic reform, what many participants of the Weiquan Movement had raised were the various negative impacts the economic reform had brought to their life. As a response, the liberals downplayed in their discussion the linkages between civil society and the market and began to acknowledge that the goal of civil society activism was plural. In this process, some liberals were even willing to incorporate some of the new leftists' concerns, such as social equity and the protection of the disadvantaged, into their political discussion.

To justify their insistence on seeing state and society as antithesis, the liberals began to argue that civil society was a precondition for many of the political goals raised by the new left. In this aspect, relevant discussions on the *Minjian* magazine provided an illustrative example. In an article published in the magazine, it was argued that, even in social issues like poverty alleviation, which had conventionally believed in China to be the state's responsibility, civil society also had a role to play. In the beginning of the article, the author acknowledged the importance of strong state capacity in redistribution. Then he switched the tone and contended that a mere strong state did not necessarily guarantee the protection of the rights of the disadvantaged. This was because an overly powerful state often tended to be very insensitive to disadvantaged people's demands; such a state might even silence the disadvantaged. Therefore, only in a civil society, where the power of the state was contained and citizens could talk freely, could poverty alleviation be realized.[27]

With these adjustments, civil society had become a rather obfuscated idea. Sometimes, it depicted an ideal situation in which the citizens' right to free and equal public discussion was perfectly protected. In other times, it was used to denote things that were already happening on the ground. When that was the case, it could refer to anything that was disturbing, or could make certain sectors of the state embarrassed. Many of the liberals had also acknowledge this obfuscation. When I was in the field in 2013, I attended an undergraduate course called "Civil Society and Philanthropy" at Sun Yat-sen University. The professor teaching the course was a liberal scholar working at the ICS. Drawing to the end of the course, one of the students in class raised his hand and asked the professor a challenging question—"Professor, the more I listen to your lectures on civil society, the more I feel confused. Before I came to this class, I thought civil society meant NGOs. But you tell me it is more than that. It seems that you argue that civil society is the antithesis of all the bad things happening in China nowadays. But this is still rather unclear to me. Could you say exactly what civil society is?" Sitting in the classroom for several months, I had the same confusion. Hence, I very much looked forward to the answer. Then, to my disappointment, the professor avoided a direct reply. He said,

> I cannot give you an answer to that question. Even if I can, what's the point of having a clear definition of civil society? The boundary of civil society, if there needs one, should be decided upon discussion attended by all participants of civil society. If we decide what counts as civil society activism a priori, we risk missing potential allies.[28]

Then I suddenly realized that it was the liberals' intention to maintain the obscurity of the concept of civil society. It was also in that class that I fully recognized that in China civil society was no longer a theoretical concept for scholarly debate; it had become an ideational instrument for alliance building.

Nevertheless, the binary thinking of state-society relations inherent to the idea of civil society had remained unchanged. In such thinking, the state was unreliable and corrupted, whereas society was seen as being indispensable for the protection of citizens' rights. In the early to mid-2000s, these ideas were expressed in various venues in the media sphere and the NGO sphere.

The Achievements of the Weiquan Movement

In the next section, I will demonstrate that the influence of the liberals was limited and that the binary thinking of state-society relations had brought new problems. However, before that, I want to talk about some of the positive legacies of the Weiquan Movement.

First, to show that Chinese people's "rights consciousness" had risen, throughout the 2000s, the liberals had enthusiastically reported various kinds of *weiquan* activisms and initiated follow-up discussions. In this way, they had rendered these activisms more visible and turned many issues into topics for public discussions. A typical example here is the liberals' intervention in urban residents' protests against the construction of garbage incineration houses. In the 2000s, with the rapid increase of garbage production in cities, many municipal governments began to build garbage incineration houses. NIMBY (not in my backyard) protests against these houses then arose. Commercially-oriented newspapers like the *Southern Metropolis Daily* offered wide coverage of the protests, in which NGO activists and experts were invited to discuss the environmental cost of garbage disposal.[29] These open discussions reminded the Chinese state, as well as the public, that the economic reform since 1992 had not proceeded without a hitch. Rather, the implementation of the reform had its costs and was full of conflicts.

Second, because of the liberals' emphasis on criticizing the state, many of the malfeasance and wrongdoings of government officials, especially those at the local level, were exposed and magnified in public discussions. The Deng Yujiao Incident was a case in point. In May 2009, Deng Yujiao, a 21-year-old hotel service worker in Hubei Province, stabbed three local township government officials who had forced her to provide sexual services, causing one death. She was then arrested and charged with homicide. With the intervention of journalists, the "rights-defending lawyers," and some NGO activists, the event quickly came to national prominence. Via action art and online discussions, people expressed their support of Deng and their anger over the corruption and immorality of the government officials. Later, in response to the public pressure, Deng was released by the court and the two surviving officials involved in the incident were removed.[30] To prevent the formation of such strong public opinions, the Chinese state had since then expended great efforts in containing corruption and disciplining its government officials.

Third, the liberals' criticism over the state had activated many laws and institutions that would otherwise be pretense. An illustrative example here was the enforcement of the regulation on public hearing (*tingzheng hui*) in the Environmental Impact Assessment Law. The Environmental Impact Assessment Law was passed in 2003. In the law, it was stipulated that a public hearing should be held in case a program might involve the environmental interests of the public. However, since the law had made no provision about the liability and the procedure for convening a public hearing, such a hearing had never really happened during the first two years after the passage of the law. Neither did most Chinese people know about the existence of such a venue for participation. Things began to change in 2005, when the management committee of the Yuanmingyuan Park started a project of paving an anti-seepage membrane at the bed of a lake in the park.[31] Because of the historical symbolic significance inherent to the park, the project aroused huge controversies. Journalists, liberal scholars, and several Beijing-based environmental NGOs launched campaigns to protest the project and demanded a public hearing be held. Facing the public doubt, the ministry of environmental protection stepped in and organized a hearing, which was broadcast live on the internet. Because of the strong dissenting opinions expressed in the hearing, the project was eventually terminated.[32] Since then, demanding a public hearing had become a repertoire in environmental protests in China.

Lastly, to establish more solid connections with *weiquan* activisms, the liberals, especially the NGO activists and the "rights-defending" lawyers, had intervened in many *weiquan* cases, offering legal aid, and helping protest leaders establish NGOs. This brought up a generation of activists who were identified with the value of social movement. With respect to turning protest leaders into professional NGO activists, the liberals had been particularly successful in the field of environmental protection. In the 2000s, with the help of the institutes for studying civil society and some Beijing-based environmental NGOs, dozens of activists who used to be victims of environmental pollution established locally based environmental NGOs. Notable instances included Greening the Huai River (*Lüman Jianghuai*) in Anhui Province, the Defender of Huai River (*Huaihe Weishi*) in Henan Province, and Pingnan Green Homeland (*Pingnan Lüse zhi Jia*) in Fujian Province.[33] The liberals had also introduced many university students to *weiquan* activisms. Through participating in online discussions of significant *weiquan* incidents, working as volunteers in NGOs, and attending various salons and lectures, some of these students had later become professional activists. In later years, although China's social and political environment had changed so much that many of the *weiquan* activisms were no longer allowed or became rather marginalized, many of the activists had chosen to stay in the field. I will come back to this point in chapter four.

The Limitations of the Counter-Hegemony

I contend that the binary thinking of state-society relations proposed by the liberals was too reductionist and that it had ignored many important things, notably the complex roles the state could play in the protection of citizens' rights, the subordinate institutions, and the power inequalities within civil society. In the following sections, I will elaborate on the negative consequences of the reductionist interpretation.

The Consequence of Ignoring the Roles of the State

The liberals stressed the importance of constraining the power of the state in the protection of human rights. This was of course meaningful in an authoritarian context. But it largely ignored the complex roles the state could play in the formation of people's rights conditions. By seeing the state as the enemy of the protection of rights, the liberals had systematically excluded many topics in public discussion. Let me use the discussion of the issue of rural migrant workers' rights in commercially-oriented newspapers in the early 2000s to illustrate this point.

Since China's participation in the neoliberal globalization, millions of peasants had left their rural hometowns and became industrial workers. In cities, these workers had constituted a disadvantaged group. Several factors were behind this situation. The first factor had to do with China's *hukou* system. The *hukou* system was a household registration system that defined citizens as legal residents in a certain region. It was a legacy of the socialist era.[34] While the mobility of China's population had dramatically increased since the market-oriented economic reform, transferring one's *hukou* registration across regions remained difficult, especially for those who lacked professional skills.[35] As I have already introduced in the previous chapter, in the 1990s and the early 2000s, to legally work in cities, rural migrant workers had to obtain a temporary living permit from the police. Those who failed to get the permit could be detained by the police and returned to their rural hometowns.

The lack of legal protection was another factor. Labor laws in China granted workers some basic rights, such as the right to safety at work and the right to social insurance. But in practice, before the late 2000s, the rules codified in labor laws were often not enforced. Since local governments tended to prioritize economic growth over labor rights, they were less incentivized to penalize corporations that violated labor laws.[36] A third factor had to do with the fact that the reconstruction of the welfare state in China had lagged behind the economic reforms. China's welfare system was established during the socialist period, when most people worked in the same place for their whole life. Hence the system was rather fragmented, decentralized, and locally based.[37] Until the late 2000s, transferring one's retirement pension across provinces was rather difficult. Moreover, many public services, such as public education, were provided to residents whose *hukou* was locally registered only. Rural migrant workers and their children thus had very limited access to various social programs.[38]

From the above discussion, we can see that the problems of the state with respect to the issue of rural migrant workers' rights were multifarious. On some occasions, it was the excessive state intervention in society and market (the *hukou* system and the "custody and repatriation" law) that had violated rural migrant workers' rights. Yet on other occasions, the failure in the pro-

tection of rural migrant workers' rights had to do with insufficient state regulation over the market (the weak enforcement of labor laws and the lack of
welfare programs).

However, when discussing rural migrant workers' rights, commercially-
oriented newspapers like the *Southern Weekly* and the *Southern Metropolis Daily* were almost exclusively interested in criticizing the excessive state
intervention. Specifically, columnists and liberal scholars associated with
these newspapers blamed the *hukou* system and the "custody and repatriation" law for obstructing the free movement of labor. They argued that the
negative impact brought by these institutions was a vivid example showing
that state intervention in the market could only harm the poor.[39] Criticism of
problems caused by insufficient state regulation was hard to find. In another
word, the liberals were only concerned with rural migrant workers' civil
rights, or the right to become free labor in the market; seldom did they consider these workers' social rights or welfare rights.

On rare occasions, the commercially-oriented newspapers discussed
rural migrant workers' limited access to welfare programs. But the focus of
the discussion was usually on showing the exhaustion of the state and the
superiority of the market. For example, commenting on the phenomenon of
rural migrant workers' children being ineligible to attend public schools, articles published in the *Southern Weekly* suggested that the root of the problem
was the state's monopoly on education. It was also argued that, if the state
opened the education market and let different kinds of schools freely compete, the market would quickly provide enough educational resources.[40] As a
matter of fact, in the early 2000s, there were already many private schools in
coastal cities that enrolled migrant children. But lacking financial resources,
these schools were not able to hire qualified teachers and construct school
buildings that met the safety standards. What these schools needed were subsidies from the state, rather than competition.[41]

What needs to be added here is that, although the liberals had downplayed the relationship between market and civil society in their discussion
of the Weiquan Movement, they had not been able to seriously criticize the
dehumanizing impact brought by the market. Many of the liberals still firmly
believed that the market was the foundation for liberty. Hence, when public
discussions touched upon core institutions of the market, such as the private
ownership of property, the liberals often quickly changed their seemingly
ambiguous attitude.

The liberals' commentaries on the New Rural Reconstruction Movement in commercially-oriented newspapers was a case in point. The New Rural Reconstruction Movement, also known as the "school of rural construction" (*xiangjian pai*), was formed in the late 1990s. Its major participants were a group of social science scholars who were critical of the Chinese state's rural policies. These scholars pointed out that the urban-rural gap in China had become increasingly wider since the 1980s and argued that the market-oriented economic reforms since 1992 had only favored urban regions.[42] In fact, in the late 1990s and early 2000s, many of the strategies the scholars had employed were quite like those of the liberals. To disseminate their ideas, the scholars studying rural issues had also established many NGOs with the help of international foundations.[43] However, because the major political agenda of the school at that time was to oppose land privatization in rural areas, the liberals expressed strong aversion to its activism. In commercially-oriented newspapers, scholars studying rural issues and their various activisms, such as the experiment on helping peasants establish co-operatives, were portrayed in very negative terms.[44] Some commentaries even described the scholars as "a group of outdated scholars who had no idea how the market economy worked" and blamed them for "bringing a horrible revolutionary culture back to China."[45] These negative commentaries remained prominent until the late 2000s.

The Consequence of Ignoring Subordinate Institutions

During my fieldwork, I discovered that many liberals, especially the "rights-defending lawyers," tended to ignore subordinate institutions. By subordinate institutions, I refer to those more concrete and specific rules that shape human actions and behaviors. I see subordinate institutions as a contrast to those principal institutions that set more fundamental rules. Many liberals paid more attention to issues of principal institutions, such as the establishment of a constitutional democracy that protected individual liberty and competitive elections, while regarding subordinate institutions as of secondary importance. However, in practice, it was often subordinate institutions that resistance activisms of this period engaged with. The liberals' disregard for these institutions had thus led them to the misunderstanding of the dynamics of many activities of the Weiquan Movement, and their intervention in the homeowners' movement in the 2000s serves as an example here.

With the commercialization of housing in China, homeowners and private housing communities began to emerge in cities since the mid-1990s.

Beginning in 1998, to reduce the government's burden in managing neighborhood properties, the state began to allow homeowners to establish homeowners' associations. In private housing communities, homeowners' associations were supposed to represent homeowners to negotiate with property management companies and manage the maintenance funds.[46] Because of the lack of legal rules in the newly emerging real estate market and the property management market, conflicts between homeowners, real estate developers, and property management companies often occurred. These conflicts sometimes evolved into homeowners' collective resistance activism.[47]

Homeowners' identity as property owners as well as the relatively autonomous homeowners' associations aroused the liberals' interest. Some liberal scholars commented that homeowners' associations were the "pioneer of China's civil society."[48] Columnists at the *Southern Weekly* even suggested that homeowners' practice of self-organization in neighborhoods may lead to more profound changes in China's political system.[49] Since the early 2000s, the "rights-defending lawyers" and intellectuals in the NGO sphere had attempted to intervene in homeowners' *weiquan* activism.

However, the evolution of homeowners' activism had largely diverged from liberals' expectations. As a matter of fact, since different municipal governments had adopted diverse strategies for coping with homeowners' activism, the development of the activism in different regions had taken divergent paths. In Shanghai, the municipal government aggressively promoted the formation of homeowners' associations. As early as 2000, to alleviate the increasingly intense conflicts between homeowners, developers, and property management companies, the municipal government issued a policy that required neighborhood party committees to help homeowners establish homeowners' associations.[50] Although this policy had lent the state the opportunity to extend its power to homeowners' self-organization, it had nonetheless backed up homeowners. By the late 2000s, homeowners' associations had been established in about 80% of the private housing communities in Shanghai, while the figure for other big cities, like Guangzhou and Beijing, was only around 20%.[51] Besides, most local level state agencies in Shanghai saw the relations among homeowners, real estate developers, and property management companies as commercial relations. When conflicts emerged among these players, the state agencies encouraged stakeholders to employ market means, such as competitive bidding, to resolve disputes. When the conflicts could not be resolved through market means and were taken to the courts, district level courts usually gave judgements out of the concern of protecting homeowners' rights.[52]

In such a context, homeowners' activism in Shanghai tended to be moderate. In the early 2000s, organizations seeking to unite homeowners from different communities emerged. A notable instance was an NGO called the Harmonious Community Salon (*Hexie Shequ Shalong*), which was established in 2003. In the activities initiated by the Salon, participants seldom discussed political issues and the project of building civil society. Instead, they saw homeowners' associations as business organizations and communicated with other homeowners on the knowledge of how to maintain and increase the value of their property.[53]

In southern cities like Guangzhou, local government's support of homeowners' associations was much weaker than that in Shanghai. The legal system for coordinating the relations between homeowners, real estate developers, and property management companies also tended to be less comprehensive. Homeowners in Guangzhou were thus in a disadvantaged position when they came into conflicts with developers and property management companies.[54] Recognizing that their property rights were not institutionally guaranteed, homeowners in the city engaged in advocacy activism. In 2005, activists from different communities co-established an NGO called the Homeowners' Club (*Yezhu Lianyihui*). Working closely with the liberal scholars at the ICS, the Homeowners' Club openly claimed that it was practicing the political ideal of civil society.[55] Besides, the organization also regularly submitted policy suggestions to the provincial people's congress.

Nonetheless, the property management market in Guangzhou was open and competitive. When homeowners in a community decided to change property management companies through market means, local state agencies usually held a laissez-faire attitude. Therefore, the political demands raised by the Homeowners' Club were still relatively moderate. What the organization had proposed to the provincial people's congress was simply that the state kept the order of the property management market so that homeowners could have more space for self-organization.[56]

Lastly, in Beijing, homeowners had been trapped in the most difficult situation. On the one hand, in the 2000s, the municipal government lent almost no support to the formation of homeowners' associations. On the other hand, local state agencies in Beijing tended to see homeowners' collective resistance activism against developers and property management companies as a threat to the political stability. Therefore, their suppression over homeowners' activism was the most proactive. Such an institutional environment had brought up a group of radical activists. In 2006, these activists founded an NGO called the Applicant Committee for Homeowners' Society

(*Yezhu Xiehui Shenban Weiyuanhui*).[57] The activists in the Applicant Committee believed that the difficulties homeowners had encountered revealed a fundamental problem in China's political system—the lack of constitutional democracy. They also believed that it was only when China became democratized could homeowners' rights be protected.[58] Apart from initiating nationwide advocacy campaigns, many of the activists had attended political activism that went beyond homeowners' interests, such as the participation in the election of the people's congress as independent candidates.[59] These activists also liked to associate their activism with China's democratization. One of these activists even told me in an interview that the Applicant Committee could become a political party representing the interests of urban property owners if one day in the future the ban on parties were lifted in China.[60]

The contrast between the homeowners' activism in the three regions clearly shows that the idea that the private ownership of property leads to the formation of an independent civil society is a myth. Homeowners, as property owners, had not been "essentially" against state intervention. Rather, the state's strategy for coping with the homeowners' activism and the condition of the property management market shaped the homeowners' political attitude. But the liberals intervening in the homeowners' activism had not seen the issue in that way. When I was in the field in the early 2010s and talked with these liberals about the development of the homeowners' movement, many of them still suggested that the homeowners' *weiquan* activism was a kind of civil society activism against the state. When I mentioned the case of Shanghai as a case that had diverged from their imagination, a liberal scholar in Guangzhou turned to the analytical framework of state-society dichotomy and offered me an explanation.

> The homeowners' movement in Shanghai has become conservative because the government in Shanghai is more authoritarian and repressive. In contrast, the government in Guangzhou is more open and liberal minded. That's why civil society develops the fastest here.[61]

A "rights-defending lawyer" in Beijing, who had often attended homeowners' activism, attributed the moderateness of homeowners' activism in Shanghai to the culture and ethos of Shanghainese. He said,

> Living in a commercial society, Shanghainese has become prudent and meticulous. They are not like homeowners in the north, who are still bold enough to challenge the government.[62]

The problem here is not only that the liberals had not been able to do good sociological analysis, but that the way they understood the activism had prevented them from sustaining their intervention. Around the early 2010s, to institutionalize homeowners' activism, many municipal governments in China began to learn from the experience of Shanghai. As a result, the regulations for coordinating the relations between homeowners, developers, and property management companies became more formalized.[63] Against such a background, the liberals' interest in the homeowners' movement quickly subsided. However, in fact, even after the state updated its strategies for governing the homeowners' associations, various problems still widely existed in communities. An example was corruption in the use of the maintenance fund.[64] Another example was the shortage of financial resources in those communities that used to be public housing communities supported by government funds.[65] Resultantly, housing-related resistance activisms still now and then occurred.[66] While these resistance activisms may not necessarily lead to the formation of an independent civil society, their existence implied that homeowners' associations, as a form of neighborhood-based organization, still had the potential to expand the space for citizens to practice self-organization and build solidarity.

Nevertheless, in the new situation, intervening in homeowners' activism required a more detailed understanding of how the institutions of the state and the market could shape homeowners' associations. In the eyes of many liberals who had presumed that civil society would spontaneously emerge in middle class property owners' communities, this was too trivial. When I was in Beijing in 2012 and discussed the trend of the homeowners' movement with a "rights-defending lawyer," he said with regret,

> I am glad to see that many homeowners are still trying hard to defend their own right. But I don't see how activisms like this could promote democracy in China. The government has enacted too many laws and policies to regulate homeowners' associations and the power of the state has also extended to commercialized housing neighborhood. Nowadays homeowners can only struggle for their parochial interest.[67]

The case of the homeowners' movement also revealed that the alliance between the liberals and the Weiquan Movement had been highly unstable. Many liberals were only interested in those issues that could bring up wide, agitational activities. When the state stepped in and to a certain degree institutionalized the activities, the liberals' enthusiasm began to diminish.

The Consequence of Ignoring Power Inequalities Within Civil Society

Finally, the liberals' discussion of the participants of civil society was rather abstract. It assumed that all citizens, regardless of their socioeconomic status, could benefit from the formation of a space that was independent of the state. In the discussion of civil society in the 2000s, some liberals began to recognize that participants of civil society were different from each other and that their concerns were concrete and plural. But the concretization of the discussion of civil society had been limited because the formation of an independent space was still seen as the precondition for the articulation of demands. In such a framework, people's concrete concerns easily became subordinated to the grand political project of fighting the authoritarian state. The conflicts between the "rights-defending lawyers" and some socioeconomically disadvantaged participants of the Weiquan Movement were a case in point.

As I have introduced above, some of the liberals like the "rights-defending lawyers" and the NGO activists had directly intervened in various kinds of *weiquan* activisms. These interventions had brought to participants of *weiquan* activisms valuable resources, such as media coverage, legal service, and foreign funds. Yet on the other hand, these interventions had also brought many unexpected troubles. First, regularly attending people's *weiquan* activisms and receiving financial aids from international foundations like the Open Society Institute and the National Endowment for Democracy, many of the "rights-defending lawyers" and NGO activists had already become figures of special concern for the authoritarian regime. Their presence at an activism per se could increase the political sensitivity of the activism.

Second, quite a few "rights-defending lawyers" and NGO activists had sought to radicalize *weiquan* activisms. In their interventions, they encouraged participants of *weiquan* activisms to employ more agitational strategies, establish wider connections, and propose sharper criticism over China's political institutions. Studies on contentious collective actions in China have repeatedly shown that, compared to those activisms that were loosely organized and focused on short-term economic interest, the Chinese state had been less tolerant and lenient with the activisms that attempted to establish formal organizations and raised political demands.[68] This implied that the process in which the lawyers and NGO activists tried to "transform" a *weiquan* activism was also the process by which the activism was exposed to higher risks of state suppression. Under special circumstances, (e.g., a *weiquan* activism drew wide attention in the public, either domestic or international), participants of the activism could be protected from the arbitrary state power. But the attention offered by the public, both the domestic and the international, tended to be limited and erratic, while the number of *weiquan* activisms happening in China each year was huge. For the vast majority of *weiquan* activisms that were by no means dramatic, winning wide attention was almost an impossible mission. After radicalizing their activities as the intervening lawyers and NGO activists wished, participants of these activisms to different degrees became the victims of authoritarian repression. Some of them were harassed by the security police. Some lost their jobs or were even detained.

Early reflection upon these negative impacts came from the liberals who had intervened in the *weiquan* activism. Recognizing that some participants of the *weiquan* activism had been trapped in worse situations after receiving aid from NGO activists and the "rights-defending lawyers," these liberals proposed that there existed an "ethical dilemma" in the Weiquan Movement—if NGO activists and the "rights-defending lawyers" wanted to prioritize the protection of participants of *weiquan* activisms, they needed to avoid mentioning the various political agendas inherent to the Weiquan Movement, such as criticizing the authoritarian state power and advocating an independent civil society. If the activists and the lawyers insisted on advancing these political agendas, they might endanger the participants of *weiquan* activism and harm their immediate interests.[69]

When I was in the field in the 2010s, I discussed the ethical issue with many liberals who had attended the *weiquan* activism. Some of them identified with the idea of the "ethical dilemma" and were more sympathetic to the real difficulties the participants of *weiquan* activism encountered. An NGO activist shared with me his thinking of the issue in an interview.

> Weiquan participants' concerns are usually simple. They want their corrupted village head to be penalized. They want to stop the factories that pollute their environment. As intellectuals, what we can do is to help them achieve their goals. We can of course tell them that the problem lies in China's political institution and that democracy is the solution. But we should not impose our will on them.[70]

But more NGO activists and "rights-defending lawyers" tended to negate the existence of the dilemma. When I mentioned the ethical issue in an interview with a "rights-defending lawyer" in Shanghai, the lawyer responded,

I don't think the intervention of the 'rights-defending lawyers' has any ethical problem. We always communicate with our clients when we decide to transform a case into a political campaign. We tell them the pros and cons of employing radical strategies, and we employ these strategies only when they say 'yes.' In fact, many ordinary people are not that unwilling to sacrifice part of their quiet life to expose the evils of the authoritarian regime.[71]

For me, the views offered by both sides sounded, at least partially, reasonable. When I was in the field, I could not judge which side was more correct. Therefore, I closely followed a few *weiquan* cases attended by the "rights-defending lawyers" and NGO activists. Here is what I observed. First, the situation in which the lawyers and NGO activists prioritized the advocacy of political ideals did exist in their interventions. But this mainly happened in politically sensitive cases, such as those cases that involved the issue of the freedom of speech and religion. Even without the attendance of the lawyers and the activists, people involved in these cases were very likely to experience harsh state suppression. There was little evidence showing that the involvement of the lawyers and the activists had made things worse.

The subtleties of the issue were revealed in those cases in which the participants of the *weiquan* activism were the disadvantaged and their demands were mainly about economic interests. In those cases, the "rights-defending lawyers" and NGO activists did try to help the *weiquan* participants. They also did communicate with these participants about the possible consequences of employing radical strategies, as what the lawyer in Shanghai had told me. Yet what these lawyers and activists had largely overlooked were that different people's perceptions of resistance movements and state repression tended to be divergent and that these divergent perceptions were largely shaped by different life experiences.

Many "rights-defending lawyers" and NGO activists had engaged in social movement activisms like the environmental movement and the AIDS movement since they were university students. Instead of struggling for their own interest, they had attended these activisms to advance the general interest. The universities had provided them with a relatively safe environment and thus prolonged the period in which they could think over the meaning of becoming a professional activist, and more importantly, the price they were willing to pay. In my fieldwork in Beijing in 2012, I met an NGO activist who had graduated from Peking University. I asked him about his experience of confronting the authoritarian state. His answer illustrated well my point here.

At first, it was within the campus. The party secretary of my department came to talk with me and asked me to write a self-criticism report (xie jiancha). Then someone from the state security department called me. As I attended more of these activities, the police invited me to have tea. Whenever the harassment from the state was upgraded, I asked myself: Is this what I can withstand? How much more can I take? When I gave positive answers, I continued and deepened my participation in these activities. When I detected fear and hesitation in me, I took a rest until I accumulated enough strength to go on. It is through this long and tortuous process that I have become a professional activist.[72]

But the *weiquan* participants who came from socioeconomically disadvantaged groups were often involved in resistance activism by accident. Compared to the NGO activists and the "rights-defending lawyers," these socioeconomically disadvantaged resisters did not have the process through which they could, bit by bit, experience how it was like to confront an authoritarian power. Moreover, these resisters, as the disadvantaged, usually lacked social prestige in their daily life. Through working with the "rights-defending lawyers" and the NGO activists, many socioeconomically disadvantaged resisters for the first time in their life felt that they were esteemed and that they were empowered to promote changes in wider society. Because of these factors, the NGO activists and the "rights-defending lawyers" tended to have great influence over the socioeconomically disadvantaged resisters with respect to their choice of strategies in *weiquan* activism.

Hence, although on many occasions, the socioeconomically disadvantaged resisters did show willingness to employ radical strategies after communicating with the activists and the lawyers, their decision-making process tended to be hasty, without thorough consideration of all the possible negative consequences. Talking about how he had been persuaded into using radical strategies in a *weiquan* activism, a rural migrant worker told me in an interview:

At the time, they [activists in the NGOs] repeatedly told us, "You guys have been suppressed to such an extent. You must defend your rights." Of course I was inclined to defend my rights. But I was also afraid of being beaten by the police. I was not certain how far I could go. Motivation and pressure coexisted in me. But if I told them so, they would deny me and ask, "Can't you just have more courage and ambition?" It was under such pressure that I took bold actions.[73]

After being suppressed by the state, many of the socioeconomically disadvantaged resisters experienced a huge mental loss. Some of them regretted their choice and turned against the NGO activists and the lawyers. Some had a nervous breakdown.

What had reinforced the conflicts between the professional activists and the socioeconomically disadvantaged resisters was this fact: While the NGO activists and the lawyers deeply influenced the strategies employed by the socioeconomically disadvantaged resisters, they were not able to share risks with the latter group, and it was often the latter group that felt the negative consequences. A *weiquan* case I had followed in Guangzhou illustrated this problem. In 2011, with the help of two NGOs, migrant workers in a jewelry processing plant in the city organized a protest, demanding that their employer pay social insurance arrears. At the time, because migrant workers had seldom won social insurance payments, the NGOs involved were keen to make a success of this case. They therefore expended great effort pushing the workers to take more radical actions. After discussing with the NGO activists, workers laid siege to the human resource department in the corporation and confined the human resource manager to his office for over 30 hours. In the end, the confrontation between workers and the manager proceeded from words to blows. Police came and detained the leaders among the workers. These leaders were not released until a month later. Eventually, workers at the plant won the social insurance payment. The NGOs involved began to use the case as a model to show how workers' *weiquan* activism could make a difference. But the leaders and major activists of the activism were either fired or suffered salary downgrades.

When I was in the field in 2013, I interviewed one of the leaders. By then, the leader had already gotten a new job and begun to work as a volunteer in an NGO that had been involved in the event. Nonetheless, the past experience still constituted a trauma for him. My original plan was to discuss with him his work as a volunteer in the NGO. But in the interview, he spent most of the time talking about the various harms the event had incurred on him and his family. Recalling the whole procedure of the *weiquan* activism, he said,

> If these things [detention and unemployment] had not happened, I would feel that these NGOs are pretty good. But in that half year, I really lost tens of thousands of yuan. My wife and children were also scared to death. I know when you want to have a revolution or promote social reform, some people in society must sacrifice. But here, all success is counted as the NGOs' merit, while all loss is on me personally. I feel that's unfair.[74]

If we scrutinize the cases in which the conflicts between the liberals and socioeconomically disadvantaged resisters arose, we may find that many of the conflicts were not necessarily unavoidable. The professional activists among the liberals and the socioeconomically disadvantaged resisters could have had better communication. People could have figured out better strategies for apportioning risks. There could have been more emotional support for the *weiquan* participants. But in a framework that tended to prioritize the confrontation with the state, it was hard for people to elaborate public discussions on the abovementioned topics. The interpretation of a "rights-defending lawyer" in Beijing of the ethical issue well illustrated this point. When I asked the lawyer in an interview how he balanced between the long-term goal of the Weiquan Movement and *weiquan* participants' short-term interest, he said,

> I think you tend to exaggerate the conflicts between the 'rights-defending lawyers' and the clients. The most fundamental contradiction in China nowadays is between the Chinese citizens whose 'rights consciousness' is rising and a public power that has not yet been constrained. It is the public power, not the 'rights-defending lawyers,' that violates citizens' rights. In my opinion, the so-called 'ethical dilemma' reveals nothing but a simple fact—the only way to improve the human rights condition in China is to fight with the authoritarian regime and build a more open and fair judicial system.[75]

The negative consequence of ignoring the inequalities between the "rights-defending lawyers" and socioeconomically disadvantaged resisters was not only that people from the latter group were harmed, but also that the two groups could not build rapport with each other. After witnessing the cost of working with these professional activists, some socioeconomically disadvantaged resisters became astute. Rather than wholeheartedly supporting the political project of building civil society, they began to see "rights-defending lawyers" and NGO activists as a kind of resource they could draw on. An NGO activist who had been actively involved in the AIDS movement offered me a vivid description of the situation.

> Some people have criticized us for making use of weiquan participants. But it is not only that we are using the weiquan participants. On many occasions, the weiquan participants are also using us. My organization had received quite a few such people. Initially, they came to us, saying that they wanted to fight to defend their rights, and asked us to contact lawyers, journalists, and

human rights organizations in the international community. Then we spent a lot of efforts, doing what they wanted us to do. It was until later that we figured out that these people had seen us merely as an instrument for pushing local government. After they got their money, they asked us to withdraw the lawsuit and never showed up again.[76]

From these discussions, we can see that, although the liberals had managed to use the discourse of *weiquan* to discursively unify the fragmented resistance activisms and create a counter-hegemonic movement, the movement had been hastily formed. While the liberals claimed that they wanted to incorporate disadvantaged groups into the project of building civil society, their political discussions had often failed to substantively take the concerns of disadvantaged groups into account. Resultantly, the solidarity formed in the liberals' intervention in the *weiquan* activism tended to be fragile.

Conclusion

This chapter investigates how the liberals had projected their imagination of politics onto people in wider society. I first trace how the liberals transformed the discourse of *weiquan* into a counter-hegemonic discourse. Then I analyze liberals' efforts in discursively unifying the fragmented contentious collective actions and building the Weiquan Movement. I suggest that, to render the idea of civil society more relevant to real world politics, the liberals had obfuscated the participants, the organizational basis, and the goal of civil society activism in their public expressions. During this process, the meaning of civil society had in many ways diverged from the original discussion of the concept in the "thought sphere." But the emphasis on the antithesis between state and society had remained unchanged. In the latter half of this chapter, I elaborate the problems of reducing the *weiquan* activism to the antithesis between state and society. I argue that liberals' ignorance of power and subordinate institutions had reproduced inequality and domination. Conversely, the existence of such inequality and domination had also harmed the sustainability of the working alliances the liberals had established during their intervention.

By going into the details of history, this chapter and the previous chapter intend to offer an alternative interpretation of the vibrant public discussions and social movements happening in China in the early to mid-2000s. In examining this period of history, some scholars have highlighted the expansion of the public sphere and the rise of "rights consciousness" among Chinese citizens. For example, Lei Ya-wen has argued that a "contentious public sphere," or a "counter public sphere," had risen in China in the 2000s and that a resistance community based on common values had been built.[77] In my opinion, this interpretation is more of what the influential actors in the public sphere during that period, that is, the liberals, had wanted people to think of China's politics. It was simply not the reality. In responding to this view, I emphasize that it was in various kinds of interstitial spaces that the liberals had emerged and that the liberals' relations with the state had been far more complex than what they had often claimed. Moreover, I point out that, although the liberals had tried hard to build alliances with different actors, the inclusivity of these alliances had been limited and the solidarity formed in this process had been fragile.

Some other scholars have held a more critical attitude toward the exercise of power in China's public sphere. A notable instance here is Zhao Yuezhi, who has argued that China's public sphere embodied state's neoliberal control and that the so-called critical news media like the *Southern Weekly* only represented middle class interests.[78] I am sympathetic to this view, especially its sensitivity to class issues. I also acknowledge the influence of neoliberalism on liberals' interpretation of civil society during this period. However, in my opinion, this view also tends to simplify the complex relations between the state and the emergent public sphere. Since the space out of which critical public opinions emerged was interstitial space, where the exercise of power was not fully institutionalized, public discussions in the space contained a certain degree of uncertainty. Some of the topics brought up by public discussions in the space, such as anti-corruption, could be tolerated or even encouraged. But there were also topics the state was reluctant to engage in, such as the restriction of public power.

Moreover, I suggest that this view exaggerates the controlling capacity of major actors in China's public sphere. First, the potential of the liberals in forging organizations and alliances had been limited by the authoritarian state. Second, in the 2000s, with the deepening of China's market economic reform, Chinese people's interests had already become rather pluralized. The power of the Chinese state had also become decentralized in the economic reform. While the number of contentious collective actions happening each year was huge, most of these actions had targeted localized state agencies. Based on these conditions, many liberals had also recognized that it had

become increasingly difficult to launch a comprehensive resistance movement and perform as the leaders of the movement. Therefore, the strategies
the liberals had taken in the 2000s tended to be more submissive. To incorporate the spontaneously emerging *weiquan* activisms into their ideological camp, the liberals had continuously adjusted their interpretation of civil
society. In other words, while it was the liberals that had set the agenda for
public discussion, their agenda setting process had not been resistant to the
transformation of demands making in wider society.

Nevertheless, during the first term of the Hu-Wen regime, the liberals
had expanded their influence in China's interstitial publics and discursively
unified the fragmented *weiquan* activisms by projecting their imagination of
civil society onto people in wider society. It was largely under liberals' efforts
that many social problems and conflicts arising during China's economic
reform were thematized. Without these efforts, the Chinese state might have
lacked motivations to invest resources to deal with these problems and conflicts. For me, this constitutes the most important reason for documenting
the history of the civil society project.

PART TWO

The Contradicting Institutionalization of Civil Society as an Ideational Movement

CHAPTER 4

The Structural Transformation of Interstitial Publics, 2008–2013

During the second term of the Hu-Wen regime, the political, social, and technological environment of China's public sphere altered again. A series of public events happening in 2008, including the uprising in Tibet, the Wenchuan Earthquake, and the opening of the Beijing Olympics, ignited patriotic enthusiasm among the younger generation. On the internet, public expression of nationalist emotion began to rise. The Arab Spring, which took place in 2011, alarmed the Chinese state of the possibility of advancing regime change through social movement activism in civil society. After that, the state's control over NGOs and critical news reports became increasingly intensified. Additionally, during this stage, China's rapid development of information technology brought new impacts to the organization of public discussion. With the rise of mobile devices for getting online and the emergence of social network media, the threshold for participating in discussions on the internet was significantly lowered. These changes led to a structural transformation of the interstitial publics that had existed since the 1990s. New players arose, while the domination of major players in the previous stage, that is, the liberals, was destabilized.

It was during this stage that the idea of civil society was widely contested in China's public sphere. Among the various kinds of naysayers, three groups of actors proposed coherent and methodical criticism over the liberal interpretation of civil society. These three groups were activists from the New Rural Reconstruction Movement, labor scholars as public sociologists, and the feminist activists. These actors challenged the liberal discourse that dichotomized state and society and questioned whether an independent space, where the state power could not legitimately interfere, was the precondition for democracy and social justice. I suggest that it was during these contestations that fissures began to grow within the project of building civil society. Nevertheless, critics of the liberals during this stage, especially the labor scholars and the feminist activists, were still largely sympathetic to the concept of civil society. They took the concept seriously and explored, through social movement activism, alternative approaches for realizing the many political ideals inherent to the concept. I hence argue that the vitality of the civil society as an ideational movement was largely maintained during the second term of the Hu-Wen regime.

This chapter (chapter four) and the next chapter (chapter five) are both dedicated to the condition of interstitial publics between 2008 and 2013. While chapter four describes the transformation of the organizational structure of public discussions, chapter five focuses on the debates between the liberals and several social movements that advocated rights and interests of subaltern groups of people. The rest of this chapter will be arranged in the following way. In the next section, I introduce the social and political background during the second term of the Hu-Wen regime. This is followed by a section that analyzes how the media sphere and the NGO sphere had become partially institutionalized due to the intervention of the state and the upgrade of information technology. Then I write a section that elaborates how the transformation of the two spheres impacted the participants of the public discussion. In this section, I first discuss the emergence of a new generation of participants. Then I discuss how some of the liberals managed to maintain their influence in the public sphere.

The Transformation of the Social and Political Environment in the Late 2000s

After a failed bid in 1993, Beijing was elected as the host city for the 2008 Summer Olympics in July 2001. Since then, in its various propaganda campaigns, the Communist Party had celebrated Beijing's success as a symbol of the resurgence of the Chinese nation. It was argued that the holding of the Olympic Games would signify China's "return" to a strong and influential nation in the international community after a long and humiliating modern history during which China fell behind in its social and economic development.[1] Many ordinary Chinese people tended to think of the sports gathering in similar ways. In 2008, the fervor for the Olympic Games was high around the country.

However, looking back, we may discover that the year of 2008 was also a year in which crises of different kinds emerged. In March, hundreds of protests and demonstrations were held in Tibet to commemorate the 49th anniversary of the Tibetan Uprising Day, when the 14th Dalai Lama went into exile. Clashes occurred between protestors and China's security forces, leading to the destruction of many Han and Hui buildings and stores and the injury and death of numerous civilians. The use of force by Chinese police and army in the suppression of the resistance activities triggered widespread protests in North America and Europe, many of which called for a boycott of the Beijing Olympics.[2] In May, an earthquake measuring 8.0 M_s hit Sichuan Province located in southwestern China, killing nearly 70,000 people and leaving at least 4.8 million people homeless. What had caused public anger was the fact that thousands of children died in the earthquake due to shoddy construction of school buildings.[3] The occurrence of these events largely provoked enthusiasm for public participation. On traditional paper media and the internet, people vehemently expressed opinions. Controversies were prominent with respect to issues like social justice in the economic reform, the accountability of government, and the relationship between China and the West.

In these public debates, people witnessed the rise of a new wave of nationalist emotions. Grassroots, bottom-up expressions of nationalist emotions had long existed in China's public sphere since the 1990s. Typical examples included the publication of *China Can Say No* (Zhongguo Keyi Shuo Bu) in 1996, a bestseller that strongly criticized US foreign policies, and university students' protests over US bombing of the Chinese embassy in Belgrade in 1999. In expressing nationalist sentiments, participants of these activisms had mainly talked to the Chinese government, calling on Beijing to take a more assertive stance in a new era of global competition.[4] While these nationalists' understanding of the problems facing China had in many ways diverged from that of the liberals, open and direct confrontations between the two groups had seldom occurred in previous years. But after 2008, the situation gradually changed. With the fast development of the information technology in the country, people were granted more opportunities to publicly express their concerns and encounter those who held different opinions. As a result, the conflict between the liberals and the nationalists became more conspicuous.[5] On some occasions, the conflict even evolved into personal attacks.

An illustrative example was the debate centering on the public expression of Chang Ping during the Tibet unrest in 2008. Chang Ping was a columnist and an associate editor at the *Southern Metropolis Weekly* (Nandu Zhoukan), a newspaper affiliated with the *Southern Metropolis Daily*. Regarding his political stance, Chang Ping was a typical liberal. During the Tibet unrest, many Chinese students studying overseas found the reportage of the event on western media inaccurate and biased.[6] For instance, the *Washington Post* used pictures of baton-wielding Nepalese police in clashes with Tibetan protestors in Kathmandu, claiming that the officers were Chinese. CNN selectively reported Chinese government's military repression, without mentioning the protestors' violent behaviors. In response to the reportage, some students studying abroad set up a website called Anti-CNN to demonstrate evidence of the one-sidedness of western media. Articles posted on the website tended to be widely spread and well received among internet users within China. On April 3rd, Chang Ping published a short essay titled "Tibet: Truth and Nationalist Sentiment" in *Financial Times China* (FT Zhongwen Wang).[7] It was this essay that had trapped him in controversies.

In the essay, Chang Ping criticized the Anti-CNN activism from two aspects. First, he pointed out that, while criticizing western media for its biased reporting, supporters of Anti-CNN had also lacked knowledge on what was going on in Tibet; behind this ignorance was the Chinese government's long-term monopoly of journalism and news reports. Therefore, according to Chang Ping, the problem with the Anti-CNN activism was that it had failed to recognize that the greatest source of biased reporting was the authoritarian state, rather than Western media. Additionally, Chang Ping contended that, while criticizing westerners for their "superiority complex" (*youyue gan*) in judging issues happening in the East, the supporters of Anti-CNN, most of whom were Han Chinese, had failed to reflect upon the fact that they too were a privileged group vis-à-vis China's ethnic minorities. At the end of the essay, he suggested that criticizing the hegemony of the West did little to help improve national solidarity in China and encouraged readers to search for alternative interpretations of problems in Tibet. While Chang Ping wrote in a cautious tone, dissenting voices became rampant on the internet immediately after the publication of the essay. Supporters of the Anti-CNN activism blamed Chang Ping for not being patriotic. Some even labeled the columnist and the newspapers he was associated with "traitors of China" (*hanjian*).[8] The public opposition eventually led to the dismissal of Chang Ping from the position of associate editor of the *Southern Metropolis Weekly*.

Another example was more subtle. After the Sichuan Earthquake, the Chinese government invested huge amounts of resources to the rescue work. Premier Wen Jiabao flew to the earthquake area just 90 minutes after the first quake. Within one day, 50,000 troops were dispatched to help with the disaster relief work in the epicenter. The horrification of the disaster, together with the government's quick response, incurred a "rally 'round the flag" effect. During the first few days after the earthquake, some of China's political leaders, especially Wen Jiabao, obtained increasing popular support. Rather than overseeing the government's rescue work and criticizing the school building problems, many Chinese people posted entries on various online forums to pay homage to the leaders and express their love of the regime.[9] These discussions largely irritated the liberals, who had often advocated to hold a more critical stance toward the authoritarian state. On May 14th, two days after the earthquake, Zhu Xueqin, a historian in Shanghai, who was also a major exponent of liberalism in China, made a commentary on the *Southern Metropolis Daily*, suggesting that the disaster was "a punishment sent by the heaven" (*tianqian*).[10] Compared to that in Chang Ping's case, Zhu's commentary aroused even greater public anger. Many readers of the *Southern Metropolis Daily* criticized Zhu for lack of sympathy toward victims of the disaster and demanded an apology. Zhu never apologized for his commentary. But the column that carried the commentary was suspended.

Random as the two incidents appeared to be, they largely changed the public image of liberal intellectuals and the southern newspapers these intellectuals were associated with. As I have discussed in chapter two, the southern newspapers, especially the *Southern Weekly*, used to be noted for their populist writing style. In revealing the dark side of China's reform and criticizing corrupted government officials, journalists and editors of these newspapers claimed to represent and stand with socioeconomically disadvantaged groups. This was also how the newspapers had established themselves as the "conscience of the media sphere." But what the two incidents had shown was that the liberals associated with the southern newspapers were a group of intellectual elites who had a "structure of feeling" that diverged from that of many ordinary people. In addition, through the two incidents, many participants of online discussions suddenly discovered that the liberals were not that invincible; satires and criticisms on the internet could easily turn them into targets of public attack.

Meanwhile, the Chinese state's attitude toward critical discussions in the interstitial publics was also changing. Two events had urged the state to strengthen its control. The first event was the publication of the Charter 08, a manifesto for constitutional democracy. The drafters of the Charter 08 were a group of dissident intellectuals who had attended the 1989 Student

Movement. Adopting its name and style from the anti-Soviet Charter 77 in Czechoslovakia, the manifesto challenged one-party rule and advocated a series of principles in a constitutional democracy, notably the separation of powers and independent judiciary. Initially, 303 people signed to support the activism. These people were mainly the liberal intellectuals in the "thought sphere" and the "rights-defending" lawyers who had achieved national influence in the early 2000s. The organization of the signing activism made it clear to the Chinese state that the liberals who talked about human rights issues in the '90s and '00s were not separated from the intellectuals who had demanded democracy in the '80s and that it was not impossible that the seemingly trivial and moderate *weiquan* activism later grew into a movement threatening the regime. Hence the repression came swift and fierce. Liu Xiaobo, a major organizer of the activism, who was also one of the authors of the charter, was detained even before the text of the charter was published online. He was later sentenced to eleven years of imprisonment for "inciting subversion of state power." The police interrogated many of the signatories, while discussions of the document were strictly prohibited on media.[11]

The other event was the rise of the Arab Spring at the end of 2010. Unlike many commentators from the West, who had regarded the popular protests in the Arab world as constituting a democracy movement, from the very beginning, the Chinese state had seen the uprising as a threat to social and political stability.[12] The state became even more vigilant when evidence was revealed that some organizations in the resistance activism had been associated with international foundations from the West, notably the National Endowment for Democracy and the Open Society Institute, as these foundations had also been working with various activists in China.

Because of these issues, the state's attitude toward the discussion of the concept of civil society dramatically changed. Before the Arab Spring, the state's attitude toward the discussion of civil society, at least in the academic field, was rather ambiguous. The studies of civil society had never been promoted. But nor had they been prohibited. The positive mention of the concept had even been seen in works published by those scholars who were very close to the state power. A notable example was Yu Keping, who was the associate director of the Central Compilation and Translation Bureau, an organ directly under the Central Committee of the Chinese Communist Party.[13] But after the uprising in the Arab world, this ambiguous space was gone. As the state's propaganda began to describe civil society as a space in which agents of overseas forces spread Western ideology, or even prepared for subversive activism,[14] talking about the concept gradually became politically sensitive.

With these changes, the public sphere in China went through a series of structural transformations.

The Partial Institutionalization of Interstitial Publics

I suggest that, during the second term of the Hu-Wen regime, the spaces in which alternative public discussions took place in the early to mid-2000s, namely the media sphere and the NGO sphere, became partially institutionalized. By institutionalization, I refer to the process in which the interstitially emergent activisms became so regulated that they no longer constituted a challenge to the dominant power of the state and the market. Behind the partial institutionalization was the fact that the state power and the market power became increasingly pervasive. However, I also want to emphasize that the influence of the two powers on alternative public discussions was still constrained during this stage. Due to the development of new technologies and the introduction of new resources, social movement activism in some areas became even more proactive. In the following sections, I scrutinize the changes of the abovementioned two spheres.

The Partial Institutionalization of the Media Sphere

The Decline of Newspapers as a Venue for Critical Public Discussion
In the late 2000s, the Chinese government's censorship over the production of critical news reports was intensified, especially on newspapers. This had been enabled by two factors. The first one was the fact that the proactive news media that had critically reported social issues in the 1990s and early 2000s were by no means independent media. As I have introduced in chapter two, all newspapers and publishers in China had to be registered under a recognized institutional sponsor, that is, party committees, government departments, and mass organizations. This meant that the head of a newspaper or a publisher, no matter how commercialized it appeared to be, was always a state cadre whose career development was largely dependent upon the wills of higher bureaucratic authorities. When the political environment was relatively open, the state cadres that intended to earn more revenues, or simply had very few interests in defending communist ideologies, became "delinquent" in supervision responsibilities. News reports that appeared to diverge from official discourses thus emerged. But when the state began to see critical news reports as a threat to the stability of the regime and finally

decided to regulate the practice of journalism, it had never lacked the leverage for achieving its goals. A most used tactic was to remove the cadre who was in charge of editorial supervision and appoint a new one. This happened to the *Southern Weekly* since the early 2000s.[15]

A second factor was the conglomeration of news media, which had started in the late 1990s and accelerated in the mid-2000s.[16] By 2011, under the guidance of the state, newspapers and magazines that engaged in the reportage of "current events" (*shizheng*), including those spin-off newspapers and magazines that were more commercially oriented, were integrated into over 120 publishing groups. These publishing groups were usually led by official newspapers or publishers at the provincial level. While the purpose of the conglomeration was to liquidate the assets of those newspapers that were directly run by party organs—which had suffered from a relative decline in circulation in the 1990s and early 2000s—the rise of these publishing groups had also largely altered the previously fragmented censorship system. Whereas in the previous stage the responsibility of supervision was spread over a diverse array of sponsoring institutions, in the new system, state cadres at the publishing groups were supposed to be directly accountable to propaganda departments and the state's news supervision institutions.[17] By conglomerating the news media, the state had lessened the power and influence of local and departmental government officials and created a censorship system that was more coherent. In such a system, many strategies that had been employed by journalists in the previous stage, such as the "cross-regional supervision," became ineffectual.

The increasingly stringent censorship over newspapers led to numerous conflicts between journalists, editors, and the state's propaganda departments, which was epitomized in the *Southern Weekly* New Year's Greeting Incident. The *Southern Weekly* had published a new year's greeting (*xinnian xianci*) on its front page of the first issue of each year since 1999. It was a tradition that the chief editor of the newspaper talked in the greeting about some political ideals shared by the editorial board. At the end of 2012, the editorial board decided that they would critically adopt Xi Jinping's discourse on the China dream (*Zhongguo meng*) and talked about the possibility of a dream of constitutionalism (*xianzheng meng*). The original version of the greeting went through the standard censorship procedure, with some of its critical content being removed. However, in the eyes of Tuo Zhen, the newly appointed head of the Guangdong Propaganda Department, the revised version was still far away from the official discourse of the China dream. He then personally wrote a commentary that glorified the Communist Party and added it to the new year's greeting without informing the editorial board. Many editors and journalists at the *Southern Weekly* had not recognized that the greeting had been interpolated until January 3, 2013, when the special issue was released, and readers discovered that the greeting contained multiple miswritten words and grammatical mistakes. This provoked the editors and journalists. As a response, they posted criticisms of the state of free speech in China online and went on a four-day strike. These activities also sparked public demonstrations against press censorship, which took place outside *Southern Weekly's* headquarters in Guangzhou.[18] Widespread and proactive as they were, these resistance activities were later suppressed. Tuo Zhen, whose intervention had directly caused the conflict, was even promoted to deputy head of the Propaganda Department of the Communist Party of China two years later.

What had reinforced the impact of the increasingly intensified censorship was the development of the internet technologies. In 2009, internet users in China witnessed the rise of a series of websites that provided social network service. These included the Sina Weibo, which later evolved into one of the biggest microblogging platforms in the world. In 2012, mobile phones for the first time surpassed personal computers and became the most commonly used devices for getting online.[19] I will talk more about how these new technologies transformed the organization of online public discussion in the next section. For this section, what I want to highlight is that these new technologies had negatively influenced the vitality of traditional media, especially newspapers. As I have introduced in chapter two, in the 1990s and early 2000s, most journalists and editors at newspapers generally welcomed or even celebrated the rise of the internet in China, as the internet technology helped them circumscribe censorship. However, in the late 2000s, these journalists and editors had to face an inconvenient fact—as more and more people turned to the internet for reading news, the circulation of newspapers dropped. Since 2012, almost all major commercially-oriented newspapers in China, including the *Southern Weekly* and the *Southern Metropolis Daily*, experienced a plummet in their advertisement income.[20] As the revenues continued to decline, many newspapers were no longer able to support investigative journalism, which was rather costly.[21]

It is a universal phenomenon that the rise of digital media brings negative impact on traditional paper media. Many prominent newspapers in the West also need to figure out strategies for coping with problems like the draining of readers and the decline of revenues.[22] In response to the changing technological environment, commercial newspapers in China adjusted their orientation. For example, since the late 2000s, the *Southern Weekly* had tried to get rid of the sensational, populist writing style and establish itself as a "high-quality" media that offered "professional" and "in-depth" interpretations of news, in the hope that readers would be willing to pay more for subscriptions.[23] However, the increasing state censorship over the reportage of social and political issues had thwarted this attempt. Additionally, the state had also thwarted the newspapers' attempts at cooperating with the newly rising internet media by categorizing articles published on commercially-oriented newspapers as "abnormal sources" (*feiguifan gaoyuan*), which were in principle prohibited from being reissued on portal websites that engaged in news reports.[24] With these constraints imposed by the state, the shock experienced by Chinese newspapers during the rise of digital media had been especially acute.

By the late 2000s, the relative decline of newspapers as a venue for producing critical public opinions had already become salient. In the early to mid-2000s, newspapers were the site where muckraking reports were published and heated discussions on controversial social issues were ignited, whereas discussions on the internet were only the follow-ups. However, since the late 2000s, the role of the two forms of media exchanged. Commenting on the exposition of significant events, Lu Hui, a senior editor who used to work for the *Southern Metropolis Daily* said in an interview, "Paper media had already got no business here."[25]

Some optimistic observers have suggested that we should not see the decline of newspapers as the end of critical public discussions, because, as many experienced journalists give up their jobs at newspapers and turn to the digital media, the spirit of critical journalism may spread to a new terrain.[26] But from my point of view, the decline of newspapers had severely hurt the liberals, because newspapers used to be an important "stronghold" in which the liberals gathered, met their fellows, and projected their political ideal onto wider society. The liberals could of course criticize the authoritarian state and advocate the idea of civil society on the internet. But the internet constituted a much more complex environment. This is what I am going to explain.

The Rapid Expansion of Social Network Media as a Venue for Public Discussion
In 2008, the number of internet users in China exceeded 300 million. This made China the country having the largest population of internet users in the world.[27] Behind the fast growth of the internet users were the Chinese

state's industrial policies that prioritized the development of digital technologies. With the synergy between the state and corporations, infrastructure for broadband network and mobile network was expanded from coastal regions to inland regions and the cost for getting online had continuously been decreasing.[28] The rise of domestic brands like Huawei, Xiaomi, and OPPO offered consumers alternatives to the expensive iPhone. Socioeconomically less advantaged people, such as rural migrant workers, were now able to buy smartphones.[29]

Alongside the advancement of the infrastructure was the emergence of large-scale, comprehensive social network media for public discussion. Platforms for discussing public issues, such as BBSes, online forums, and blogs, had existed on China's internet since the 1990s. But these previous platforms had either targeted specific social groups or categorized participants according to their interests and concerns. For example, prominent BBSes like SMTH and YTHU had mainly targeted university students and well-educated people. Commercially-oriented online forums like Tianya had set up multiple boards to differentiate topics for discussion. In contrast, many social network media emerging in the late 2000s intended to build a comprehensive platform on which people with different interests and concerns could meet and all sorts of topics could be discussed. Among these social network media, the most influential one was Weibo (literally meaning microblogging), a platform launched by Sina in 2009. Many of Weibo's functions resembled those of Twitter. A user may post messages, mention other people using "@ username" formatting and repost and comment on other users' messages. To attract users, Sina invited many celebrities, such as entertainment stars and business executives, to join Weibo and granted them a "V" logo, which appeared after their account name. These celebrities were later called the "big Vs." Weibo enjoyed an exponential growth immediately after it was founded. By February 2011, the number of its registered users had already surpassed 100 million.

Another social network media worth mentioning was WeChat, a mobile phone app launched in 2011. Unlike Weibo, WeChat was not designed for holding public discussions in the beginning. Instead, it provided instant messaging service between individuals. But because of the many functions the app had developed later, such as voice messaging, video conferencing, and digital payment, it eventually became the "app for everything" in China, with its active users surpassing 100 million in 2012. In such a context, some of WeChat's functions began to play roles in the public sphere. A typical example was the function of "public account" (*gongzhong hao*), on which users could post entries and push feeds to subscribers. With friends sharing, both in WeChat groups and the social feed of friends' updates, entries on some "public accounts" could reach a large audience within a rather short period of time.

These new technologies brought the online public sphere in China to a new era. On new platforms like Weibo and WeChat, participants, many of whom now used smartphones, proactively discussed social, political, and cultural issues. Compared to the situation in the previous stage, the configuration of online discussions had changed in at least three ways.

First, the new technologies had largely lowered the threshold for participation. In this aspect, Weibo offered an illustrative example. Compared to blogs in the earlier years, Weibo was much easier to access. To set up a blog that reached a wide range of readers, one needed to have good writing skills as well as skills in composition and photography. One probably also needed a laptop to write a blog. But to post entries on Weibo, one only needed a smartphone. Additionally, Weibo set a word limit for each post at 140 characters,[30] which was around five sentences in Chinese, an amount that people without much rhetoric could also write. Because of these features, Weibo attracted many people who were previously marginalized or even excluded from public discussions. Scholars studying the use of the internet in China have been debating whether the development of technologies had enlarged or lessened the "information gap" between different social classes.[31] Some of them have argued that influential users on Weibo are still those who have more resources in the real world, such as celebrities in the entertainment industry, university professors, and government officials (or the "big Vs").[32] I cannot argue against this. Yet what I want to highlight is a process through which some forces came into existence from non-existence. Inconspicuous as they were, socioeconomically less advantaged people like rural migrant workers could now use the media to talk about their concerns.

Second, as large-scale, comprehensive social network media drew wide attention, many small-scale, fragmented forms of online discussions began to be marginalized. An illustrative example here was the decline of blogs in the 2010s. As I have introduced in chapter two, in the 2000s, dozens of blog service providers emerged in China and blog writing became an important constituent in critical public opinions. In the 2010s, many blog websites that used to be quite active in previous years, such as the MSN Space, Blogbus, and Blog China, closed their service. This was not because in the new age people were no longer interested in writing or reading long posts. Many people still liked to produce and share these posts. The critical point here is that the way people got access to these posts had changed. As large-scale, comprehensive social network media like Weibo and WeChat commanded the most developed channels for disseminating information, any blogger who had more than a tiny ambition in popularizing his or her posts had to get connected with these media—either through writing directly on these platforms, or through pushing the feeds of their blogs onto these platforms.

The trend that most participants were centralized to a small number of platforms had an important implication to the practice of censorship. In the previous stage, the practice of censorship took place in multiple sites. All blog service providers had their own department for censoring blog contents, while the standard each provider followed varied greatly according to the value of the provider and its relationship with the state. Because of the existence of market competition, quite a few blog service providers had tried to make the censorship process less arbitrary. For example, some service providers had kindly reminded users about the occurrence of "sensitive words" (*mingan ci*) in their blog posts and allowed them to publish the posts after minor revisions. In such a context, many politically sensitive posts, such as those discussing protests, constitutional democracy, and the history of the Communist Party, got to survive on the internet.[33] During the 2010s, with the rise of comprehensive platforms like Weibo and WeChat, the structure of the practice of censorship became more centralized. For the sake of survival and profit making, these platforms were usually highly cooperative with the state. Instead of negotiating with users on the choice of words in discussing politically sensitive issues, these platforms tended to completely remove the content seen by the state as inappropriate.[34] To put it simply, while censorship had always existed on China's internet, with the emergence of large-scale, comprehensive social network media, the efficiency of censorship had increased.

The third transformation of the configuration of online public discussions was related to the first two. As the population of internet users vastly expanded and state censorship became more effective, participants of online public discussions in China became further differentiated. On discovering that the domestic online environment had become increasingly unfriendly to the discussion of politically sensitive issues, internet users who were dedicated to the advocacy of liberal ideals—many of whom were dissident intellectuals and the "rights defending" lawyers—turned to western platforms, such as Twitter and Facebook. On these western platforms, these internet users posted messages that exposed human rights abuse in China and expressed their hatred of the authoritarian rule. However, these activities were cut off from the vast public discussions happening on domestic websites, where participants willy-nilly mobilized society-wide concerns within the framework set up by the Chinese state.[35] This differentiation had been reinforced by the Chinese government's decision around 2010 to block a series of western social media websites, including Facebook, YouTube, and Twitter, and Google's decision to withdraw from China.[36]

In a word, seeing from the perspective of domestic online discussions, a more expansive and plural public sphere, which was also a public sphere whose relations with the state was more institutionalized, came into view during the second term of the Hu-Wen regime.

The Partial Institutionalization of the NGO Sphere

State's Attempt at Regulating NGOs

Since the late 2000s, the state's regulation over the NGO sphere had also become intensified. A couple of NGOs that engaged in "rights defending" activities were targeted and repressed. Among the cases of state repression, what had attracted the widest public attention was the close of *Gongmeng*, an NGO that advocated constitutional democracy and unified the "rights defending" lawyers in Beijing. As I have introduced in chapter two, *Gongmeng*, also known as the Open Constitution Initiative, was an NGO that relied on financial support from international foundations; its leader, Xu Zhiyong, had played an important role in the Sun Zhigang Incident. In 2008, *Gongmeng* sponsored a research project that investigated the uprising in Tibet, which resulted in the publication in 2009 of a report on the "social and economic causes of the 3.14 Incident." Rather than attributing the uprising to the intervention of Dalai Lama and Western forces, the report revealed the failure of Beijing's policies in promoting economic development and social equity in Tibet.[37] The report aroused wide international attention. In July 2009, *Gongmeng* was fined 1.46 million yuan for tax evasion and Xu Zhiyong was arrested. Through crowdfunding online, *Gongmeng* quickly raised the money for paying the fine. As Xu Zhiyong was released on bail in August, the organization had continued many of its activities under a new name, *Gongmin* (literally meaning citizens).[38] However, for many NGO practitioners, the signal released by the state in the case was clear—many practices that used to fall into the "grey area," such as engaging in human rights activism, would no longer be safe.

Apart from targeting specific organizations, the state had also sought to govern NGOs through making laws. The pressure for creating a more regularized institution for governing NGOs had come from multiple groups. The first group was local government officials who shouldered the responsibility to supervise NGOs, notably those officials in civil affairs departments. As I have discussed in chapter two, rather than prevent people from establishing NGOs, the previous registration system that set many hurdles in the registration procedure had simply forced activists to register their organizations as enterprises or remain unregistered. This brought huge difficulties to officials in civil affairs departments, as they tended to lack the information of those organizations that had not been properly registered—which had actually constituted the majority of NGOs in Chinese society. Officials in these departments who were relatively open-minded eagerly hoped that the registration procedure would be simplified so that more NGOs could become visible to the state and incorporated into the state's governance framework.[39]

The second group was, of course, activists from various kinds of voluntary associations, such as non-governmental rescue teams, mutual help groups established by patients of rare diseases, and community-based organizations for helping disabled people. These activists wanted their associations to be formally recognized so that they could raise funds, enjoy tax exemptions, and recruit volunteers in the wider society. While these associations had long existed in Chinese society since the 1990s, it was during the Sichuan Earthquake in 2008 that they were recognized by the public and the government.[40]

Lastly and surprisingly, those intellectuals who worked for research centers for studying civil society had also constituted an important force for promoting the enactment of NGO laws. As I have introduced in chapter two, many of these intellectuals had a strong belief in the idea of civil society that is based on an independent space in which the state power cannot legitimately interfere. In the early 2000s, some of them argued that it was OK—if not a better choice—for voluntary associations to remain unregistered, because these associations, as "non-governmental forces" (*minjian liliang*), did not need to merge with the state.[41] In the late 2000s, these intellectuals' interest in promoting NGO laws had come from very pragmatic concerns. After working with many NGO activists, they gradually discovered that, without a relatively stable institutional framework for registration and fundraising, only a small group of people were able to run NGOs in the long run. Talking about these concerns, an activist who had engaged in NGO activism since the late 1990s explained to me in an interview,

> I have established a couple of NGOs. None of them have been registered as "private non-enterprises." The government now and then closes my organizations and invites me to "have tea." I don't really care this sort of thing because I believe in democracy and civil society. But I also know that this is too much for ordinary people. I have counted the people who are as courageous as I am in China. I believe that the number does not exceed 200. If one day the government decides to arrest all of us, our cause is over. That's why I think we need a better institutional environment for NGOs.[42]

In the late 2000s and early 2010s, through submitting policy suggestions to the people's congress, both at the local and national level, these intellectuals actively participated in the making of several laws relevant to NGOs, notably the Philanthropy Law.

The state's attempt at institutionalizing NGO activism started from the local level. Since the late 2000s, several provincial-level governments, such as Beijing and Guangdong, began to carry out reforms to simplify the registration procedure. Instead of requiring NGOs to find a "supervisory agency," these governments now asked NGOs to directly register at the departments of civil affairs. Later, the central government adopted some of the local policies. In 2011, the ministry of civil affairs announced that it intended to lower the threshold for the registration of those organizations that "engaged in philanthropy activities and provided social service."[43] In the following years, the state council announced that "social work organizations" (*shegong zuzhi*) having the capacity to "help the disadvantaged" should be promoted. Several administrative orders were issued, requiring local governments to financially support the "social work organizations" through "government purchasing service" (*zhengfu goumai fuwu*) programs.[44]

The state's attempt at regulating NGOs coincided with the withdrawal of international foundations. Because of China's rising economic influence in the global community, since the late 2000s, many international foundations that invested money in areas like poverty alleviation, rural development, and the prevention of AIDS, began to reduce their financial support in China.[45] What had filled in the gap were many domestic foundations that were supported by domestic entrepreneurs or enterprises.[46] Unlike many international foundations—notably the Ford Foundation and the Gates Foundation—that had eagerly wanted to help Chinese people build civil society, the newly rising domestic foundations were usually more interested in philanthropy. Instead of performing the role of granters and supporting grassroots-based NGOs, these domestic foundations often preferred organizing philanthropy projects of their own.[47]

Still Limited Influence of State's Regulation
The increasing state intervention as well as the rise of domestic foundations had led many watchers of China's NGOs to the conclusion that the state would incorporate the NGO activism: through establishing the registration procedure and offering funds, the state, together with domestic foundations as its allies, would be able to encourage those organizations providing philanthropic service and eliminate those engaging in agitational activities, criticizing government policies, and advocating human rights.[48] However, based on my observation of those NGOs that worked with rural migrant workers in the Pearl River Delta in 2012 and 2013, I would argue that the effect of the state policies had been rather limited during this stage.

NGOs working with rural migrant workers had emerged in Chinese cities since the 1990s. Receiving funds from various international foundations, these NGOs engaged in a variety of activities related to rural migrant workers' rights and welfare. While some of them had organized cultural and recreational activities in workers' residential communities, others had been involved in more agitational activities, such as launching campaigns advocating for workers' collective rights or attending workers' strikes and protests. I will provide more details of these organizations in chapter five. In the early 2010s, in response to the central state's policy of "social work organizations," quite a few state agencies at the provincial and municipal level, including the ACFTU, ACWF, and the Communist Youth League (CYL), began to engage with some of the NGOs in rural migrant workers' communities and provided them with funds through the "government purchasing service" programs.[49] These state agencies expected that, through providing funds, these NGOs would get away with the international foundations as well as various agitational activities.

However, the implementation of the state policies had been full of contradictions. First, at this stage, state's rules on what kind of organizations could get registered and what kind of organizations were eligible for state funds were far from unequivocal; their enforcement at the local level was still largely dependent upon the local social and economic conditions, or even local government officials' personal understanding of the issues. For example, it was rather unclear what kind of activities could be accounted as "providing service." While some local government officials confined the referent of the term to very moderate activities like providing childcare in rural migrant workers' communities, others included those activities that might induce conflicts, such as offering legal aid. A typical figure in the latter group was Chen Weiguang, the leader of the municipal branch of the ACFTU in Guangzhou and a member of the standing committee of the municipal people's congress. Chen used to work at a chemical fiber plant in the 1970s. Because of this experience, he had often been sympathetic toward workers. On many different occasions, he openly criticized the staff at the ACFTU for being "too bureaucratic" and praised NGOs for their activities in helping workers defend rights.[50] In practice, he did maintain connections with several NGOs in Guangzhou that were involved in workers' factory-based collective actions.[51]

This kind of divergency among government officials led to inconsistencies in state repression, which constrained the state's capacity to contain the NGO activism emerging from the rural migrant workers' community. The effect of the repression on NGOs in Shenzhen in the early 2010s was a case in point. In 2012, nine NGOs in the city claimed that they were harassed by some local gangs. Multiple lines of evidence revealed that these gangs were associated with the government. While many of these NGOs had never been involved in any agitational activities, they were forced to leave the community in which they provided service to workers. Meanwhile, in Guangzhou, a city neighboring Shenzhen, some NGOs often intervened in workers' protests; yet they were largely tolerated and experienced no suppression. The contrast made activists in Shenzhen extremely confused. Some of them began to think that it was simply the problem of the municipal government. Some began to believe that keeping a low profile did no good for increasing the survival chances of NGOs. Eventually, angry activists publicized the harassment on the internet and won wide sympathy.[52] As a result, the harassment failed to tame the NGOs. According to my research on the historical transformation of labor NGOs in China, among the nine labor NGOs that had experienced suppression, only two had been disbanded. Four had returned to the field one year after and continued their previous activities, while the rest of the three turned to even more radical activities like organizing advocacy campaigns.[53]

In addition, during this period, local state's capacity to distinguish and supervise NGOs was still quite limited. When I was in the field in Guangzhou and Shenzhen in 2013, I discovered that quite a few NGOs were able to keep their connection with international foundations and attend advocacy activism even after they got registered and received state funds. For the sake of expanding funding sources, activists from these NGOs quickly learned to speak two languages. When they were in front of the state, they emphasized that they were "social work organizations" providing service to the disadvantaged. When the activists were with labor scholars or granters from some international foundations, they became more critical and talked about issues like raising workers' rights consciousness. Because of the existence of this kind of loopholes, many NGOs serving rural migrant workers chose to enter the regulation system set up by the state. With the state funds, these NGOs hired more full-time staff and refurbished their office place, which facilitated their interactions with workers. From this angle, the state's intervention during this period had even, to some extent, empowered the NGOs based in rural migrant workers' communities.

In a nutshell, while the state's intention in institutionalizing the NGO sphere had significantly increased during the second term of the Hu-Wen regime, due to various obstacles in the implementation of policies, the effect of the state's intervention had been limited and activism in the sphere at this stage was still far from being fully institutionalized.

The Structural Transformation of the Interstitial Publics

The Rise of a New Generation of Activists

The partial institutionalization of the media sphere and the NGO sphere significantly influenced the way ideological debates were organized in the interstitial publics. As I have introduced in chapter two and chapter three, it was the liberals who had dominated the formation of critical public opinions in China's public sphere in the early to mid-2000s. However, since the late 2000s, because of the state's increasing vigilance toward the critical discourses that challenged the legitimacy of the regime and the introduction of new opportunities and resources, a new generation of activists began to rise. Compared to the liberals in the previous stage, the new generation had more interest in criticizing and discussing specific social problems and concerns. While the new generation still employed various ideological discourses, like what the liberals had done, they employed the discourses instrumentally;

demonstrating the truthfulness of these discourses was no longer the focal point in their public expression.

Some of these activists had emerged from those thematic fields that used to be dominated by the liberals. A typical example here is the field of environmental protection. As I have introduced in chapter one, many early environmental activists in China were intellectual elites who had attended the 1989 Student Movement. These activists had turned to the cause of environmental protection in the 1990s because they had regarded it as a politically less sensitive issue—an issue that was relatively safe for the expansion of an independent space for citizens' participation vis-à-vis the state. Because of this origin, the public expression of environmental activism in China had often echoed the liberals' interpretation of state-society relations. In influential environmental campaigns in the early 2000s, such as the campaign for protecting the Nu River and the campaign for protecting the Yuanmingyuan Lake, the state and its bureaucracies at different levels had been portrayed as the destroyer of the environment, whereas civil society—which was supported by NGOs—was presented as an important force for supervising and checking the misbehavior of the state. However, since the late 2000s, as the Chinese state gradually recognized that the environmental movement could perform as the precursor of a democracy movement, the previously politically insensitive issue quickly became sensitive.

On the other hand, since the mid-2000s, the environmental campaigns led by the liberal-minded activists began to encounter challenges from a newly rising social group in the public sphere, the science students and researchers. This group's activism can be traced to Fang Zhouzi's criticism of the environmental activists in the campaign for protecting the Nu River in 2005. Fang Zhouzi is a biochemist who had received his PhD degree in the United States. He had been a popular science writer since the 1990s, being well-known for his criticism of various practices of "pseudoscience" in Chinese society. During the Nu River campaign, Fang Zhouzi stood in opposition to the environmental activists and suggested that the activists' objection to the construction of a dam on the river had "lacked scientific evidence."[54] In the late 2000s, with the rapid development of the internet infrastructure and social network media, many science students joined Fang Zhouzi's camp. The most important organization emerging during this process was the Science and Squirrel Association (*Kexue Songshu Hui*), an NGO founded by a group of science students studying abroad and in top universities in China. During a series of protests against the construction of PX plants, members of the Science and Squirrel Association wrote popular science essays online, claiming that PX was not a toxic substance and blaming participants of the protests for being irrational.[55] Most liberal-minded environmental activists disagreed with these criticisms. However, as these activists usually had an art or humanity background, they were not in an advantageous position when debating with the science students on technical issues like the "lethal dosage of PX."

Facing the increasing political risk and challenges from other social groups in the public sphere, the environmental movement began to change. In the mid-2000s, a new generation of environmental activists emerged. Notable examples included Ma Jun, the director of the Institute of Public and Environmental Affairs (*Gongzhong yu Huanjing Yanjiu Zhongxin*), an NGO that provided the first public database of water pollution information in China; Mao Da, one of the founders of the Zero Waste Alliance (*Ling Feiqi Lianmeng*), a loosely organized network that focused on the issue of garbage disposal; and Zhang Boju, the new director of the Friends of Nature. Many of these activists had entered the field following very specific issues, such as water pollution and the saving of endangered birds. In contrast to the environmental activists in the 1990s, who had seen the environmental movement as a means to the end of a greater goal (i.e., political democratization), this new generation of activists tended to see the environmental movement as an end in itself. Additionally, many activists in the new generation had an academic background in environmental-related science or social science. For example, Mao Da has an MS degree in environmental science and a PhD degree in environmental history. Zhang Boju has an MA degree in political science. In contrast to an earlier generation of activists, who had mainly appealed to emotions when talking about environmental problems, the new generation tended to emphasize data and scientific evidence.

With respect to the concern of expanding the space for public participation, the new generation of environmental activists generally supported the idea of civil society. For instance, most of them also hoped that environmental NGOs in China had more power and autonomy so that citizens could have more space for expressing their concerns on environmental issues and checking the misbehavior of government and corporations. This had been illustrated in the campaign for advocating NGOs' litigation rights in environmental public interest litigation, which lasted for several years before the passage of the new Environmental Protection Law in 2014.[56] However, the attitude of the younger generation of environmental activists toward the state tended to be more pragmatic and less influenced by the liberals' dichotomous interpretation of state-society relations. These activists were critical of the state when its bureaucracies at different levels failed to perform the duties of environmental protection. But when they believed that the state should play greater roles in certain environmental-related issues, they never hesitated to publicly express the opinion. An illustrative example here was activists' advocacy that the state popularized the practice of garbage classification through legislation.[57]

A similar transformation had also taken place in other fields, notably the labor movement and the feminist movement. In these fields, new actors, such as student activists and scholars representing subaltern interests, utilized the new resources and opportunities brought by the changing political and technological environment and articulated critical discourses that were an alternative to those of the liberals. I will elaborate on the public discussions initiated by these movements in the next chapter.

The Maintenance of the Liberals' Networks

As I have already mentioned in the previous sections, the increasing state intervention and the development of new digital technology since the late 2000s severely destabilized the domination of the liberals in the public sphere. As the influence of several important "leading organizations" among the liberals, such as the *Southern Weekly* and *Gongmeng*, was weakened, the previously loosely organized liberals' networks now became even more fragile. But I still want to emphasize that it was not during this stage that the liberals became completely marginalized in public discussions. Since the state's regulation over the interstitial publics was still in many ways porous and diplomatic, the liberals were left with sufficient space in which they could adjust their strategies and adapt to the changing environment.

In the NGO sphere, the liberals who used to work at centers for studying civil society proactively kept up with the state's agenda of reforming NGOs and adopted new discourses like "social work" and "philanthropy." Among these people, those who had been the most successful in the adaptation were the liberals at the ICS. Incisively capturing the changes in the political environment, in 2011, major organizers of the ICS founded another research institute affiliated with Sun Yat-sen University—the School of Philanthropy (*Gongyi Cishan Yanjiuyuan*). Compared to the ICS, the School of Philanthropy tended to talk about the idea of civil society less frequently. Instead, it more often used moderate and neutral terms like "community development" and "social innovation." But with respect to promoting the NGO industry in China, the School of Philanthropy had performed roles that were approximately the same as those of the ICS. The school had also worked with international foundations, such as the Rockefeller Brothers' Foundation, and helped these foundations search for proper grantees. In various capacity-building programs, scholars at the school had also discussed with trainees the possibility of expanding an autonomous space for participation. To introduce new resources to the field, the school had even established working alliances with several newly rising domestic foundations, notably the Narada Foundation (*Nandu Gongyi Jijinhui*).

Because of these new connections, those liberals who used to work for the ICS maintained their influence among NGOs during the second term of the Hu-Wen regime. I worked as a visiting fellow at the School of Philanthropy when I did fieldwork in the Pearl River Delta in 2013. When I visited various local NGOs, I had always received the warmest welcome whenever I mentioned my connection with the school. This provided partial evidence of how influential the school was among NGOs in southern China at that time.

The transformation of the liberals in the media sphere was even more illustrative. As I have introduced in chapter two, in the early to mid-2000s, China's public sphere witnessed the rise of a group of media-based public intellectuals, who used a more amiable language to advocate the liberals' political agenda. These liberal public intellectuals usually attributed various social problems rising during China's economic reform to the "maladies of the system" (*tizhi wenti*) and suggested that the solution was to learn from the West, especially the United States of America. Coming to the late 2000s, with the rapid expansion of the population of internet users, these public intellectuals began to encounter increasingly more challengers. Some of the challengers, such as the "fifty-cent army" (*wumao dang*), were nationalists who tried to defend the authoritarian state.[58] Yet there were also challengers who were simply dissatisfied with the liberals' over-reductionist interpretations. These controversies pushed many scholars in the liberal community to reflect upon their discourses.

Then, around 2010, a new generation of liberal public intellectuals who had more refined strategies for disseminating their political ideal emerged. The most typical example among them was Liu Yu, a political scientist who received her PhD degree from Columbia University. Liu was in the beginning a blogger who wrote political commentaries. Later, as she became rather influential on the internet, some of her blog entries were compiled and published. These included the famous *The Details of Democracy* (Minzhu de Xijie), a book introducing democracy in America to a Chinese audience. Like the liberals in the early years, Liu advocated the rule of law, checks and balances of power, and the idea of civil society. But compared to her predecessors, she had a more modest tone when praising the American political institutions. She did not avoid talking about some of the "dark side" of American democracy, such as the lack of social welfare, inequalities, and the US hegemony in international politics. Some of her essays even had lengthy discussions on these issues. It was usually at the end of these essays that she revealed her core argument—despite the "dark side," the democratic institutions in America still provided the best chance for people to participate in politics and check the powerful.[59] The book achieved great commercial success immediately after it was published in 2009 and became one of the best sellers of the year.

Another example was Chai Jing, a journalist who used to work for CCTV. Chai had established herself as a journalist who dared to resist the government authority in her reportage of the outbreak of SARS in Beijing in 2003. In 2015, Chai re-entered the public horizon with a self-financed documentary film called *Under the Dome* (Qiongding zhi Xia). The 104-minute documentary concerned the problem of air pollution in China. With respect to its ideological position, the documentary did not diverge too much from the liberals' understanding of politics. It attributed the air pollution problem in urban China to the state's monopolies in the energy industry. Apart from advocating that citizens raise their rights consciousness in the issue, the documentary also proposed privatization and the introduction of market mechanisms as the solution to the problem. Yet, on the other hand, in articulating this ideological position, Chai and her team demonstrated very high techniques of persuasion. Learning from another environmentalist documentary film, *An Inconvenient Truth* by Al Gore, *Under the Dome* invoked great amounts of data, scientific evidence, and interviews with experts. To appeal to the audience's sensations, Chai even implicitly suggested that a tumor found in her newly born daughter had something to do with the hazardous air in China.[60] After the issuance of the documentary online, except for a few scholars and students interested in new leftist theories, most audiences simply ignored the ideological stance behind the documentary and applauded Chai and her team for exposing a problem that was so important to the environment and public health.[61] Although the documentary was later censored and removed, it had already aroused huge public anger toward the government's failure in curbing pollution.

These cases show the vitality and flexibility of the liberals. Through adjusting their strategies and discourses and utilizing new resources, some of the liberals managed to maintain their influence in the public sphere.

Conclusion

This chapter offers a general sketch of the structural transformation of the interstitial publics in China since the late 2000s. I start with introducing the changes in the social, political, and technological environment. Then I scrutinize the transformation of the media sphere and the NGO sphere. I argue that the transformation of the two spheres brought intricate yet subtle influence on the participants of public discussions. On the one hand, the state's suppression of proactive liberal activists as well as the development of digital technologies provided new actors with opportunities to publicly express opinions. It was during this stage that a new generation of activists, who had focused on more specific issues and employed ideological discourses more instrumentally, began to arise. On the other hand, since the institutionalization of the interstitial publics was still partial, some of the liberals were able to maintain their influence in public discussions. As a result, the interstitial publics in China entered a stage in which old and new actors coexisted.

A question concerning scholars studying the decline of human rights activism in China is—when did the shrinkage of the space for the resistance movement happen? In answering the question, some scholars trace to a series of state interventions in the media sphere and the NGO sphere during the second term of the Hu-Wen regime.[62] While I recognize all the negative impacts brought by these interventions, what I want to demonstrate in this chapter is a more complex picture. First, I suggest that the state was far from capable during this stage to bring all critical public discussions under its control. Second, by establishing a more routinized system for governing non-governmental forces like NGOs, some of the state interventions had even offered opportunities to those who were previously excluded from public participation. This "equalizing effect" had also been amplified by the development of digital technologies and the introduction of various kinds of new resources.

It will become clear to readers as I analyze the condition of critical public discussions in the next stage (2014–2019): with respect to the participants of interstitial publics, the stage this chapter describes (2008–2013) constituted a very special stage in the ideational movement of building civil society in China. Before this stage, although many issue-oriented activists had already emerged, it was the liberals—a group of actors with a strong belief in an ideological discourse and a package plan for democratizing China—that dominated alternative public discussions. After this stage, as state suppression over the interstitial publics increased, the liberals became too marginalized to initiate any influential, nation-wide public discussions. It was only during this stage—when the power of the liberals was destabilized yet not fully undermined—that many serious debates on the relevance and applicability of the idea of civil society came into being. This is what I am going to explain in the next chapter.

CHAPTER 5

The Increasing Contestation over the Project of Building Civil Society, 2008–2013

Various critical thoughts that were alternatives to liberalism had existed in the interstitial publics in China since the 1990s. As I have discussed in chapter one, around the turn of the century, the debate between the liberals and the new left introduced to the Chinese audience different kinds of social and political theories. Apart from liberalism, scholars in the "thought sphere" also discussed critical theories like neo-Marxism and post-colonialism. However, because it was mainly the new leftist scholars—a group of intellectuals who had lacked interest in attending non-governmental organizations and social movements—who were talking about the alternative critical theories, in the early to mid-2000s, these theories had rarely been heard in the wider public. Since the late 2000s, with the structural transformation of the interstitial publics, this situation began to change. As new participants arose, some of the old debates were revitalized and alternative critical discourses were brought forward to public discussions in the wider society. This chapter is dedicated to elaborating on this process as well as discussing its impact on the community of resistance movements in China.

In analyzing the emergence of new critical discourses, I focus on three groups of social movement actors who claimed to represent some form of subaltern interest. These three groups were rural scholars and activists from the New Rural Reconstruction Movement, labor scholars and activists, and feminist scholars and activists. In the late 2000s and early 2010s, all three groups of actors debated with the liberals on various political ideals the liberals had raised, including the project of building civil society. Unlike the debate between the liberals and the new left, which happened in the "thought sphere" and mainly focused on theories, these newly rising debates were saturated with considerations over concrete social issues and problems. As I will elaborate, during these debates, the new participants of the interstitial publics had not only brought in information on the many specific difficulties facing socioeconomically disadvantaged groups but also challenged the liberal understanding of civil society theory that regarded state and society as antithesis.

I emphasize that, although the three groups had all contested the liberal interpretation of civil society, their degree of willingness to openly confront the liberals varied (see Table 4). As I have discussed in chapter three, in the early to mid-2000s, the liberals had often dismissed the rural scholars on commercially-oriented newspapers. However, in public debates happening since the late 2000s, except for expressing their own opinions, the rural scholars tended to avoid confronting the liberals. In contrast, the labor activists and the feminist activists were more proactive in articulating how their agenda had diverged from that of the liberals. I suggest that this had to do with the different conditions of the three movements, or more precisely, the degree to which these movements had been institutionalized by the state during that period. During the second term of the Hu-Wen regime, as the Chinese state partially adopted the New Rural Reconstruction Movement's policy suggestions on tackling rural problems, the rural scholars gradually became uninterested in expanding their influence in the interstitial publics as well as confronting the liberals. In contrast, both the labor activism and the feminism had become more grassroots based and more alienated from the state since the late 2000s. In articulating their political ideals, they frequently encountered the liberals, who used to have hegemonic influence over the production of critical opinions. It was these encounters that had facilitated the heated debate on the idea of civil society.

Moreover, I suggest that the confrontation between the liberals and these movements led to the formation of different kinds of relations. Both the labor activists and the feminist activists at this stage expressed that they believed that the concept of civil society had intrinsic value; it was simply that they disagreed with the liberal interpretation of the concept. However, after articulating their opinions, while the labor activists built a cooperative relationship with many liberals, the feminist activists gradually discovered that their conflicts with the liberals were irreconcilable. I contend that the variation across the two groups can only be explained by the nature of their topic they had raised.

What the labor scholars and activists had focused on since the late 2000s was mainly rural migrant workers' social rights. Their major concern in this issue was that the Chinese state had failed to provide workers with sufficient

Table 4. The Three Social Movements Representing Subaltern Interest, 2008–2013

	Institutionalization by the State	Willingness to Openly Confront the Liberals	Major Topics Challenge State/Society Dichotomy	Relations with the Liberals after Confrontation
New Rural Reconstruction Movement	Yes	Low	Yes	Not applicable
Labor Activism	No	High	Not quite	Selective cooperation
Feminist Activism	No	High	Yes	Antagonism

safety networks to counteract the dehumanizing effect brought by the neo-liberal market economy. In discussing the problem, most labor scholars and activists were highly critical of what the state had done. Additionally, these scholars and activists regarded civil society—or an ensemble of organizations, voluntary networks, and movement activism emerging from workers' communities—as a crucial force that was able to push the state to change its attitude toward workers. This "society versus state" mindset had enabled the labor scholars and activists to build alliances with those liberals who were sympathetic to the socioeconomically disadvantaged. In contrast, what had initiated controversies between the liberals and the feminist activists were women's rights in the family planning policies. In this issue, the role played by the Chinese state had been more subtle and difficult to be generalized in a "black or white" manner. To bring forward a more comprehensive understanding of the issue, the feminist scholars and activists had not only criticized what the state had done but also questioned the liberal interpretation of civil society that dichotomized the public and the private. This more thorough criticism over the project of building civil society eventually ruined the possibility that the feminist activists cooperated with the liberals.

The rest of this chapter will be arranged in the following way. In the next three sections, I discuss, respectively, the debate between the liberals and the three social movements that claimed to represent the disadvantaged. In each section, I introduce the historical origin of the three movements first. Then I elaborate how they had criticized the liberal interpretation of civil society and what kind of relations they had established with the liberals. After these three sections, I discuss the multiple, contradicting consequences brought by the debates. While acknowledging the value of the new information brought in by the debates, I highlight the many divisions emerging in the resistance movement in China during this stage.

The New Rural Reconstruction Movement and Its Criticism over the Liberals

A Brief History of the New Rural Reconstruction Movement, 1996–2013

Since 1978, a series of political and economic changes took place in China's rural areas. The most important one was the emergence and eventual prevalence of the household responsibility system, which restored the individual household and replaced the production team system as the unit of production and accounting. It was widely believed, especially among economists, that this reform had largely improved agricultural productivity and peasants' income.[1] Because of these changes, coming to the 1990s, many people began to think that the rural part of China's market economic reform had already succeeded. Hot spot issues for public discussion then turned to various reforms in urban areas, notably the privatization of state-owned enterprises. However, the really existing rural areas in the '90s were far from being prosperous. With the restoration of economic reform in urban areas after Deng's southern tour, the income gap between China's urban and rural areas was quickly widened.[2] The rise of town and village enterprises since the 1980s caused severe environmental pollution.[3] Because of the withdrawal of state power, social service programs including education and medical care were underfunded.[4] Moreover, at the village and town level, corruption was rampant.[5] It was against this background that the New Rural Reconstruction Movement emerged.

The de facto leader of the movement, Wen Tiejun, is a state-endorsed agricultural economist. Wen was born in the 1950s and went to college after the Cultural Revolution. After graduating from college, he was dispatched by the Chinese government to study abroad, first at the University of Michigan, Ann Arbor, and then the World Bank. In the 1990s, he served at several state sponsored research institutes and think tanks, including the Research Center for Rural Development (*Nongcun Fazhan Yanjiu Zhongxin*) and the Office for Rural Reform Experimental Zones (*Nongcun Gaige Shiyanqu Bangongshi*), both of which were directly led by the State Council. It was during this period that Wen proposed the discourse of the "three rural issues" (*sannong wenti*). The discourse of the "three rural issues" was used to refer to a series of problems facing peasants, rural areas, and the development of agriculture in China. These problems were later generalized as "peasants are miserable, rural areas are impoverished, and agriculture is risky" (*nongmin zhen ku, nongcun zhen qiong, nongye zhen weixian*).[6]

In advocating for the discourse of the "three rural issues," Wen met and allied with different kinds of actors who were dissatisfied with China's rural conditions. Apart from a few social science scholars who studied rural issues in universities, these actors included some lower-level government officials in rural areas and university students coming from rural families. In the early 2000s, these actors established three advocacy organizations.[7] The most important one among these organizations was the editorial board of a magazine called the *China Reform: Rural Edition* (Zhongguo Gaige: Nongcun Ban). Another one was an NGO called the James Yen Institute (*Yan Yangchu Xueyuan*). Established in 2003 in Hebei Province, the organization provided training programs to peasants and helped peasants organize cooperatives. A third one was the Liang Shuming Center (*Liang Shuming Zhongxin*), which was also an NGO. Established in 2001 in Beijing, the organization aimed to train student activists.[8] In various situations, these organizations exposed social problems in rural areas, opposed further land privatization, and demanded that the state pay more attention to rural development.

What is worth mentioning here is that the emergence of these organizations had also relied upon various interstitial spaces in the state. The issuance of the *China Reform: Rural Edition* was a case in point. Established in 1986 by the Development and Reform Commission, a subordinate of the State Council, the *China Reform* magazine had functioned as a think tank for China's top leaders. When Wen Tiejun became the chief editor of the magazine around 2000, he proposed to increase the proportion of those articles discussing rural issues. But his proposal had not been supported by many associate editors, who then believed that urban issues were more important.[9] To circumscribe these associate editors, in 2002, Wen turned the previously monthly magazine into a fortnightly magazine. The issue published in the first half of a month was left to the editors who were interested in discussing urban issues, while the one in the second half was renamed the *Rural Edition*. Being financially supported by an international foundation, the Oxfam Hong Kong, Wen convened a new editorial board for the *Rural Edition*, which had mainly consisted of scholars and student activists who were sympathetic to the discourse of the "three rural issues." The magazine eventually became a platform in which the New Rural Reconstruction Movement publicly expressed its concerns.

The Chinese state positively responded to the rural scholars and activists' advocacies. In 2003, the state formally adopted the discourse of the "three rural issues" and claimed that promoting economic and social development in rural areas had now become one of the government's core missions.[10] To alleviate the peasants' burden, the central government issued many social welfare policies, among which the most influential one was the full cancellation of the agricultural tax in 2005.[11] Scholars have been debating the extent to which these policies solve the rural problems.[12] Nevertheless, many would acknowledge that the issuance of these policies indicated that the Chinese state had begun to pay more attention to rural development.

Meanwhile, the political environment that tolerated advocacy organizations was also changing. As I have introduced in the previous chapter, the state's regulation over NGOs had become intensified after the Arab Spring. For the New Rural Reconstruction Movement, the timing was even earlier. In 2004, the publication of the *Rural Edition* was suspended. In 2007, the James Yen Institute was shut down. Some scholars and activists in the movement had attributed the fall of these two organizations to the manipulation of the liberals within the state,[13] while others simply saw it as a signal of an increasingly suppressive political environment.[14] One way or the other, the state's suppression of the two organizations thwarted many activists who had hoped to organize a more proactive and profound movement for changing China's rural conditions.

Facing these changes, since the late 2000s, many scholars and activists in the New Rural Reconstruction Movement began to employ new strategies. First, the movement decreased their criticism over the state. In the early to mid-2000s, albeit their dislike of the liberals, scholars and activists at the *Rural Edition* and the James Yen Institute now and then employed the "rights-defending" discourse.[15] However, since the late 2000s, these scholars and activists began to discourage peasants from attending rights-defending activism like lodging complaints to higher-level government.[16] In discussing the causes of rural problems in the public, rural scholars tended to talk more about "neoliberal globalization," or the "hegemony of the West," while the problems of state policies were largely bypassed.[17]

Second, some scholars and activists in the movement, mainly those who had worked at the James Yen Institute, began to turn to food issues. In 2008, activists from the James Yen Institute left Hebei Province and started in

Figure 3. Little Donkey Farm Selling Books on Leftist Theories in a Farmers' Market. Photo taken during author's fieldwork in Beijing, July 16, 2011.

Beijing an alternative food network project called the Little Donkey Farm (*Xiao Maolü Nongyuan*). The farm avoided using chemicals in cultivation and required consumers to participate through either labor quota or prepayment. The activists claimed that this kind of practice could not only benefit the farming environment but also increase peasants' income.[18] This idea was later generalized as the model of "community supported agriculture" (*shequ zhichi nongye*, or CSA). To broadcast the model, activists from the New Rural Reconstruction Movement later established an organization called the CSA Alliance for Social and Ecological Agriculture (*Shehui Shengtai Nongye CSA Lianmeng*).[19] The alliance mainly supported activisms like farmers' markets and consumers' cooperatives.

Continuities existed between activists' practices in establishing alternative food networks and their advocacy of the "three rural issues." For example, in organizing and attending various farmers' markets, activists from the Little Donkey Farm often discussed with customers the importance of rural reconstruction. Sometimes, these activists even tried to sell books of leftist theories to the customers (see Figure 3).[20] Nevertheless, with the "urban turn," the New Rural Reconstruction Movement began to work with various new

players, such as middle-class activists in urban communities and small agricultural business owners interested in concepts like organic food.

The Debate on Food Safety Issues

As I have introduced in chapter three, scholars in the New Rural Reconstruction Movement used to debate with the liberals on the issue of land
privatization in the early to mid-2000s. During that period, many prominent liberal economists in China advocated to further privatize land in rural
areas.[21] Leading scholars in the New Rural Reconstruction Movement, on
the other hand, argued that China's per capita agricultural land was quite
limited and that most peasants were the "small peasants" (xiaonong) who
lacked capital and risk-resistance capacity; under such a condition, further
land privatization would only lead to large-scale land annexation and the
emergence of many displaced peasants.[22] As an alternative, the rural scholars
suggested that the state should support peasants' cooperatives.[23] While the
rural scholars were in a disadvantaged position vis-à-vis the liberals in those
debates appearing on commercially-oriented newspapers, the Chinese state
seemed to adopt the rural scholars' refutation against privatization. In 2006,
the National People's Congress passed the Farmers' Specialized Cooperatives
Law, which provided a relatively stable institutional framework for the oper-
ation of cooperatives.

In the late 2000s, with the "urban turn" of the New Rural Reconstruction
Movement, the focus of the contention between the rural scholars and the
liberals changed. What had aroused interest among both the rural scholars
and the liberals in the late 2000s was the issue of food safety in China. Since
the 2000s, muckraking reports on various food scandals, such as poisonous
ham, fake liquor, and tainted dumplings, had emerged in China's newspapers
and television programs. The influence of these food scandals reached its
zenith in 2008, when some social network media accounts exposed that large
amounts of milk and infant formula in the domestic market had been adul-
terated with the chemical melamine and that the contaminated dairy products had already resulted in kidney stones and other forms of kidney damage
in infants.[24] After the exposure of the milk scandal, public anger was rampant.
In multiple sites for online discussions, such as the Tianya Forum and Weibo,
people criticized not only the dairy corporations involved but also the Chinese government.[25]

Although the influence of the liberals in the public sphere had already been weakened in the late 2000s, many of them still proactively intervened in the issue. The "rights defending" lawyers, mainly those from *Gongmeng*, offered victim families legal aid and launched advocacy campaigns.[26] Journalists and liberal public intellectuals wrote commentaries in newspapers and on the internet to criticize problematics inherent to China's political regime. Like what they had done in the early to mid-2000s, these liberals tried to use the food scandal case to demonstrate the rightness of their political ideal of building civil society. During the milk scandal, a prominent voice in many online discussions was that the root of food safety problems was the malfunction of government's supervision departments. The popular cry was high that state bureaucracy at different levels shoulder more responsibility in regulating the food production market.[27] Yet many liberals suggested that government was the problem, rather than the solution. For example, a commentary published in the *Southern Weekly* argued that the cost of government supervision was too high and that the cost could eventually transfer to consumers.[28] Another commentary revealed that in China the government departments involved in the supervision of food production were already many and various; the problem was that these departments were accountable to their higher authorities only, instead of to citizens. This commentary then concluded that the real solution to the food safety problem was to create a space in which citizens could participate and check the government.[29]

Some liberal scholars, especially the economists, advocated to introduce more "market force" (*shichang liliang*) to tackle the issue. What is worth being mentioned here is that, when using the term "market force," these scholars usually pointed to big corporations that could integrate upstream and downstream firms in the food production industry. In these scholars' opinion, only the big corporations, which valued their brand image, had the motivation and capacity to establish and enforce rigid food safety standards; food production firms controlled by the "small peasants," on the other hand, were usually shortsighted and opportunistic; the fragmented nature of these firms also increased the cost of supervision.[30]

Interestingly, many rural scholars agreed with the liberals on the opinion that mere state supervision could not guarantee food safety. They argued that the whole process through which food was produced was too complex to be fully monitored by the state. Like the liberals, these rural scholars also advocated the involvement of a wider society.[31] However, the rural scholars tended to have different opinions on what constituted "society" and how citizens' participation could help to cope with the social ills. The divergence between the two groups lay in their different understanding of the nature of the issue of food safety.

As early as 2006, rural scholars like Wen Tiejun began to publicly talk about the relationship between food safety and agriculture. In these rural scholars' discussions, the idea of food safety tended to be more broadly defined. When the liberals discussed the food safety issue, they usually pointed to the toxic or harmful substance produced during food processing and its negative impact on human health. Yet the rural scholars and activists believed that the issue of food safety was embedded in a larger system that involved not only the production of food but also food's exchange and consumption; while the defense of human health was certainly a desirable goal, to talk about food safety, one also needed to take the protection of the environment and fair trade into consideration.[32] Based on these concerns, the rural scholars proposed two alternative opinions.

First, the rural scholars and activists doubted the big corporations' motivation and capacity to enforce rigid food safety standards. They highlighted that many corporations involved in the milk scandal like Sanlu were exactly big corporations with famous brand names—this illustrated well that under the pressure of profit seeking big corporations could also produce and sell contaminated food. They also revealed other potential problems brought by the monopoly of big corporations, such as "small peasants'" gradual loss of bargaining power in the market.[33]

Second, the rural scholars and activists emphasized the externalities in the food safety issue. On the one hand, they pointed out that the overuse of fertilizers and pesticides had already caused irreversible harm to the farming environment in China. On the other hand, they highlighted the difficulties "small peasants" faced—decreasing the use of the chemicals, or employing the so-called "organic farming" method, would make the farming process more labor-intensive; the uncertainties inherent to the new farming method could also introduce more risks to cultivation. These scholars and activists argued that it was unjust to ask the "small peasants" to deal with the pollution problem all by themselves and that urban consumers needed to share risks.[34] More specifically, they suggested that the model of CSA was particularly useful for tackling the food safety issue—through paying higher prices for ecologically friendly food and establishing a cooperative relationship with peasants, consumers could take up their responsibilities in building a more sustainable food system.[35]

In private conversations, the rural scholars and activists often complained about the prominence of the liberal view. In one of my interviews, an activist from the New Rural Reconstruction Movement criticized that the liberal interpretation of civil society had ignored the many negative impacts brought by the capitalist market economy.[36] Another interviewee suggested that the liberals' understanding of participants of civil society was too "abstract"—by ignoring the different identities involved, that is, producers and consumers, the liberals reduced the food safety issue to the question of power balance between government and citizens; yet in fact, the issue also involved how citizens from different social groups should treat each other, or more precisely, how social solidarity was possible.[37]

However, these criticisms had mainly been circulated among food activism activists. In the wider public, the activists had seldom articulated their divergence from the liberals. A major reason was that, beginning in the 2010s, the New Rural Reconstruction Movement had gradually lost interest in attending any confrontational public debates. By turning to the food issue and working with the urban middle class, the movement had found a domain in which it could insert influence and sustain its organizational networks. As the rural scholars and activists decreased their criticism over state policies and withdrew their support of peasants' "rights-defending" activism, state suppression of their organizations had also largely been lessened. By claiming that the CSA model helped consumers get safe food, the Little Donkey Farm grew fast after the contaminated milk scandal. Within a few years after it was established, the farm had already become one of the most influential organic farms in northern China, enrolling nearly 700 members. The farm had also offered a training program to those peasants who wanted to start their own organic agribusiness. Talking about these achievements, an activist said to me in an interview, "State policies are quite good now, which provides space for our CSA practices. Hence, the time for those endless ideological debates has passed. Now we only want to focus on our own business."[38]

The Labor Activism and Its Criticism over the Liberals

A Brief History of Labor Activism, 1996–2013

China's participation in neoliberal globalization since the 1990s remade the Chinese working class. In the Northeast, workers were deprived of their social compacts in the privatization of state-owned enterprises. In coastal regions in the East and the South, as I have introduced in chapter three, millions of peasants became industrial workers; because of the lack of legal protection and the constraints set up by the *hukou* system, they were usually trapped in a socioeconomically disadvantaged position in cities. Both processes released a great many social conflicts. As early as the 1990s, workers in different regions rose to resist. Through collective actions like wildcat strikes, protests, and demonstrations, they demanded higher wages, better working conditions, and more comprehensive welfare benefits.[39]

However, for a long time, labor rights issues as a topic for public discussion were rather marginalized in China's public sphere. Because independent unions were strictly prohibited in China, workers' resistance had lacked organization and most of the labor insurgencies had remained factory-based and fragmented.[40] In the media sphere, as I have elaborated in chapter three, commercially-oriented newspapers dominated by the liberals interpreted labor rights as civil rights, or the right to become a free laborer in the market; the labor rights issues thus became subordinated to the political agenda of promoting the market economic reform. In the "thought sphere," as I have elaborated in chapter one, new leftist intellectuals like Wang Hui and Wang Shaoguang mentioned labor rights issues when they criticized the increasing inequality brought by China's participation in neoliberal globalization. However, since these new leftist intellectuals had placed their hope on a strong state, they had seldom considered the possibility of combining their theoretical criticism with workers' on-the-ground struggles.

It was not until the mid-2000s that this situation began to change. Several significant transformations took place during that period. First, seasonal labor shortages occurred in the manufacturing industry in the Pearl River Delta, which granted workers more bargaining power.[41] Second, with the transformation of the state's development pattern during the Hu-Wen regime, several laws that aimed to provide better protection to workers were passed. These included the Labor Contract Law, the Labor Dispute Mediation and Arbitration Law, and the Social Insurance Law. The changes in the labor market and state policies largely encouraged workers to struggle for their rights. In the late 2000s, workers' collective actions surged.[42] In some well-known strikes, notably the Honda Strike happening in Nanhai in 2010, workers began to raise demands that went beyond their immediate interest.[43]

In response to these transformations, several groups of actors who were associated with labor rights issues came onto the stage of public discussion. The first group of actors were social science scholars specializing in labor studies, or the labor scholars. These labor scholars were mostly sociologists and political scientists from top universities and research institutes in China and Hong Kong, namely Tsinghua University, Peking University, Sun Yat-sen University, the Academy of Social Sciences, and Hong Kong Polytechnic University.[44] Among them, the most important group were sociologists from Tsinghua University. The department of sociology at Tsinghua was not founded until 2000. But immediately following its establishment, leading scholars in the department, such as Shen Yuan and Guo Yuhua, decided that the sociology of labor should be the department's major research area. In the following years, these scholars not only advised graduate students to conduct ethnographic research on labor issues but also translated numerous Western academic works on labor into Chinese.[45] Many of these labor scholars were strong advocates of Michael Burawoy's idea of public sociology, believing that social science knowledge could be employed to make public interventions.[46]

The second group of actors were labor NGOs. Various community-based NGOs serving rural migrant workers began to emerge in Beijing and the Pearl River Delta in the 1990s.[47] But before the late 2000s, these organizations seldom contacted each other and did not have a common identity. NGOs based in Beijing were mostly established by intellectual elites who had connections with government officials. Organizing cultural and recreational activities among women rural migrant workers, these NGOs usually emphasized feminist discourses. Most of the NGOs based in the Pearl River Delta, on the other hand, were established by rural migrant workers who were relatively well educated (e.g., those who had received high school education). In migrant communities, these organizations provided workers with affordable legal service. Working with the liberals at the ICS, they advocated the idea of civil society and regarded their own activism as a practice of expanding an independent space for self-organization.[48]

Beginning in 2007, with the help of some international foundations, such as the Oxfam Hong Kong, and the labor scholars, a series of workshops and communication camps for training labor activists were held. Many activists serving at the community-based NGOs were invited. Besides familiarizing trainees with theories in labor studies, the workshops and communication camps also invited labor activists from abroad to talk about their labor-mobilizing experiences.[49] These kinds of activities popularized the idea that NGOs could play a more proactive role in workers' resistance and promoted the formation of a community of NGOs serving rural migrant workers. It was during those years that "labor NGOs" became a common identity for these different organizations.

The third group were student activists. University students' participation in labor activism also had to do with labor scholars' intervention. In 2009, the labor scholars started a program called the "New Generation Project" (*Xinshengdai Jihua*). In the program, students recruited were advised to do research on labor-related issues first, and then encouraged to intern in factories and plants. Many of the students later became activists in NGOs led by rural migrant workers or founded their own NGOs for serving rural migrant workers. A notable example was an NGO called Safety Helmet (*Anquan Mao*). Established by a group of students from Peking University and Tsinghua University, the organization disseminated the knowledge of safety production among construction workers.

The last group were labor lawyers. Since 2009, a group of labor lawyers based in Shenzhen launched a campaign for advocating workers' rights to collective bargaining. Working with some of the labor NGOs in the Pearl River Delta, the labor lawyers intervened in workers' factory-based collective actions and helped workers initiate collective bargains with the management. Policy-wise, they also advocated that workers have more collective rights.[50]

Being facilitated by the lowered threshold for NGO registration, the increase of state funds, the still porous NGO regulation system, and the rapid development of social network media, these different actors formed a loosely organized advocacy network. In the late 2000s and early 2010s, this network played an important role in unifying workers' otherwise fragmented resistance activism and in magnifying workers' voices in the public sphere. It problematized a series of difficulties rural migrant workers encountered, such as industrial injuries and the lack of social insurance.[51]

The Debate on Workers' Social Rights

In contrast to the New Rural Reconstruction Movement, in the late 2000s and early 2010s, the labor activism was far from being incorporated by the state. To galvanize support and promote common concerns, the labor scholars and their colleagues (hereafter labor activists) had to work with organizations and institutions in the interstitial publics, where the liberals had a huge influence. To articulate their agenda, the scholars had to explain to the public how their understanding of politics and society was different.

Labor scholars' intervention in the Foxconn event was a case in point.

Foxconn was a contract electronic manufacturer that supplied goods to Apple. In 2009 and 2010, more than a dozen rural migrant workers who were around the age of twenty committed suicide at its plants in Shenzhen and Chongqing. In the beginning, the labor scholars wanted to initiate public discussion on the event in the newspapers. However, many commercially-oriented newspapers at that time interpreted the event as individual workers' failure to be assimilated into urban life and suggested that the suicide problem could be cured by improving the workers' psychological health condition.[52] To propose an alternative interpretation, the labor scholars turned to their students and organized fieldwork research at several plants of Foxconn. The research activism was eventually crystalized into an 87-page report, which described workers' real living conditions and associated the suicide event with the social, economic, and political structure that had put rural migrant workers into the disadvantaged position.[53] To ensure the dissemination of the report, the labor scholars and their students even held a press conference to discuss the Foxconn event.[54]

During the second term of the Hu-Wen regime, labor activists' major concern was rural migrant workers' social rights. Unlike the liberals who had seen workers as freely moving labor power in the market, the labor scholars and their colleagues emphasized that workers were citizens and human beings who had the full right to enjoy all the fruits brought by the development of economy and society. In advocating workers' social rights, the labor activism had challenged the liberal interpretation of civil society in at least two ways.

First, by bringing the discourse of class back in, the labor activists challenged the liberal interpretation that saw participants of civil society as unitary and homogeneous. As I have emphasized in chapter three, the liberals assumed that all citizens, regardless of their socioeconomic status, would be benefited if the state power was constrained; therefore, seldom did they consider the inequality and difference generated by structural forces, such as the capitalist market economy. As a matter of fact, to legitimize its various policies in the market economic reform, the Chinese state had also intentionally played down in its propaganda many socialist discourses, including the discourse of class.[55]

The public discussion over the class issue was initiated by a Beijing-based labor NGO called the Workers' Friendly Society. In 2006, some activists from the organization announced that they would like to use the term "new working class" (*xin gongren jieji*) or "new workers" (*xin gongren*) to substitute the term "peasant workers" (*nongmingong*), which was commonly used on the then mainstream media. According to these activists, "peasant workers" was a pejorative term. By calling rural migrant workers "new workers," they hoped to revive a socialist culture in which laborers were respected.[56] In the first few years after it was coined, the term was usually associated with subcultural activities. An art troupe consisting of activists from the Workers' Friendly Society made a concert tour and released a CD called "Sing for Laborers." Several other labor NGOs, notably Little Grass (Xiao Xiao Cao) and Hand in Hand (Shou Qian Shou), held programs that supported workers to express their feelings through artistic creations, such as poems and fictions.

The labor scholars later theorized and intellectualized the discussion of the "new working class." These scholars used the term "new working class" to distinguish rural migrant workers from those workers who were employed by state-owned enterprises during the socialist period, or the so-called "old workers" (*lao gongren*). They argued that whereas the power of the socialist state almost exclusively determined the condition of the "old workers," both state policies and the dynamics of a more globalized market economy shaped the life of the "new working class."[57] Labor scholars' public discussion of the term usually contained two layers of meanings, one for criticizing the reality, and the other for pointing out the direction for future actions. On the one hand, it was emphasized that rural migrant workers were a socioeconomically disadvantaged group; while this group had made tremendous contributions to China's economic miracle, they were still marginalized in society and often excluded from enjoying the benefits of economic growth. On the other hand, it was highlighted that various kinds of resistance among rural migrant workers, such as wildcat strikes and the organization of labor NGOs, were already rising and that the resistance activism would eventually promote the formation of a class.[58]

While scholars in the academic community had debated whether rural migrant workers in China did constitute a "new working class,"[59] for many people who were involved in workers' on-the-ground struggles, the term simply provided a useful framework for making public interventions. In the late 2000s and early 2010s, many NGO activists, and even some leaders in workers' wildcat strikes, claimed that they were trying to raise workers' class consciousness.[60]

Second, the labor scholars elaborated a more sophisticated discussion of the role of the state. As I have discussed in chapter two and chapter three, most liberals' attitude toward the state was a critical one. However, when talking about concrete social problems, except for arguing that the authoritarian state should be constrained, the liberals had seldom articulated any detailed suggestions on how the state power could be restructured to cope with the problems.

The labor activists had more to offer in this aspect because they tended to consider more about the possibility of promoting policy changes. Labor activists' policy advocacies on the issue of rural migrant workers' access to social insurance programs was a case in point. As I have introduced in chapter three, China's social insurance programs, as part of the welfare system that was reconstructed during the economic reform, had been rather fragmented, decentralized, and locally based. In the early 2000s, because of the difficulties in transferring one's social insurance accounts across regions, many rural migrant workers had chosen to be excluded from the programs. Targeting this problem, several labor scholars argued that, had the central government had more power to make overall planning for the social insurance program, the cross-regional transfer of payment would have been much easier, which would have benefited those workers who were not able to settle down in one place. In policy suggestions submitted to the National People's Congress, these scholars also proposed that the administrative power of the Ministry of Human Resources and Social Security should be expanded, because that would enable the state to penalize those enterprises that had failed to offer social insurance payments.[61] Through these advocacies, the labor scholars developed a set of critical discourses that were different from those proposed by the liberals. Whereas the liberals advocated the withdrawal of state power, the labor scholars suggested that, to provide better protections to workers, the state had to reestablish its power.

Nevertheless, many labor scholars had intentionally kept their debate with the liberals as a "debate within family." A major reason behind this was the labor activists' distrust of the new leftist scholars and their sympathy toward the civil society project. Many labor activists agreed with the new left on the idea that, to protect workers' rights, the state should intervene in the market and take more responsibilities. But these activists did not think that these were what the Chinese state had done. On the contrary, these activists were highly critical of the state. In their opinion, during the economic reform, the state had often collaborated with the power of the capitalist market in the commodification of labor. In such a situation, it was only when a strong civil society being constituted of social movements arose that the capitalist logic could be constrained and the state could be pushed to enact policies and laws that offered better protections to labor rights.[62]

On many occasions, the labor scholars clearly expressed that they also wanted to promote civil society in China; it was simply that their understanding of civil society was somewhat different. For example, in a public lecture held in Beijing, Guo Yuhua, a sociologist from Tsinghua University, explained to the audience,

> Whereas the liberals advocate the restriction of state power, the new leftists more often criticize the capitalist market. In my opinion, this kind of divergence is unnecessary, because both the state and the market need to be criticized. . . . Civil society should become a common ground.[63]

These expressions largely shortened the distance between the labor activism and those liberals who were sympathetic to socioeconomically disadvantaged groups. During my fieldwork in Guangzhou, I met a liberal intellectual who had engaged in NGO activism and had advocated the idea of civil society since the 1990s. His attitude toward the labor scholars was typical among that of his colleagues. When I asked him about his opinion of the labor scholars' interpretation of civil society, he said,

> I disagree with their criticism of the market, as I believe that the market economy and the private ownership of property are the basis for liberty. I also believe that the growth of the market economy is the key to the development of civil society in China. However, civil society is still different from the market. It is supposed to be a place where everyone, including rural migrant workers, can participate and speak. From my point of view, what the labor scholars advocate is that workers enter civil society. This does not diverge too much from our project. Hence, I see them more as friends than as enemies.[64]

The media sphere also showed a much friendlier attitude toward the labor scholars, compared with their attitude toward the rural scholars. In 2007, the *Southern Weekly* invited sociologists from Tsinghua University to write an ongoing column on "constructing society" (*jianshe shehui*). In the column, the labor scholars systematically explained their political project and used plain language to introduce to the public new theoretical perspectives for understanding the concept of society, such as Polanyi's theory of countermovement.[65] In 2011, the ICS even published an edited volume called *Public Life Review: The New Working Class*. Many labor scholars were invited to write on topics like labor protests and labor NGOs.[66]

In a word, at this stage, while raising criticism over the liberal interpretation of civil society, the labor scholars and the labor activism they had initiated had largely maintained a cooperative relation with the liberals.

The Feminist Activism and Its Criticism over the Liberals

A Brief History of the Feminist Activism, 1996–2013

Since the Communist Party came to power in 1949, the Chinese state has always been claiming that gender equality is one of its principal national policies. The first constitution of the People's Republic of China, which was enacted in 1954, stipulated that men and women should have equal rights. To liberate women from traditional roles in family and society, the party and the government promoted the slogan of "women hold up half the sky" (*funü nengding banbian tian*). During the socialist era, many laws and policies were issued to ensure equal pay for equal work and equal opportunity in political participation. To facilitate the implementation of the policies, the party and the government also founded the ACWF, a "mass organization" representing women's interest. Major leaders of the organization were mostly activists in those women's movements initiated by the Communist Party during the republican era.[67] These state-supported feminist practices had enlarged employment opportunities for women. However, they were far from successful in empowering all Chinese women. As women were transformed into state subjects, the feminist agenda was forgotten, and the public sphere of labor and politics kept its masculine order.[68]

Coming to the reform era, the unaccomplished cause of gender equality in China met new challenges. For example, as the labor market shifted from an administratively regulated wage system to a market oriented one, the gender wage gap continued to be widened in the 1990s.[69] The one-child policy introduced in the 1980s substantially increased the incidence of sex-selective abortions and female infanticide.[70] However, due to the transformation of the cultural and ideological environment for public discussions, the socialist discourses for gender equality quickly subsided during the first two decades of the economic reform. In the academic community, famous sociologists like Sun Liping and Zheng Yefu criticized the gender-equal policies during the socialist era as being "too radical" and "unnatural."[71] In various articles they published, it was argued that the situation of "women hold up half the sky" had been achieved at the cost of erasing gender difference. These articles also advocated that to comply with the "natural instincts" of gender women should go home and leave job opportunities in the market to men.

In the 1990s, women intellectual elites within the state system organized social movement activisms to express alternative opinions. A common practice among them was to establish centers for feminist studies and research.[72] These centers had not only introduced various kinds of non-Marxist feminist theories to the Chinese audience but also promoted the reflection upon the essentialist understanding of gender issues, which, as I have just mentioned, was rather prominent in the then public discussions. Another common practice was to establish NGOs. As I have introduced in chapter two, intellectuals and cadres in the ACWF system founded the first wave of NGOs engaging in women's rights issues after the World Women's Conference in Beijing in 1995. Working with the legislature, these NGOs tackled issues like domestic violence. However, while informing the policymakers of the many problems women encountered during the economic reform, the abovementioned activisms had achieved very limited influence in the wider public. In the 1990s and early 2000s, public discussions of gender roles had been saturated with the capitalist consumerist culture.[73] In the interstitial publics, many participants who were at the front line of producing critical opinions, such as the liberal public intellectuals and journalists, had very low awareness of gender inequality in society. Among this group, the employment of masculine or even misogynist discourses was not uncommon.[74]

Feeling dissatisfied with the approach of working within the state system, in the late 2000s, some women intellectuals began to explore new social movement strategies. Among these women intellectuals, the one who later had the greatest influence in China's feminist movement was Lü Pin, a freelancer who used to work as a journalist at *China Women's News*, a newspaper sponsored by the ACWF. Lü joined the feminist movement in China in the 1990s. In 1996, she founded the Women's Media Monitor Network, an NGO I introduced in chapter two. Seeing the NGO activism in the 1990s as being too elitist, she resigned from her position in the state-sponsored institution in the mid-2000s. In 2010, immediately after the launch of Weibo, Lü turned the Women's Media Monitor Network into a social network media account, which had later established itself as the Feminist Voices on China's internet.

In the 2010s, the Feminist Voices offered feminist discourse analysis in public discussions and was closely associated with many grassroots-based advocacy campaigns on women's rights. In 2011, Lü and her friends founded another NGO called the One Dollar Commune (*Yiyuan Gongshe*). The organization offered training programs to feminist activists and a public space in which activists from different places communicated.

In these new organizations, women intellectuals met a younger generation of activists. This younger generation of activists had mainly consisted of women university students and graduates. Many of these activists had come from urban middle-class families and were around twenty when they got involved in the feminist activism. Being raised up as the only child in a family during a period in which China's urban economy grew at an unprecedented rate, these women had enjoyed relatively abundant financial and social resources. Many of them had excelled at academic performance and received education in China's top-tier universities. However, when these women began to prepare to join the labor force, they suddenly discovered that gender-based discrimination was prevalent in the job market and that women were far from being empowered in their career development. This kind of shock urged the young women to express their discontent in the public sphere.[75]

Two forms of activisms had played crucial roles in thematizing the issue of women's rights in the public sphere in the 2010s. Both forms had largely benefited from the rapid development of the information technologies in China. The first form was the "action-art" (*xingwei yishu*) activism, in which activists engaged in "out-of-line" behaviors to problematize various hidden gender inequalities in society. The most well-known case in this category was the "Occupy Men's Toilets" protest. During the annual meeting of the people's congress in 2012, women activists and volunteers in several cities posted on Weibo photos of their occupation of men's toilets and criticized that the arrangement of men's and women's toilets in many public places had failed to consider gender differences. This eye-catching strategy turned out to be a huge success in initiating public dialogue. As activists' posts received millions of comments and reposts within a rather short period of time, many traditional paper media—including even the *People's Daily*—began to report the issue.[76] The second form of activism was media criticism. On social network accounts like the Feminist Voices, activists exposed and criticized gender-based discrimination in movies, TV programs, and news reports. Among these criticisms, the most influential one was an online campaign against misogynist expressions in CCTV's New Year Gala show, which was held in 2015.[77]

In the first few years after the younger generation of activists arose, the feminist activism mainly engaged in topics that urban middle-class young women felt interested in.[78] But this situation had gradually changed around 2015, as some of the young women activists began to attend labor activism. Working with labor NGOs led by university students, the young women activists organized campaigns to tackle issues like sexual harassment at the workplace and advocated women workers' social rights.[79] During this stage, the feminist activism had also intersected with the lesbian movement in China. In the 1990s, China's lesbian movement used to work closely with China's gay movement. However, in the 2000s, as the focus of China's gay movement turned to the issue of AIDS prevention, state bureaucracies largely incorporated the movement.[80] In response to this transformation, activists in the lesbian movement found their new allies among young feminist activists. Around 2010, the lesbian activists had attended many advocacy campaigns organized by the feminist activists, notably the campaign against domestic violence. The feminist activism had also addressed the issue of sexuality.[81]

The Debate on Family Planning Policies

Looking back, we may discover that the relationship between China's feminist activism and the liberals' project of building civil society should not have been an uncooperative one. As I have mentioned in chapter two, a large part of NGOs established in the 1990s were NGOs engaging in the issue of women's rights, while the founders of these NGOs were mostly women intellectuals who had been influenced by the World Women's Conference. On the one hand, these women intellectuals organized NGOs to empower socioeconomically disadvantaged women and promote changes in laws and policies. On the other hand, they saw their activism as an attempt at expanding an independent space for citizens' participation.[82] These ideas went well with liberals' political agenda and could be perfectly incorporated into the project of building civil society. As I have elaborated in chapter three, in principle, the liberals had also supported all social groups to struggle for their rights.

However, in the late 2000s and early 2010s, when the feminist activism for defending women's rights did flourish, many liberal public intellectuals began to feel uncomfortable. Some of them suggested that "women's rights" were a political agenda set by intellectuals in the West; in China, since women and men were already very equal, the advocacy of women's rights was far less important than some grander causes like the struggle for constitutional democracy. Some argued that it was unnecessary to emphasize "women's rights," since the term "human rights" was already comprehensive and could cover "women's rights."[83]

Liberal public intellectuals' commentaries on feminist activists' performance art activism best illustrate the attitude of the liberal camp. In the summer of 2012, the official Weibo account of the Shanghai Metro posted a photo of a young woman wearing a sheer blouse, suggesting that this kind of apparel was likely to incur sexual harassment in subways. In response to this suggestion, feminist activists got on trains in subways and held boards with the slogan "I can be slutty, but you can't get dirty" (*Wo keyi sao, ni buneng rao*). Later, these activists also posted articles on Weibo, pushing the Shanghai Metro to take substantive measures to prevent sexual harassment, instead of blaming the victims.[84] While the feminist activists framed their activism as a "rights-defending" activity, it aroused huge controversies in the public sphere. On the *Southern Metropolis Daily* and the *Southern Weekly*, liberal public intellectuals wrote several articles to question the legitimacy of the activism. For example, Qiu Feng, a scholar studying economic thoughts, who was also a famous columnist, argued that those who wore little in the public were releasing a signal suggesting that they served in some "special industries" (*teshu hangye*) where sex was casual. He also contended that women should not put their right to choose clothes before the etiquette (*lisu*) of a society.[85]

Many feminist scholars and activists also recognized that their advocacies were unwelcome among the liberals. In an article titled "Why Don't the Liberals in Mainland China Support Feminism" (*Zhongguo Dalu Ziyou Zhuyi Zhe Weihe Bu Zhichi Nüquan Zhuyi*), Li Sipan, who was then a feminist scholar studying at the University of Macau, summarized the liberals' discontent with the feminist expressions and offered several explanations of the phenomenon.[86] In Li's opinion, the liberals' unsupportive attitude toward feminism had to do with both their academic background and their position in society. With respect to the liberals' academic background, Li suggested that many of the liberals had been under the influence of classical liberalism, whose core subject was the protection of citizens' negative liberty; these liberals had lacked understanding of political theories of social liberalism, such as those articulated by John Rawls. Moreover, Li contended that the liberals were mostly men occupying advantageous positions in society. As beneficiaries of China's market economic reform, these liberals became unwilling to reflect upon their positions and thus lacked sympathies over the disadvantaged.

While I am sympathetic to Li's arguments, I still want to point out that they cannot explain why, among the many and various alternative activisms emerging during the second term of the Hu-Wen regime, the liberals had been particularly inimical to the feminist activism. If not reading Rawls and lacking self-reflection would necessarily lead to an unsupportive attitude toward disadvantaged groups' social movement activism, the liberals should also have turned their back on labor activism. Yet as I have just introduced in the previous section, this had not happened, at least around 2010.

My explanation is that the breakup between the feminists and the liberals had to do with the nature of the topics the feminists had proposed for public discussion. The liberals had been particularly uncomfortable with the rise of the feminist activism because it was the feminist activism that had best illustrated the problems inherent to the many dichotomies advocated by the liberals, such as the public vs. the private, and state vs. society. The controversies raised by public discussions on China's family planning policies were a case in point.

Introduced in the 1970s, China's family planning policies—among which the most influential one was the one-child policy—had long been controversial. As I have just mentioned, because of the existence of son preference, the incidence of sex-selective abortions and female infanticide had significantly increased since the 1980s. The enforcement of the policies at the local level had also encountered resistance and caused a great many social conflicts, especially in rural areas. In the early 2000s, many activists in the liberal camp—mainly the "rights-defending" lawyers—had protested the one-child policy and intervened in cases in which state bureaucrats used violence to enforce relevant laws. A major discourse the liberal activists had employed was that childbearing was an individual freedom and that the state should not interfere.[87] During this stage, the issue of gender was seldom mentioned.

It was in the late 2000s that the gender issue and women's rights became a focus of the public discussion of the family planning policies. In 2007, Yi Fuxian, a Chinese-born American obstetrics and gynecology researcher, who claimed that he had long been studying China's demography issues, published in Hong Kong a book titled *Big Country with an Empty Nest* (Daguo Kongchao). In generalized terms, the book argued that the one-child policy should be abandoned because it would ruin China's economic growth in the long run.[88] The Chinese government banned the circulation of the book almost immediately after its publication. But the major argument of the book had spread on the internet and was recommended by many liberal public intellectuals, such as Mao Yushi. Yi was also allowed to give lectures in several universities and research institutes. In these lectures, Yi often advocated for the "traditional value" of big families and suggested that the women's major responsibility was to procreate and take care of their families. These expressions had incurred discontent among the feminist scholars and activists. Some of them went to the lectures and openly debated with Yi, arguing that the critics of the one-child policy had only wanted to transfer the discretion in childbearing from the state to the patriarchal family, without considering whether women could obtain more freedom or become empowered in this process.[89]

The conflict between the liberals and the feminist activism became more confrontational and visible when the debate on the family planning policies was brought to the internet. Since the late 2000s, because of the continuously decreasing fertility rate, many provincial level governments began to adopt some more relaxed forms of the one-child policy.[90] For example, in cities like Shanghai, those parents who were single children in their original families were allowed to have a second child.

On the internet, many women, especially those who were urban born and well educated, began to express their concerns over the social implications of the new policies.[91] Some of them suggested that urban-born girls were the greatest beneficiaries of the one-child policy in the past two decades, because the policy had made these girls the only "investment" in the family. These people worried that the relaxation of the one-child policy would revive the traditional Chinese culture that "viewed sons as better than daughters" (*zhongnan qingnü*) and deprive girls of their educational opportunities. Others suggested that the one-child policy had to some extent reduced the "motherhood penalty"—while women in the workforce still had to, compared to men, spend more time and energy in child rearing, they at most needed to bring up one child. These people worried that, in a situation in which two or more children became the norm and the welfare support for child rearing fell short, women would need to sacrifice more in their families and the job market would become even more unfriendly to women. The liberals harshly criticized these views. Some of the liberals hastily generalized women's questions and concerns as a proposal for supporting the one-child policy. Some even blamed the feminist voices on the internet for complying with the authoritarian regime.[92]

In response to these criticisms, feminist activists made clarifications. In an interview, Lü Pin claimed that she and her colleagues did not support the one-child policy; moreover, to fight for women's rights in China, feminist activism had to struggle with both the authoritarian state and the patriarchal family—as the two powers were largely homologues.[93] In the interview, Lü also encouraged women participants of online discussions to find alternative languages to express their concerns, instead of pinning their hope on the state.

But these clarifications seemed to do little in changing the liberals' impression of the feminist activism. Here the tricky thing was this—even though feminist activists emphasized that the authoritarian state was not able to guarantee gender equity, the role of the state involved in the issue of women's rights, as exemplified in the public discussion on family planning policies, was far more complex. As the online criticisms over the relaxation of the one-child policy had demonstrated, in a certain historical context, the advancement of women's interests had been associated with the state's arbitrary intervention in the patriarchal family—though the advancement had been achieved at great cost and benefited only some women. Conversely, when the arbitrary state intervention was lessened, women's interests could be harmed.

If the feminist activism had adhered to the "state vs. society" framework held by the liberals, many of the women's concerns would have been deemed private issues and would thus lose legitimacy to become topics for public discussion. Therefore, the strategy employed by the labor activism—accepting the "state vs. society" framework and revising the framework from within—did not work; to raise many gender-related issues in the public sphere, the feminist activism had to challenge, in a more thorough fashion, the fundamental assumption of the project of building civil society. As a matter of fact, many feminist scholars had argued that the boundary between the public and the private, which had been set by the liberals, needed to be criticized and that more attention should be paid to the various power inequalities in the so-called private sphere.[94] It was this kind of challenge that had dismantled the foundation on which the feminists and the liberals could work together.

Divisions Brought by the Ideological Debates

Before the concluding section, I would like to highlight that the various debates happening in the interstitial publics during this stage had incurred divisions in the social movement community. The conflict between the liberals and the feminists, as I have just introduced, was a case in point. Divisions had also occurred within single social movements. The conflict among activists from different labor NGOs provides an illustrative example here. During the early 2010s, labor NGOs in China had already differentiated into several groups. The first group were those organizations engaging in subcultural activities. Activists from this group were often heavily influenced by Marxist and Maoist discourses. Organizations in the second group provided legal aid service to individual workers. Because of their historical cooperation with the liberals, these organizations more often emphasized the idea of civil society. The last group were the so-called "collective bargaining" organizations. Working with the labor lawyers, these organizations intervened in workers' factory-based collective actions.

When I was in the field between 2012 and 2015, I discovered that, working in a highly contested ideological environment, labor NGO activists engaging in different forms of activism employed multiple critical discourses to dismiss others and valorize their own activism. For example, those from the "collective bargaining" organizations argued that their organizations were the truly "workers' movement organizations" (*gongyunxing zuzhi*), while those organizations that engaged in workers' subcultural activities were too moderate and docile.[95] On the other side, activists engaging in the subcultural activities argued that, by reconstructing a working-class culture, they were able to raise workers' class consciousness and promote workers' transition from a "class-in-itself" to a "class-for-itself." Therefore, only labor NGOs organizing cultural activities were the truly revolutionary, while the "collective bargaining" organizations were "neoliberal," because they still sought to resolve the conflict between capital and labor within the framework of law.[96]

These conflicts had not been kept private. Activists sometimes openly attacked each other. As I have mentioned in chapter three, because of many different reasons, the activists' intervention in the "rights-defending" activities often ended up trapping the disadvantaged in a worse situation. Similar things had also happened in labor NGOs' intervention in workers' factory-based collective actions. On some occasions, activists from the "collective bargaining" organizations failed to explain to workers the potential risks inherent to their actions, and then workers lost their job after confronting the management. To demonstrate that the "collective bargaining" organizations were "neoliberal" and could only harm workers, activists from those organizations that emphasized Marxist and Maoist discourses videotaped complaints from those workers who had received aid from the "collective bargaining" organizations and posted the recordings on video-sharing websites in China, such as Youku.

In an interview with an activist who had harshly criticized the "collective bargaining" organizations, I tentatively asked, "Isn't solidarity in the labor NGO community a desirable goal?" My interviewee, who was then a student activist, simply avoided answering my question and suggested that it was only through political and cultural struggles that the labor movement in China was able to find its way to establish "workers' subjectivity" (*gongren de zhutixing*).[97] However, online quarrels like this made people in the wider public feel very confused about the role of labor NGOs in labor rights issues. As I will show in the next chapter, these quarrels had also made these organizations more vulnerable to state suppression.

Conclusion

In this chapter and the previous chapter, I discuss the condition of China's interstitial publics between 2008 and 2013. In chapter four, I argue that the transformation in China's political, social, and technological environment had changed the way public discussion was organized. While the domination of the liberals was destabilized, new participants who were more interested in issue-oriented discussion arose. In this chapter, I demonstrate how the structural transformation of the interstitial publics had shifted the way civil society was debated in public discussion. I analyze and compare three social movements that had claimed to represent subaltern interests, which were the New Rural Reconstruction Movement, the labor activism, and the feminist activism. All three social movements had challenged the liberal interpretation of civil society. I emphasize that, because of the different extent to which these movements had been institutionalized by the state and the diverse nature of the topics they had proposed for public discussion, the three movements had eventually ended up having divergent relations with the liberals.

At the end of the chapter, I talk about the "dark side" of the ideological debates by highlighting the divisions emerging in China's social movement community. Nevertheless, I contend that these new participants' debates with the liberals had largely enriched the public discussions in China's interstitial publics. On the one hand, these debates brought in important information with regards to the concrete difficulties the disadvantaged encountered.

In the previous stage, the liberals had also claimed that they hoped to advance disadvantaged groups' rights. However, because the liberal understanding of civil society was too reductionist, the real difficulties facing the disadvantaged were often ignored. By talking about issues like the externalities in defending food safety, the rise of the "new working class," and the perplexities facing working women in childrearing, activists in the three social movements complicated the public criticism over China's politics and society. On the other hand, since the three movements had emerged and established themselves out of the debate with the liberals, their articulation had also complicated people's understanding of the idea of civil society. Many topics that had been marginalized in the previous stage, such as the power inequalities within civil society, the multiple roles the state could play in the development of civil society, and the conflicting relationship between civil society and the market, were brought back to the public view.

But the time left for the activists was limited. Coming to the end of the Hu-Wen regime, the state's regulation over the interstitial publics had become more intensified. As both the media sphere and the NGO sphere were constrained, the space for ideological debates was quickly shrinking. This is what I am going to elaborate in the next chapter.

CHAPTER 6

The Fragmentation of Public Discussion, 2014−2019

Once again, significant changes took place in China's social and political environment after Xi Jinping became president in 2013. The occurrence of the Umbrella Movement in Hong Kong in 2014 forbode the approach of a new era. After that, the state's intervention in public discussion became more arbitrary and frequent. The influence of commercial power in the media sphere and the NGO sphere also became more pervasive. Resultantly, many interstitially emergent actors who had been active in various public debates in previous stages, including both the liberals and those who had challenged the liberals, were put in a more constrained situation.

I suggest that, during this stage, as the liberals were further marginalized in public discussion in wider society, the political project of building civil society eventually disintegrated. However, the disintegration of the project had not brought "peace" to China's public sphere. Nor had it implied that all resistance activisms had now been under state's control. The contrary was true. With the decline of the liberals, various kinds of new actors and new forms of activisms emerged, especially in the field of labor rights and women's rights. Like their predecessors, some of these new actors and new forms of activisms also drew on ideological discourses in their public expression and proposed grand political project. However, the public sphere had become too fragmented to allow any concerted efforts that brought the grand project and grassroots resistance activism together. As a result, the new forms of social movement activisms appeared to lack a package plan. Their impact on China's politics and the stability of the regime also became more unpredictable.

This chapter is dedicated to elaborating on the transformation of the interstitial publics between 2014 and 2019. I choose 2019 to be the ending point of my historical documentation, because at the end of that year, COVID-19—a pandemic that had later altered many people's political and social lives—hit

China and the world. Nevertheless, many of the social movement activisms emerging before 2019 have lasted after the pandemic. This implies that some of the subjects I am going to discuss in this chapter are currently still changing and evolving. I will thus try to keep my discussion and analysis open.

The rest of the chapter will be arranged in the following way. In the next section, I briefly introduce the changing social and political environment in China since the mid-2010s. Then I describe the further decline of existing interstitial spaces, namely the media sphere and the NGO sphere. After that, I discuss the fragmentation of the liberal camp during this stage. I also report on the transformation of the three social movements I analyze in the previous chapter—the New Rural Reconstruction Movement (or the food movement), the labor activism, and the feminist activism. In the conclusion section, I discuss the political implications of the disintegration of the project of building civil society.

The Changing Political and Social Background Since the Mid-2010s

For major actors in the community of resistance movements in China, the most influential political event happening in 2014 was the Umbrella Movement in Hong Kong. Being sparked by Beijing's decision to pre-screen candidates for the election of the special administrative region's chief executive, on September 26, tens of thousands of Hong Kong citizens started an occupation campaign demanding a more transparent election. The campaign was later named the Umbrella Movement, or the Umbrella Revolution, referring to the umbrellas used as a tool for passive resistance to the Hong Kong police's employment of pepper spray in dispersing the crowd.[1] Compared to a later movement happening in Hong Kong—the movement against the Extradition Law Amendment Bill in 2019 and 2020—the Umbrella Movement had aroused very few interests in China's public sphere. Because of stringent state control over media coverage, discussion of the event had been limited to various intellectual elites, such as scholars, liberal journalists, the "rights-defending" lawyers, and some youth activists.[2]

However, the rise of the Umbrella Movement had made Hong Kong a politically sensitive place.[3] Since 2014, many interactions between social movement activists in Hong Kong and those in mainland China were constrained. The experience of political activist Chan Kin-Man was a case in point. Chan was formerly an associate professor of sociology at the Chinese University of Hong Kong and one of the co-founders of the ICS at the Sun Yat-sen University. In the 2000s, he had often been invited by various government departments and research institutes in China to give lectures on topics like "civil society and the building of a harmonious society."[4] In 2013, to call for universal suffrage in Hong Kong, Chan initiated a campaign called "Occupy Central with Love and Peace," which sowed the seeds for the Umbrella Movement. In 2019, he was sentenced to 16 months in prison for his role in the movement.[5] As the Umbrella Movement gained its momentum in 2015, no organizations and institutes in mainland China dared to openly invite Chan anymore. After the Umbrella Movement, because of its close association with Chan, the ICS became an organization of special concern to Beijing. In 2016, the ICS was closed. ICS's connection with Hong Kong even influenced the School of Philanthropy at the Sun Yat-sen University. Eventually, in 2017, the school was also closed.

This kind of disconnection was particularly harmful to the various social movement organizations in the Pearl River Delta. In the early to mid-2000s, interstitially emergent actors in the Delta had benefited from their geographical proximity to Hong Kong. For many organizations, it was through their interaction with Hong Kong that they obtained resources and information from the international community and eventually achieved national influence in China. The ICS was a typical example.[6] Another example were labor NGOs. According to my research on the history of labor NGOs in China, about two-thirds of these organizations received funds from Hong Kong-based organizations. Major supporters of labor NGOs included the Oxfam Hong Kong, China Labour Bulletin, Labour Education and Service Network, and Worker Empowerment. Many of these Hong Kong-based organizations had regularly received funds from labor rights-related foundations all over the world.[7] As social movement organizations' interactions with Hong Kong were constrained, so was their capacity to launch proactive campaigns in mainland China. As I have mentioned in chapter two, the city of Guangzhou used to be one of the dual centers—alongside Beijing—of the liberal camp. But after 2014, no social movement organization with national influence had been formed in the Delta. Inadvertently, the Umbrella Movement had transformed the configuration of the interstitial publics in mainland China.

Meanwhile, with Xi Jinping's rise to the highest leader of the country in 2013, the domestic political atmosphere in China was also slowly but steadily changing. On the one hand, the Xi regime launched a series of campaigns that aimed to solve some of the most severe problems in Chinese society.

Two notable examples were the anti-corruption campaign, which had started in 2012 and removed more than two million government officials at different levels, and the "targeted poverty alleviation" (*jingzhun fupin*) campaign, which started in 2014, aiming to lift over 70 million rural population above the poverty line by 2020. Scholars have been debating the real intentions behind these campaigns and the extent to which these campaigns could eliminate problems like corruption and poverty.[8] But many agreed that, through political mobilization in these campaigns, the Xi regime had reversed the tendency of the decentralization of state power that had started in the mid-1990s and increased the state's capacity to penetrate society.[9]

On the other hand, the state's ideological control over public discussion had continued and become even more intensified. In 2013, Lu Wei, the director of the State Internet Information Office, urged media professionals to spread "positive energy" (*zheng nengliang*), implying that online discussions should focus on the positive side of China's social and economic development, while expositions of the dark side should be avoided.[10] This had largely reversed the atmosphere formed during the first term of the Hu-Wen regime that encouraged citizens to openly discuss and criticize social problems. Additionally, as China gradually built up its economic power in the global market, the West had lost some of its leverage to influence China in issues like human rights. As I have mentioned in chapter one, to save its image in the international community after the 1989 Student Movement and take part in the neoliberal globalization that was then dominated by the West, the Chinese government had released quite a few political dissidents in the 1990s. But in the 2010s, on many occasions, the government simply disregarded Westerners' demands to release political dissidents in China.[11] With these transformations, the social and political conditions that facilitated the emergence of interstitial space in the 1990s were almost gone.

Nevertheless, although the Chinese state's capacity to regulate society had significantly increased, it was not able to solve all social problems. Nor could it eliminate all expressions of discontents. Since 2012, China's economic growth had shown a marked slowdown, with growth rates declining from double digit levels before the global financial crisis in 2008 to around 7% in 2014. The slowing growth of the economy incurred many problems, such as the shrinkage of new job opportunities and the increasing pressure for commodifying labor. Facing these problems, Chinese people, especially the younger generation, felt a lot of anxiety and depression. As the mainstream public discussion now allowed "positive energy" only, people turned to alternative channels. In society, various forms of subcultural activities, such as live houses, street dances, and talk shows, flourished. In these activities, people expressed negative feelings about the dim reality and the uncertain future.[12] With these transformations, the ethos of public expression took on a new look.

The Decline of Interstitial Spaces Emerging in Previous Stages

The Further Disintegration of the Media Sphere

As I have discussed in chapter four, during the second term of the Hu-Wen regime, commercially-oriented newspapers as a venue for producing critical public opinions had declined due to increasing state interventions and the rapid development of digital technologies. Because of the rise of mobile phones as devices for getting online, users of the internet expanded. The emergence of comprehensive platforms lowered the threshold for participating in online discussions, while at the same time facilitated the practice of censorship. As the state's regulation over the domestic cyberspace became more stringent, "radical" activists like the "rights-defending" lawyers turned to platforms overseas, which made the online public sphere more segregated. Since the mid-2010s, all these tendencies had been reinforced.

In the Xi regime, because of the slumping circulation and advertisement revenues, the income of investigative journalists at commercially-oriented newspapers continued to drop. So did their professional prestige. Under such a circumstance, many investigative journalists changed their profession.[13] Because of the development of digital technologies, participants in cyberspace continued to increase. With the rise of a series of video sharing apps, notably Kuaishou, the population who participated in the activities of online content generation now expanded to an even larger population, including people like rural migrant youth, peasants, and housewives in lower class families.[14] Meanwhile, on these newly rising platforms as well as on some "old" platforms like Weibo, the influence of commercial power became more pervasive. Internet companies began to place more emphasis on the idea of network flow (*wangluo liuliang*) and the possibility to liquidate. Great numbers of users on platforms thus turned to profit-seeking activities.[15]

The practice of censorship also became more institutionalized. To unify the previously fragmented regulation system, a new department, the State Internet Information Office, was established within the State Council Information Office in 2014. Under the auspices of the new office, municipal-level rules targeting online public discussion were introduced, information censorship demands were detailed, and a real-name registration system was established.[16] What is worth mentioning is that, during this stage, various market forces had been involved in the practice of censorship. Employing advanced technologies like big data, hundreds of profit-driven internet opinion companies had helped their government clients at different levels to analyze the development trend of online opinions, eliminate anti-government information and boost pro-government discourses.[17] This had made the censorship more efficient and impersonalized.

To circumscribe state censorship and the prominent consumerist/commercial culture, people holding critical and alternative political opinions turned to various new interstitial spaces. Some, like the liberals in the previous stage, began to use platforms or tools that were only available outside the Great Firewall. For example, instead of using WeChat, activists engaging in human rights activism began to use Signal or Wire as their major instant message app. Instead of writing a blog or posting entries on Weibo, activists now documented and discussed critical social events on Matters.

Some others turned to channels where state censorship was still porous, such as podcasts. Since the mid-2010s, listeners in China witnessed the emergence of several podcast programs focusing on politics and history. Notable examples included the Left Right (*Hu Zuo Hu You*) and East Asia Observatory (*Dongya Guanchaju*). These podcast programs were usually run by scholars, journalists, editors, and enthusiasts of history, political science, and sociology. Unlike many content generators on comprehensive platforms who aimed to maximize the network flow to make profit, the producers of the podcasts saw their activities as a social intercourse that could help them attract fellows with similar interests and concerns. To avoid becoming too influential—which might incur more intensive state censorship—the podcast programs usually discussed political issues in very sophisticated ways and required listeners to have a relatively abundant knowledge of relevant topics.[18]

Naturally, these new interstitial spaces all had relatively high thresholds. To use platforms and tools outside the Great Firewall, one needed not only the money to buy Virtual Private Network (VPN) but also the technical know-how to use it. To participate in the discussions initiated by the podcast programs and decipher the political messages hidden in the scholarly talks, as I have just said, one needed to be very knowledgeable in politics and history. Public discussion on China's cyberspace had started from small, well-bounded communities. As I have mentioned in chapter two, major platforms for online discussion in the 1990s were the university-based BBSes, whose participants were mostly university students, professors, and alumni. In the 2000s, what had broken the boundary were the rapid development of the internet infrastructure and the intervention of commercial power. But in the 2010s, with the increasing pressure brought by the state and the market, many participants of online discussion began to, passively or proactively, build new boundaries.

Another relatively new phenomenon emerging since the mid-2010s was that, to ensure that "positive energy" prevailed on the cyberspace, the Chinese state now proactively intervened in many online discussions. Traditional party media like the *People's Daily* employed languages that young people liked and refurbished their online contents. Some fandom groups among the youth echoed this effort. As young people in fandom groups fervently embraced nationalist discourses, the boundary between political discussion and entertainment was blurred.[19] This further marginalized those serious discussions that sought to expose social problems and criticize state policies.

To clarify, by elaborating how the state power and the market power had become more pervasive in the media sphere since the mid-2010s, I am not suggesting that the space for criticism had been fully eradicated and the chance to articulate alternative opinions had decreased to zero. As I have just discussed, people were still trying to find new interstitial spaces. Empirical studies on fandom also show that, even when the expression of nationalist discourses seemed to be rather prominent, the alliance between the state's propaganda departments and the fandom groups was rather fragile.[20] However, I do want to suggest that the media sphere featuring the critical reportage of and commentary on news and current affairs had become fragmented. In all the previous stages, there were one or a few leading platforms on which people with alternative political agendas gathered and influential critical public opinions were produced. In the early to mid-2000s, these platforms were the southern newspapers, being facilitated by a few commercially-oriented online forums like Tianya. In the late 2000s and early 2010s, the major platform became Weibo. But since the mid-2010s, the articulation of critical public opinions was scattered on many different platforms. Criticism still existed. But it had become highly disorganized.

The Re-Elitization of the NGO Sphere

As I have discussed in chapter four, the state's efforts in institutionalizing the NGO sphere had started during the Hu-Wen era; however, because of various discrepancies within the state and bureaucracies' limited infrastructure power to enforce rules, the state's regulation system had been rather porous. This situation was eventually changed in the Xi regime. In 2016, two laws relevant to NGOs were passed, which were the Charity Law and the Law on the Administration of Activities of Overseas Non-governmental Organizations within the Territory of China. These laws specified the rules on the registration of NGOs, the management of charity funds, and domestic NGOs' interaction with international foundations. After that, the Ministry of Civil Affairs also issued several enforcement regulations, detailing how local governments should evaluate NGOs and supervise the use of funds.[21] For example, it was required that relevant government departments routinely investigate the activities of NGOs and establish a blacklist to document those organizations that engaged in "abnormal activities." Those organizations that had been put on the blacklist would be deprived of the opportunity to compete for the "government purchasing service" funds. In practice, activities like receiving funds from unregistered international foundations and organizing agitational activism could all be categorized as "abnormal."[22] With the passage of these laws, local governments' influence was lessened, and the state power for regulating NGOs became more unified.

The transformation of labor NGOs in the mid-2010s best illustrated how the increasingly stringent regulation had impacted NGO activism. In 2015, twenty years after the first labor NGO in China was established, systematic regulations aimed at labor NGO activism finally came. What raised the curtain was the crackdown on a couple of labor NGOs in the Pearl River Delta. On December 3, fifteen activists in four labor NGOs were detained.[23] All four organizations were internationally funded and had been involved in workers' protests and strikes. Although this was not the first time the state suppressed labor NGOs, the repression was different from the previous instances in several ways. First, the order of repression was issued by the central government, rather than any local government. Second, the crackdown on labor NGOs and the arrest of activists were quickly publicized, while in previous years, these were usually done surreptitiously. On CCTV, a special program was broadcast, in which labor NGOs like Panyu Migrant Workers were labeled as "agents of overseas hostile forces" that intended to manipulate Chinese workers and intensify labor-capital disputes. The repression of the labor NGOs in the Delta made many labor activists realize that the many "loopholes" in the state's regulation system had gone.

To save their organizations, many labor NGO activists turned to service provision activities. But, as I have discussed in the previous chapter, because these organizations had been very active in a series of advocacy campaigns during the second term of the Hu-Wen regime, local governments had black-listed most of them. Even after they had completely quit the advocacy campaigns, the state's security departments continuously harassed major activists of the organizations. Raising funds also became rather difficult for these organizations. Because of their past experience of advocating for labor rights, obtaining "government purchasing service" funds became impossible. Some activists turned to newly emerging crowdfunding platforms on the internet, such as the philanthropy platform supported by Tencent. But what these platforms could offer was also limited, because the majority of donors on these platforms were the middle class who had little interest in the idea of class struggles.[24]

Under these pressures, the community of labor NGOs quickly disintegrated. According to my study of the historical transformation of China's labor NGOs, between 2015 and 2020, 21 labor NGOs—about one third of all the organizations that had been active in the field in the early 2010s—were disbanded.[25] To avoid repression, most of the remaining organizations had to de-emphasize the discourse of the "new working class" and the identity of "labor NGOs" and package their activities in other issues, such as migrant children's education.

In rare occasions, some NGOs had persisted in the field of labor rights. A notable example was the Zhicheng Legal Aid Center for Rural Migrant Workers (*Zhicheng Nongmingong Falü Yuanzhu yu Yanjiu Zhongxin*) in Beijing. Since the mid-2010s, the center had published a series of influential reports on labor rights issues on digital labor platforms and submitted relevant policy suggestions to the people's congress.[26] But the Zhicheng Center was an exceptional case. Its founder and current leader, Tong Lihua, was a deputy to the National People's Congress in 2012 and legal advisor to the Ministry of Civil Affairs and the ACFTU. The center enjoyed many political resources and connections that most other labor NGOs, especially those grassroots organizations in the Pearl River Delta, could never obtain.

Similar trends also happened in other fields, such as environmental protection and women's rights. As I mentioned in chapter one and two, in the 1990s and early 2000s, major founders of NGOs in China were various kinds of intellectual elites who were closely connected with the state power. NGOs established by people from socioeconomically disadvantaged groups, or the so-called "grassroots NGOs," did not emerge until the mid-2000s. What facilitated the rise and flourish of these "grassroots NGOs" were the training programs offered by institutes like the ICS, the lowered threshold for registration, and the state funds. But in the mid-2010s, institutes like the ICS were suppressed, the threshold for registration was raised again, and the funding environment became extremely unfriendly to the "grassroots NGOs." It hence returned to the situation that only people who were able to mobilize resources in the state and the market were eligible to establish NGOs. I call this process the re-elitization of the NGO sphere. For sure, many elites founding charity organizations today cared about the welfare of the disadvantaged and eagerly hoped to employ innovative methods to solve social problems. Zhicheng Center's advocacy of labor rights was a case in point. However, without far-flung networks consisting of actors from different backgrounds, NGOs' capacity to detect problems in society and absorb resistance activities significantly dropped. I will come back to this point later in my discussion of labor activism and feminist activism since the mid-2010s.

The Transformation of the Liberal Camp

With the decline of the media sphere and the NGO sphere, the liberal camp finally disintegrated. First, due to the state's increasing ideological control, some of the most radical actors in the liberal camp, notably the "rights-defending" lawyers, were silenced. In 2015, the Chinese government launched a campaign targeting "rights-defending" activists all over the country. More than two hundred lawyers and their assistants in 24 provinces were detained, warned, or interrogated.[27] This crackdown had ruined many activists who had hope to democratize China through the Weiquan Movement.

The transformation of the liberals with a relatively moderate political agenda varied across groups. Those who had been highly embedded in the state were mostly incorporated. Notable examples included scholars and intellectuals who had served at the research centers studying NGOs and civil society. As I have discussed in chapter four, as early as the late 2000s, some of the scholars and intellectuals, such as those at the ICS, had already begun to employ the state-endorsed discourses like "philanthropy" and "social work." But unlike the situation in the late 2000s, when training programs offered by the institutes like the School of Philanthropy still tried to discuss issues like an independent space for participation, the NGO scholars now took the state-endorsed discourses for real. Many of them employed theories from public administration or management and conducted research that aimed to help the government regulate NGOs.[28]

Those who had been less embedded in the state and relied more on the resources provided by the market, notably the internet-based public intellectuals, turned to new popular discourses in the public sphere, such as the nationalist discourses. A case in point was Lian Yue, a former journalist and columnist at the *Southern Weekly*. In the early to mid-2000s, Lian Yue was famous for his sharp criticism over government and his advocacy of civil society and the Weiquan Movement.[29] When the anti-PX protest arose in Xiamen in 2007, Lian was among the first few activists who had openly discussed the issue online. In the Sichuan Earthquake in 2008, when many Chinese people praised the government for its quick response in the rescue work, Lian hastily pushed people to pay attention to the government's failure in predicting the occurrence of the earthquake. But in the late 2010s, Lian took a U-turn. On his WeChat public account, he suggested that his participation in the anti-PX protest was stupid and his criticism over China's political institutions in early years was naïve. He also suggested that the most important thing in his career as a columnist now was to be patriotic.[30]

A couple of liberals managed to maintain their ideological position and critical attitude. However, facing the rapidly changing environment, many of these liberals had appeared to be slow to adapt to the emergence of new topics in public discussion, such as sexual harassment and gender equity. A case in point was Liu Yu's response to the MeToo Movement in China. Around 2017, being influenced by the MeToo Movement in the West, dozens of victims of sexual harassment began to tell their stories online. The alleged figures in these accusations were mostly people occupying advantageous positions in academics or the entertainment industry. In an article posted on Weibo, Liu Yu criticized the MeToo Movement in China. She contended that the movement had relied too much on populist power; without resorting to more institutionalized strategies like lawsuits, the movement could only create disturbance and disorder. She also expressed her concern that the movement would eventually destroy an atmosphere in which men and women could easily flirt with each other and establish ambiguous relationships. At the end of the article, she suggested that women who did not want to get involved in sexual harassment simply needed to put on more clothes.[31] Liu's comment infuriated many activists who had spared great efforts in problematizing the issue of sexual harassment in China's online public sphere. They argued that Liu had ignored the many power inequalities inherent to the issue and that what she had advocated was nothing but blaming the victims.[32]

A similar instance was the liberal intellectuals' defense of Feng Gang in the debate on gender discrimination in academics. Feng Gang was formerly a professor of sociology at Zhejiang University. In 2017, some feminist activists discovered that Feng's posts on Weibo contained many discriminatory remarks. For example, Feng had often complained that graduate schools had enrolled too many women and contended that women were not suitable for academic studies. Reposting these remarks on Weibo, the feminist activists asked for an apology. But Feng refused to apologize. Instead, he quarreled vehemently with the activists on cyberspace.[33] In the dispute, several liberal intellectuals chose to stand with Feng. For example, Xiao Han, a professor of political science who had long advocated for a constitutional democracy, wrote an article titled "Political Correctness and the Freedom of Speech" (*Zhengzhi Zhengque yu Yanlun Ziyou*). In the article, he blamed feminist activists' actions as being "hegemonic" and supported Feng's "freedom to express his opinion" in the public sphere.[34]

What is worth mentioning here is that, since the mid-2010s, quite a few liberals had expressed a dislike of the many policies and measures taken in the West that were intended to avoid offense to members of disadvantaged groups in society. Learning from the conservatives in the United States, these liberals had also used the phrase "political correctness" (*zhengzhi zhengque*) as a pejorative. Some of them even argued that social movements like the feminist movement and gay rights movement since the 1980s had already "ruined the foundation of western civilization" and advocated that Chinese people learn from "a more classic and liberal United States."[35] During the presidential election in the US in 2016, many of these liberals became devoted followers of Donald Trump.[36]

Taking all these facts into consideration, it may not be difficult for readers to understand that, in the eyes of a new generation of activists who had been interested in issues like labor rights and women's rights, the term "the liberals" had become a distant memory. When the term was associated with reality, what came to young activists' minds was often a group of figures who were, in many senses, conservative. In 2017 and 2018, I and my colleagues in the Pearl River Delta conducted a research project on youth activists. When talking about the liberals and their political project of civil society, many of our interviewees offered critical opinions. An activist in the feminist movement said,

From my point of view, what the liberals want was a political reform, or a reform of China's political institution. But most of them dared not say that. Then they began to say things like weiquan and citizens' actions, and presented an idealized picture, telling people that China would become democratized one day if there is a civil society. Looking back, I would say these people were very idealistic. I had also been under their influence. But I would also say they were kind of naïve.[37]

Another activist, who had worked in labor NGOs, said,

The liberals are allies of the bourgeoisie. Some of them advocate social democracy. But social democracy is just not enough for the working class. Civil society is a theory proposed in the 70s and 80s. In my eyes, it is a bit outdated. It only talks about the balance of political power. But the critical issue here is the distribution of economic resources. If you want to talk about the distribution of economic resources, you must talk about class. But the liberals here never talk about class.[38]

Except for a few young activists who had hoped to turn to academics, most activists engaging in social movements now no longer felt the need to debate with the liberals. In this way, the liberals were completely marginalized in the production of critical opinions in China's public sphere.

The Transformation of Social Movements Representing Subaltern Interests

In the last chapter, I discuss the emergence of three social movements that had claimed to represent subaltern interests and analyze how these movements had debated with the liberals on the applicability of the idea of civil society. In the following sections, I elaborate the transformation of these movements after the marginalization of the liberal camp. I argue that, since the mid-2010s, the development of the three movements had taken divergent paths. The New Rural Reconstruction Movement had largely become commercialized. The labor activism had become radicalized in the first few years and then experienced degeneration due to strong state suppression. The feminist activism, on the other hand, had become popularized. I demonstrate that the different paths taken by the three movements had to do with their interactions with the state and the liberals in the previous stage.

Commercialization: The Transformation of the
New Rural Reconstruction Movement

In chapter five, I demonstrate that the New Rural Reconstruction Movement experienced an "urban turn" since the late 2000s; as the movement withdrew their support of peasants' "rights defending" activism and turned to food issues, state suppression over the movement decreased and the survival space for the movement was enlarged. Since the mid-2010s, activists of the movement had continued their strategy. To mobilize more resources, the movement had even worked more closely with the commercial power in its practice of CSA.

As I mentioned in the last chapter, to unify the fragmented practice of CSA in China, activists of the New Rural Reconstruction Movement established the CSA Alliance for Social and Ecological Agriculture. In the early 2010s, major participants of the annual conference of the alliance were the "small peasants" and the scholars from the "school of rural construction." But since 2016, leading actors of the conference became officials in local government and corporations in agroindustry. Major e-commerce platforms in China, notably Taobao and JD, were also invited.[39] Confronting the criticism that the movement had become "neoliberal," the CSA Alliance claimed that their purpose of introducing the commercial capital to the field was to help more "small peasants" start organic farming.[40] But several empirical studies on China's CSA show that the influence of organizations like the CSA Alliance and the Little Donkey Farm on the "small peasants" had been quite limited; those who were able to benefit from the CSA model were mostly young peasants who had received a college education and once worked in cities—in China's public sphere, these peasants were often referred to as the "youth returning to rural areas" (*fanxiang qingnian*).[41]

Because of these transformations, the New Rural Reconstruction Movement had moved further away from a social movement criticizing dominant political and economic institutions.

Radicalization and Degeneration: The Transformation
of the Labor Activism

In chapter five, I analyze the emergence of labor NGO activism and its relations with the liberals. I argue that, by emphasizing the discourse of the "new working class" and elaborating a more sophisticated discussion of the role of the state in the protection of labor rights, the labor scholars and the labor

NGO activism they had initiated put forward an alternative interpretation of civil society. Additionally, because most of the labor scholars had a strong belief in the value of social movement in pushing the state, during the second term of the Hu-Wen regime, these scholars formed a cooperative relationship with some of the liberals. Together, these actors thematized many labor rights issues in China's public sphere. However, since the mid-2010s, it was just because of these wide connections the labor activism had built, that it became a special subject of state suppression. As I have discussed in a previous section, most labor NGOs had either disbanded or turned to other issues under the increasing pressure of state control. What else had been suppressed were various university-based programs for training labor activists. A case in point was the "New Generation Project," which had introduced many university students to labor activism. In 2013, the project was terminated.

Facing an increasingly suppressive environment, labor activists explored a new interstitial space. Of particular significance here were those students who had worked as activists or attended various training programs in the previous stage. Because of the experience, some of them had become quite tenacious in standing with workers. For these students, holding an NGO that refrained from criticizing the state and the capital was meaningless. In my interviews, when discussing those labor NGOs that had chosen to turn to other issues or become "social work organizations," these students often suggested that they were "too conservative," or even accused them of "betraying the labor movement."[42] To sustain the public concern of labor issues, these students began to experiment with alternative forms of activism.

Some student activists established university-based associations, such as reading groups and learned societies. Participants of these associations were usually those who were interested in Marxist political economic theories and sought to "apply" the theories into social movement practice. These associations offered night school classes to workers on campus. Sometimes they also intervened in workers' collective actions. Among the collective actions these student activists had intervened, the most influential case was the Jasic Incident in 2018, the case I introduced at the beginning of this book. When workers in Jasic, a company fabricating welding products in Shenzhen, went into conflict with management regarding their wages and working conditions, student activists from the abovementioned student associations formed an alliance called the "Jasic Workers Solidarity Group" (*Jiashi Gongren Shengyuan Tuan*). To attract public attention, the students demonstrated outside the

Jasic plant and held public speeches to criticize the company's exploitation of workers and express their belief in Marxism.[43]

Some student activists employed social media to expand the space for discussing labor issues. Typical cases included Tootopia (*Tudou Gongshe*) and Hot Pepper Tribe (*Jianjiao Buluo*), two social media accounts established around 2015. On these accounts, student activists introduced various kinds of leftist social theories, used the theories to explain real world problems, and reported labor rights issues in China and around the globe. These expressions both continued and transformed the previous discussion on the "new working class." On the one hand, student activists continued the criticism of the dehumanizing effect brought by the capitalist market economy and advocated decommodification. On the other hand, they tended to emphasize that the dehumanizing effect brought by the capitalist market economy did not just hit the socioeconomically disadvantaged class; many problems people commonly faced today, such as precarity and the long working hours, were in fact inherent to neoliberal globalization. In this way, student activists brought in new topics for public discussion. An illustrative case was the activists' online protest over the "996 system" in China's IT industry. The term "996" referred to the common requirement that IT engineers worked from 9 a.m. to 9 p.m., six days per week. In 2019, some activists organized on Github a campaign called "996, ICU," suggesting that the long working hours in the industry had almost hounded its employees to death.[44] The campaign aroused heated discussions on labor rights issues among professionals.

Compared with the labor NGO activism in previous years, the organizing structure of the students' activism became more diffuse and decentered. On most occasions, the organizations involved had been event-based concern groups, lacking formal decision-making structures. This kind of organizing structure had granted youth activists more flexibility in employing radical strategies. In the 2000s and early 2010s, many student activists either established their own labor NGOs or worked with some labor NGOs organized by workers. Considering the long-term survival of the organizations, they usually employed moderate strategies, such as publishing research reports. But in the late 2010s, as the state's regulation over NGOs became too stringent to allow any space for social movements, student activists no longer expected to establish registered NGOs. Many constraints hence went away. Student activists' employment of radical strategies had been well illustrated in the Jasic Incident. When summarizing the difference between the student activists in the late 2010s and the student activists in labor NGOs in the previous stage, an activist who had worked for several labor NGOs said to me in an interview,

> We still considered strategies—things like how to avoid state repression and how to protect leaders of a protest. But for the younger generation, the most important thing, which is perhaps also the only important thing, is resistance. When they have discontent, they express it. When they feel something is wrong, they want to immediately change it.[45]

Additionally, the diffuse and decentered organizational structure had also granted student activists more flexibility in connecting with actors from other social movements. For example, the Hot Pepper Tribe had been particularly proactive in joining the feminist movement in China and criticizing gender issues like sexual harassment in the workplace and the discrimination against women employees in the job market.[46]

Unfortunately, the student activism, like the labor NGO activism in the previous stage, invoked state repression. Immediately after the Jasic Incident, leading youth activists were detained. Those student associations that had attended the demonstration were forced to disband. Because of their connection with some labor scholars and international foundations, Tootopia was forced to disband in 2019, whereas the Hot Pepper Tribe was closed in 2021. In academics, the issue of labor rights became a politically sensitive topic. During the Hu-Wen regime, many labor scholars were grantees of China's National Social Science Foundation—a state-sponsored foundation. It was with the support of such foundations, both the financial and the symbolic, that the labor scholars held training programs for labor NGO activists and introduced university students to labor activism. But since the mid-2010s, applying for grants to support research on labor rights issues simply became an impossible mission. Many well-known research centers that had supported labor rights activism, notably the Labor Studies and Service Center (*Laogong Yanjiu yu Fuwu Zhongxin*) at the Sun Yat-sen University, were also closed.

By the late 2010s, except for a few exceptional cases like the Zhicheng Legal Aid Center, there were no organizations or organized networks in China's public sphere that were able to thematize labor rights issues. While labor protests and strikes still now and then occurred among many different types of workers, such as crane operators and meal delivery riders,[47] these workers' voices remained rather fragmented. The open discussion of labor rights issues in the public sphere thus degenerated.

Popularization: The Transformation of the Feminist Activism

In chapter five, I introduce the emergence and development of the feminist activism in China since the World Women's Conference held in Beijing in 1995 and elaborate how the advocacy of women's rights had moved from organizations highly embedded in the state to grassroots-based organizations and networks. In analyzing feminist activists' contestation over the idea of civil society, I emphasize that it was in the public debate on women's rights issues that the liberals' dichotomous understanding of the relationship between the public and the private was thoroughly challenged; that was also why irresolvable disputes emerged between the feminist activists and the liberals around 2010.

Although the feminist activism in the late 2000s and early 2010s was far less proactive than the labor activism in terms of the number of issues activists raised and the extensiveness of solidarity networks these activists built, the feminist activism nonetheless initiated controversies and created disturbances. Hence, in the mid-2010s, when the Chinese state decided to "clean up" social movement activists in the public sphere, the feminist activists had not been able to escape. On March 6, 2015, five feminist activists who had engaged in the "action art" activities (Li Maizi, Wu Rongrong, Zheng Churan, Wei Tingting, and Wang Man) were arrested in Beijing for planning a protest against sexual harassment. This arrest sparked outrage, both domestically and internationally. Confronting the backlash following their detention, the Chinese government eventually released the five activists on bail on April 13. However, for many, the arrest of the Feminist Five signified that the issue of gender equity and women's rights, which had also often been raised by the Communist Party, was no longer a "safe" topic in the public sphere.[48] To avoid political persecution, major supporters of the feminist activists, notably Lü Pin, chose to stay in the West after 2015. The "action art" activism, which used to be prominent around 2010, was then largely suppressed.

The state's increasingly stringent control over the media sphere and the NGO sphere had also influenced feminist organizations. In 2018, Feminist Voices' Weibo account was cancelled. Around 2016, the Anti Domestic Violence Network and the Women Law Studies and Service Center at Peking University, two NGOs established in the 1990s, were forced to disband.[49] Although, a few months later, major activists of the two organizations managed to register new NGOs, the new organizations became even more cautious about getting involved in confrontational or agitational activities.

Surprisingly, unlike the situation in the labor field, feminist activism in China had not disappeared from the public horizon. Instead, it had become even more popularized. Major actors in a new round of feminist activism were a group of feminist bloggers on Weibo. The emergence of the feminist bloggers had to do with the adjustment of Weibo's marketing strategy since the mid-2010s. To reduce potential political risks, Sina, the corporation launching Weibo, decided to weaken the influence of the "big Vs" who had often appealed to the "general interest" in discussions of public issues and support a new generation of content creators who were better adapted to the vertical market, that is, those bloggers who were able to offer content specific to an audience with specialized needs.[50] During this process, dozens of bloggers who focused on talking to women emerged. Notable examples included Mu Dama, Woshi Luosheng, Maiyu Xiangyi, and Lin Maomao.

These feminist bloggers had diverged from the feminist activists in previous stages in many ways.[51] As I have discussed in chapter five, since the late 2000s, a younger generation of feminist activists arose. Unlike an older generation of feminist activists, who had been highly embedded in the state, activists from the younger generation were mostly grassroots-based. Nonetheless, connections widely existed between the two generations of activists. It was from their communication with the older generation of activists that the younger generation came to know concepts like social movements, or even the political project of building civil society. For example, many feminist activists who had attended the "action art" activities were participants of the One Dollar Commune in Beijing, while the founders of the One Dollar Commune were a group of activists who had engaged in NGO activism in China since the 1990s. Before the organization disbanded, the idea of civil society was a frequently raised topic among its participants.[52] Therefore, although it was based on their reflection upon their own life that these young women became activists around 2010, they had not been unfamiliar with the many abstract political ideals the liberals and other kinds of intellectual elites had proposed in China's public sphere since the 1990s. However, the feminist bloggers arising since the mid-2010s had been disconnected from any of the intellectual groups I have discussed in previous chapters. Instead of appealing to any abstract political ideals like "civil society" and "citizenship rights," these bloggers intended to share with their followers very concrete suggestions on how women could maximize their interests in a society where there lacked gender equity.

On the other hand, while many feminist activisms in the previous stage had been organized on the street, leading participants of these activisms had often thought of the possibility of pushing the state and promoting policy changes. But since the mid-2010s, as major channels through which social movement actors could influence the state were blocked, the feminist bloggers no longer considered the possibility of transforming the larger policy environment. Instead, many of them began to argue that protecting women's interests was about women's own choice. These bloggers' discussion of marriage and reproduction was a case in point.[53] Around 2015, a frequently mentioned topic raised by the feminist bloggers was Chinese women's disadvantaged position in the institution of marriage and reproduction. On Weibo, these bloggers criticized phenomena like the public ignorance of domestic violence and the devaluation of housework. However, instead of promoting the transformation of relevant policies and laws, the bloggers advocated that the best solution for women was not to get married. These advocacies were later generalized into a widely spread slogan on the cyberspace—"No marriage or children if you want to stay safe" (*Buhun buyu bao ping'an*)! In their daily interactions with Weibo users, some of the feminist bloggers even abused women who chose to get married and called these women the "wedding donkey" (*hunlü*).

Feminist bloggers' public expressions incurred strong backlash. On the cyberspace, discontents invented various labels to stigmatize these bloggers. A notable example of these labels was "countryside feminist" (*tianyuan nüquan*) (see Figure 4).[54] Another commonly used label was "feminist fist" (*nüquan*).[55] Critics suggested that the feminist bloggers had intentionally faked the antagonism between men and women and that what these bloggers had wanted was nothing but a gender-based privilege.[56] But for many users on Weibo, especially those young women without much social and economic resources, reading content offered by these bloggers was an "enlightening" experience. According to these young women, it was through these feminist bloggers' posts that they came to understand that the current institution of marriage exploited women and that there existed alternative modes of life.[57] On Weibo and other online platforms, these young women turned the pejorative "feminist fist" upside down and built upon it a new identity, the "fem-

Figure 4. Icons of "Countryside Feminism" on Cyberspace. Source: Wapbaike.

inist boxer" (*quanshi*). Whenever gender-related issues were raised in the public sphere, the "feminist boxers" showed up to engage in an activism of what they called "boxing" (*daquan*), which usually consisted of confronting the mainstream patriarchal, masculine culture and harshly criticizing gender inequality inherent to various social institutions and practices.

The gathering of online participants being interested in gender issues eventually produced social and political consequences. An illustrative example here was the rise of the MeToo Movement in China since 2017. In the movement, although it was mainly victims of sexual harassment and their various resourceful friends that had initiated the exposition online, supportive measures by "feminist boxers," including activities like reposting and commenting, played important roles in sustaining public attention.[58] Among several events in which the alleged figures were professors at prestigious state-sponsored universities, the government's initial response to the impeachment online was to remove all relevant discussions. However, as reposts and comments of the impeachment continued to accumulate strength, government censorship was made impossible or appeared to be rather ridiculous. In those cases, the government and the universities had to conform to a certain degree, dealing with the accusations with care, or even penalizing those professors who had committed sexual harassment or misbehaved in teacher-student relationships.[59] On some occasions, the online collective actions even turned offline. In 2018, Xianzi, an intern at CCTV sued Zhu Jun, a nationally-renowned TV host for sexual harassment. As Xianzi's posts on Weibo won wide sympathies, many of her supporters gathered at the court when the trial of her case was conducted.[60]

Because of the power and strength exemplified by the new wave of feminist activists in movements like MeToo, many activists in previous stages, especially those activists who had engaged in the "action art" activities around 2010, held a relatively positive attitude toward the expansion of the feminist community in China. In the opinion of some elder activists, although feminist bloggers' discussions of gender issues were rather crude, it was through these discussions that feminist ideas became genuinely popularized in China.[61] To show their support, some of the elder activists also began to use labels like "countryside feminist" in a positive fashion. For example, Xiao Meili, a feminist activist who used to engage in the "action art" activities, launched a podcast in 2019 called "Into the Field" (*Youdian Tianyuan*, which literally meant "somewhat countryside"). The podcast mainly discussed gender issues in China.

Nevertheless, the new round of feminist activism had its limitations. As I have just mentioned, the feminist bloggers had seldom considered the possibility of promoting policy changes. Hence, fragmented feminist voices on the cyberspace were rarely crystallized into any operationalizable political agenda. In fact, most of the feminist bloggers had not even considered the existence of structural constraints that were not solely gender based, such as the many constraints imposed by the authoritarian government. In public discussions of many political issues, such as human rights in Tibet and Uygur, quite a few feminist bloggers embraced nationalist discourses, supporting state conducts, and emphasizing that they and their followers were patriotic.[62] This phenomenon made those liberals who had kept watching China's public sphere feel even more dissatisfied with the feminist activism. But many of the liberals would acknowledge that the issue of gender equity had become one of the most heatedly discussed topics in the wider public.

Conclusion

In this chapter, I discuss the transformation of the interstitial publics since the mid- 2010s. I argue that, during this stage, the liberals and their networks were further marginalized. State suppression over social movement activism and alternative public discussion played a major role in this process, while the pervasion of commercial power also helped. Consequently, the political project of building civil society eventually disintegrated. I also describe the development of the three social movements that had in different ways challenged the liberal interpretation of civil society during the second term of the Hu-Wen regime. I demonstrate that, due to their different relationships with the state and the diverse nature of the issues they had raised, the transformation of the three movements had taken divergent paths after the decline of the liberals. The New Rural Reconstruction Movement had become commercialized. The labor activism had become radicalized in the beginning and quickly degenerated after state repression, while the feminist activism had become popularized.

The impact brought by the decline of the liberals was complex. First, various competitors of the liberals, including the new leftist scholars in the "thought sphere" and several groups of social movement activists representing subaltern interests in the late 2000s, had hardly benefited from the disintegration of the political project of building civil society. As the state's control over the public sphere became more stringent, many organizations and networks formed by these competitors were also suppressed. In recent years, with increasing economic and cultural frictions between China and the West, nationalist emotions became prominent in China's cyberspace. As the economic growth slowed down, people's concern over the issue of equity and social justice rose. These sentiments echoed many topics the competitors of the liberals had proposed in the public sphere. However, because of the lack of organization, the public expressions of these sentiments were rather disorganized. In an environment in which any controversies and disturbances could be read by the state as a potential threat to the stability of the regime, the leftists—be they theorists or social movement activists—were by no means in a more advantageous position to articulate their ideas and set political agenda.

Second, ironically, even if we see the history of the rise and fall of the project of building civil society in China from the perspective of the authoritarian state, we can hardly say this is a successful story. On the surface, since the mid-2010s, the Chinese state had successfully wiped out almost all organizations and networks that were able to produce critical public opinions in previous stages. But the state was far from capable of controlling all possible expressions of discontents. As was shown in the development of the labor activism and the feminist activism, resistance activities kept emerging from new interstitial spaces. What had made things worse for the state was the following transformation: In the late 2000s and early 2010s, many organizations and networks that were critical of China's politics had very concrete goals and were willing to communicate with the government. The labor scholars who submitted policy suggestions on reforming China's social insurance system and the feminist organizations promoting the passage of the law against domestic violence were both typical examples. Yet the new interstitially emergent actors tended to have very obscure goals and lack experience (or perhaps willingness) to consider social issues from the perspective of policies and laws. In another word, by eradicating the many organizations and networks in the interstitial publics, the Chinese state had also deprived itself of the various sensors that could react to society-wide problems and stimulate constructive public opinions.

Time will tell how the new interstitially emergent actors evolve. Chances are that these actors' voices remain fragmented. Under certain conditions that we currently cannot fully predict, these actors could also gather strength and promote more profound changes. But one thing is clear: the disintegration of the project of building civil society is not the end of the story; the fall of the liberals only signifies that political and cultural conflicts in China have been pushed into a new terrain.

Conclusion

In the previous six empirical chapters, I focus on the condition of the Chinese liberals and document the rise and fall of civil society as an ideational movement in China's public sphere. I argue that the liberals' capacity to incorporate various social movements into their political agenda had to do with the structure of the publics, which had been shaped by the changing political, social, and technological environment during China's reform.

In specific terms, the liberals rose in China's public sphere during the New Enlightenment Movement in the 1980s. Although the movement was suppressed after 1989, due to the pressure from the international community and the influence of the neoliberal ideology, Chinese state's control over society had remained porous throughout the 1990s. To restart their enlightenment project, the liberals began to advocate the idea of civil society. It was argued that civil society as an independent space could constrain the state power and promote democratization. In the beginning, the discussion of the idea was limited to the circle of intellectual elites. Things began to change in the early to mid-2000s. As China entered the Hu-Wen regime, new spaces for alternative public discussion, namely the media sphere and the NGO sphere, became well-developed. This provided the liberals with opportunities to project their imagination of politics onto people in wider society. By reducing various resistance activisms to the confrontation between state and society, the liberals successfully incorporated many social issues into their project of building civil society.

During the late 2000s, the domination of the liberals in the public sphere was destabilized under increasing state intervention. The further development of digital technologies and the routinization of the NGO sphere brought in new participants for public discussion. Around 2010, several groups of activists who claimed to represent subaltern interests, such as the labor activists and the feminist activists, began to challenge the liberal interpretation of civil society that dichotomized state-society relations. Nonetheless, because the state's control over the alternative spaces was still constrained, the liberals remained influential in the formation of critical public opinions. Resultantly, many debates between the liberals and those activists representing subaltern interests had been kept within the framework of civil society. It was not until the mid-2010s, when the power of the state and the market became more pervasive in the alternative spaces, that the liberals were completely marginalized. As newly emerging actors in the public sphere no longer felt the need to debate with the liberals, the project of building civil society finally disintegrated.

In this conclusion chapter, I will summarize my empirical findings and discuss the theoretical implications of this book. The rest of the chapter will be arranged in the following way. In the next section, I summarize how my findings have in several ways diverged from extant studies on civil society and the public sphere in China. After that, I discuss three implications of the book, which are the interstitial space as a location of the public sphere, the political consequences of the global dissemination of the idea of civil society, and the paradox of an ideational movement.

Toward an Alternative Interpretation of China's Public Sphere

My presentation of the project of building civil society in China diverges from the extant literature in several important ways. First, I emphasize the continuity between the social movement activisms in the 1980s and those in the 1990s. Many extant studies on social movement activisms in China in the '90s highlight the rupture brought by the failure of the student movement. It is argued that, since the student movement was suppressed and the Chinese state commanded more techniques to control resistance activism, in the 1990s, movements advocating grand, abstract political ideals subsided and movements proposing concrete social and economic demands rose.[1] My documentation of the interstitial publics in the '90s questions the existence of the rupture. I suggest that many intellectuals engaging in the theoretical and ideological debates in the "thought sphere" in the '90s were also the "enlighteners" in the '80s; the first wave of NGO activists in the '90s were mostly participants of the 1989 student movement.

More importantly, the political project of building civil society was largely the inheritor of the spirit of the New Enlightenment Movement—the liberals in the '90s inherited the dichotomous thinking of politics and history, which had been prominent in the '80s, reflected upon it and packaged it in new discourses. If we acknowledge that the project of building civil society had become rather influential in China's public sphere before it declined in the mid-2010s, we may reach an alternative understanding of the continuity of the history of social movement activism in China after the economic reform: the spirit of the New Enlightenment Movement had not died of sudden, arbitrary state repression in 1989; rather, it faded away around the mid-2010s, under progressively intensified pressure from the state, the market, and the changing technological environment.

Second, I offer an alternative interpretation of various resistance activisms happening during the first term of the Hu-Wen regime. Analyzing activisms like the production of critical news reports, environmental campaigns, and homeowners' protests, quite a few scholars, both in China and from abroad, used to argue that Chinese people's rights consciousness was rising and an independent space being able to check the state power was in the making.[2] By seeing the dissemination of the idea of civil society as an ideational movement, I challenge this view and contend that what had arisen was only the liberals' capacity to incorporate social issues into their political agenda, rather than a popularly-based resistance movement community with common values and ideology.

I suggest that the overly optimistic interpretation of resistance activisms in China in the 2000s had to do with the way the knowledge of these activisms was produced. Many of the scholarly works on these activisms, both in Chinese and in English, had been written by those who were closely associated with the liberals, or even the liberals themselves.[3] Moreover, when scholars from abroad traveled to China to do fieldwork, they often relied on research institutes led by the liberals, such as the ICS at the Sun Yat-sen University, to search for informants. The informants with whom these scholars talked with usually only included activists who had closely worked with the liberals. Therefore, it was not surprising that the scholarly interpretations of resistance activisms in China were to different degrees under the influence of the liberals. Based on a more thorough examination over the construction of various *weiquan* activism, I suggest that the liberal argumentation that a Wei-quan Movement was rising in China lacked corroboration; the unification of various resistance activities was only at the discursive level and the solidary networks formed by the liberals were fragile.

Third, I highlight the rise of movements representing subaltern interests around the late 2000s, namely the New Rural Reconstruction Movement, the labor activism, and the feminist activism. In the recent decade, many scholarly works on these movements trace their historical origins and analyze their transformation.[4] However, while most of these works focus on the interactive relations between these movements and the state, the interactive relations between these movements and the liberals are largely bypassed. In my analysis, I pay attention to the triangular relations among these movements, the state, and the liberals. I contend that the contestations between these movements and the liberals were important because it was through these contestations that many themes that the liberals had ignored in their interpretation of civil society were brought back to the public sphere. These themes included the formation of class in civil society, the role of the state in the protection of rights, and the relationship between market and civil society. To reiterate, the New Rural Reconstruction Movement, the labor activism, and the feminist activism were not just "new forms of civil society activisms" emerging in China, alongside those activisms that had emerged earlier, such as environmental campaigns and homeowners' protests; ideologically, these activisms had brought in critical new themes for public deliberation.

Moreover, I contextualize the emergence of these contestations. I emphasize the special political, social, and technological environment in the late 2000s and early 2010s that had destabilized the domination of the liberals yet left the liberals the space for adaptation. Before the late 2000s, most grassroots-based, socioeconomically disadvantaged activists were marginalized, while the new leftist intellectuals lacked interest in attending social movements. After the mid-2010s, under an increasingly tightened political atmosphere, both the liberals and many activists representing subaltern interests were suppressed. Ideological debate over the project of civil society was thus gone. These imply that the critical articulation of an alternative interpretation of the idea of civil society had only happened in a very specific historical context.

Lastly, this study also offers an alternative interpretation of the consequence of current state's control over resistance activism in China. As the Chinese state's regulation over the media sphere and the NGO sphere became increasingly stringent in recent years, commentaries suggest that the authoritarian state has regained its power; as the state power becomes more pervasive and the government commands better techniques for supervising societal actors, any proactive social movement activism that may challenge the regime is suppressed.[5] I agree with these commentaries on the many negative impacts brought by state suppression on social movement activism. However, I also highlight the unintended consequences of the suppression. As is shown in my discussion of the labor activism and the feminist activism since the mid-2010s, it was simply because many institutions and organizations that had been able to unify people's voices and produce critical public opinions in previous stages were suppressed that the expression of discontent became increasingly fragmented, abrupt, and unpredictable.

I would even go so far as to argue that this tendency has been reinforced in the past few years. While the Chinese state has been able to suppress critical news media and NGOs engaging in agitational activism, there are still many crises the state lacks capacity to deal with, such as the continuously decreasing fertility rate, the economic growth that has been slowed down, numerous financially strapped county governments, and the deteriorating environment. When old channels for expressing anxiety and discontent are blocked, people look for new ones. It is true that suppression and regulation over new channels often immediately follow up. However, there are still two problems the state cannot solve. First, suppression and regulation over the production of critical public opinions are costly, which implies that the growth of state power in this field is not limitless. Second, as the state power becomes more pervasive and expansive, common people also get more opportunities to recognize state's incapacity to cope with crisis and the many injustices in the exercise of state power.

The online activism commemorating Dr. Li Wenliang during the COVID pandemic was a case in point. Dr. Li Wenliang was an ophthalmologist in Wuhan, the city where the pandemic started.[6] In December 2019, when both government officials and the public had not yet recognized the threat of the disease, Dr. Li shared through a WeChat group information on the emergence of several mysterious "pneumonia" cases. A few days later, Wuhan police summoned and admonished him for "making false comments on the Internet about unconfirmed SARS cases."[7] In January 2020, the outbreak was confirmed to be SARS-Cov-2, a new coronavirus. Since it became clear to the public that the new virus was even more threatening to human society than SARS, Dr. Li was dubbed a whistleblower. As the admonition letter issued by Wuhan police ordering Li to stop "spreading rumors" was disclosed, public anger was rampant. This emotion was excessively provoked on February 6, when Li tragically died of COVID. On Weibo, the hashtag "We Want Freedom of Speech" gained over two million views and 5500 posts within five hours. Research shows that many participants of the activism had never attended any political or social activism before. These people suddenly became interested in political rights issues because Dr. Li's case "visualized" not only the state's pervasive supervision over public communication but also the immensely harmful consequence of the supervision.[8]

In the 2000s and early 2010s, various social movements emerged and pushed the state to deal with the many social problems arising during China's economic reform. By allowing some forms of discussion of the problems and responding to some demands proposed by the movements, the legitimacy of the state was enhanced. But nowadays, as the space for rational and critical public discussion shrinks, the mechanism for generating legitimacy is also waning. In other words, while preempting the formation of organized resistance activism, the Chinese state's intensified control over the public sphere has also made its rule more fragile.

Interstitial Space as a Location of the Public Sphere

In his early work, *The Structural Transformation of the Public Sphere*, Habermas argues that the public sphere in western societies has originated in bourgeois spaces like cafes and table societies.[9] Later, to search for a more decontextualized, universal model for the public sphere, Habermas begins to locate the public sphere in a lifeworld that is outside systems, that is, the bureaucratic state and the capitalist market.[10] It is argued that the integration of social actions in systems relies upon the steering media of power and money, which is not open-ended; therefore, it is only in a space that is independent of the systems can the social integrative power of communication, which is also the foundation of a public sphere, prevail. This independent space has sometimes been described as civil society, or a rationalized lifeworld.[11]

I fully agree with Habermas's criticism on the overexpansion of the systemic powers of the state and the market. I also agree with his advocacy of using the social integrative power of communication to check the state and the market. But in my empirical research on the public sphere in China, I find that, with respect to how critical and alternative public discussion could emerge in a society, my case has contradicted Habermas's theory. First, many actors and organizations that had played crucial roles in promoting the formation of critical public opinions in the 1990s and 2000s were by no means independent of the Chinese state; rather, they were to different degrees embedded in the state. It was through complex interactions between forces from within the state and outside the state that social issues like environmental pollution, domestic violence, and the increasing urban-rural gap were problematized and thematized. Second, being outside the state, or even being independent of the state, does not guarantee the participation of critical public discussion. As is shown in my analysis, by stipulating the rules for registration and fundraising, the Chinese state incorporated NGO activism into its social work system by the mid-2010s. In terms of their routine activities, NGOs nowadays have already achieved a large degree of autonomy from the intervention of the administrative state. However, compared with their predecessors in the 1990s and 2000s, these organizations now show much less interest in engaging in social conflicts. While these organizations still provide services to disadvantaged groups, they have already lost their critical edge.

To conceptualize the emergence of alternative and critical public discussions in China since the 1990s and the later transformation of these discussions, I borrow from Michael Mann's discussion of interstitial space. In Mann's theoretical framework, an interstitial space is defined as a space where the exercise of power has not yet been fully institutionalized; it is often in an interstitial space that social change takes place.[12] Following the thread of this argument, I highlight that the occurrence of critical public discussions in China has been polygenetic. Some of these discussions have emerged from "new" social spaces, such as the internet space brought by the development of new digital technologies. Yet some of them have also emerged from some forms of "old" spaces, such as the many state-run universities and research institutes. I call these different activisms as constituting various interstitial publics. Moreover, I emphasize that the freedom interstitially emergent actors enjoy tends to be ephemeral; when interacting with powerful, dominant institutions, these actors and their practices could be institutionalized. This is shown in my elaboration of the transformation of the media sphere and the NGO sphere since the second term of the Hu-Wen regime.

Based on my research, I contend that, compared to civil society, the idea of interstitial space serves as a better conceptual tool for searching the location of the public sphere and describing the sphere's changing dynamics. I suggest that the concept is especially useful in places like China where the differentiation of major institutions in society is limited and the boundary of these institutions is rather unclear.

For researchers studying other regions, the idea of interstitial space also has implications. The first implication is that the location of the occurrence of critical public discussions cannot be envisaged beforehand, because there will not be any stable relations between interstitial space and major institutions in human society, notably the state and the market. The condition of major institutions in society, including the state and the market, is historically specific. In many real-world situations, the "system integration" of these major institutions is far from being total—not to mention that many regions still lack an effective bureaucratic state based on formally rational laws and a formally free and open market. Interstitial spaces that could nurture the formation of critical public opinions thus may well exist within these institutions. Readers who have looked for a more general or universal model of the public sphere may feel disappointed here. But this is exactly my point. Instead of focusing on a few seemingly independent organizations and institutions, such as NGOs, voluntary networks, and independent media, we need to broaden our scope in our empirical studies of the public sphere. Political and social actions that have the potential to check and challenge the systemic powers may arise in certain unlikely spaces.

A second implication is that the formation of a space for producing critical public opinions is not a battle that can be accomplished at one stroke. This can also be seen as a takeaway message for social movement activists. When I was in the field, I was often a bit surprised to see activists' reckless effervescence with newly emerging opportunities. In 2012, when the Chinese state's control over online activism had already become savvy, many activists still held a strong belief in the power of technology. In an interview, one activist told me, "Internet is a gift of God (*laotian geide liwu*). With such a technology that the government cannot fully control, China will sooner or later have freedom of speech."[13] Some activists had similar attitudes toward the power of market economy. In an interview, one activist said, "As long as China insists on the market economic reform and does not go back to socialism, we will have an increasingly open society and Chinese people will eventually understand the value of democracy."[14] Things happening later have already shown that these judgements are too optimistic. In my opinion, the problem lies in these activists' ignorance of the institutionalization of interstitial space. As dominant power institutions like the state gradually learn the nature of interstitial space and the necessary techniques for governing the space, practices in the space could become so routinized that they no longer constitute any challenges to these institutions.

Nevertheless, seeing this story from a different perspective, we can also say that, even when certain interstitially emergent resistance activism—in the China case, these are the NGO activism and the production of critical news on commercially oriented media—decline, we can still keep hope. Because the influence of a dominant power structure in human life can never be total, interstitial space always exists. This implies that new forms of activism may be gathering strength in those spaces that "old" activists have not yet fully recognized. Keeping hope is important because we need to be prepared—the political struggle between the state and the market as institutionalizing forces and social movements as interstitially emergent actors may have already entered a new round.

The Project of Building Civil Society: Past and Present

Since the 1980s, with the rise of neoliberal policies in the West and the political transformation in eastern Europe, people have witnessed a revival of a new round of discussions on the idea of civil society. It is argued that civil society offers an alternative to the bureaucratic state and the capitalist market economy; with civil society, people are more likely to achieve democracy, solidarity, or even sustainable development. Being influenced by this idea, governments, foundations, and corporations invest a great many resources in a rather heterogeneous field, which involves actors like NGOs, social movements, and voluntary associations. To some extent, the dissemination of the idea of civil society has become a global ideational movement. I suggest that what had happened in China since the 1990s can be seen as a part of this movement.

The development of civil society in China has often been constituted as an unsuccessful story vis-à-vis its counterpart in eastern Europe.[15] In eastern European countries like Poland and Czechoslovakia, social movement activism advocated the idea of civil society and eventually brought about regime change. In China, although many of the liberals who talked about civil society in the 1990s had learned this idea from the democratic transition in eastern Europe and very much hoped that similar things could also happen in their own country, the rule of the Chinese Communist Party has remained rather stable over the past three decades. In this book, I highlight the many "achievements" of the project of building civil society in China. I argue that the liberals' advocacy of the idea of civil society played a crucial role in sustaining China's reform. It is through the liberals' merciless criticism over state power and their tireless advocacy of an independent space for participation that many problems arising during the reform got to be revealed. Without the liberals' activism of building civil society, the Chinese state might have lacked motivation for coping with these problems.

Some critics point out that the global dissemination of the idea of civil society represents the hegemony of western neoliberal policies.[16] I have mixed concerns over this criticism. On the one hand, I find that this criticism has not been ungrounded in the empirical world. Some of the Chinese liberals who had advocated the idea of civil society did have strong beliefs in the validity of the free market and the private ownership of property. Many of these liberals did have ignored substantive inequalities in their organization of resistance activism. It is also true that the project of building civil society in China did bypass many issues that were relevant to the citizens' social rights. A notable example is the reform of state-owned enterprises since the 1990s, which had deprived millions of workers of their welfare compacts and caused a great many social unrests all over the country.[17]

But on the other hand, based on my review of the historical transformation of China's public sphere, I would argue that the partialities of the project of building civil society in China had more to do with the concrete strategies intellectuals and activists had taken than the intension of the idea itself. As is elaborated in chapter one, there used to be several different interpretations of the idea of civil society in the "thought sphere" in the 1990s. It was simply because the new left chose to support a strong bureaucratic state that the project of building civil society became the liberals' project. It was not until the late 2000s that issues the new left was concerned with, such as workers' social rights, were brought back to the civil society debate. At that time, the reform of state-owned enterprises that had created millions of "laid-off workers" had already drawn to an end, and more systemic state regulation over the public sphere was approaching. The new leftist intellectuals thus missed the historical opportunity to combine their political ideal with social movement activism and create a more leftist civil society in China.

From the China case, we can see that the "strength" of civil society as an ideational movement lies in its abstractness. The idea of communism reduces all evils to the private ownership of property and calls for a society that abandons constitutional democracy, state, political parties, families, and division of labor. The idea of neoliberalism suggests that the solution is always the omnipotent market—if the introduction of market mechanisms does not solve your problems, you simply need to introduce more. Compared to these strong ideological programs, the project of building civil society appears to be rather empty. Except for advocating the making of an independent space for participation, it does not specify any institutional arrangement. Nor does it specify any concrete actors, such as certain social classes or groups. It is this emptiness that has enabled the Chinese liberals to build allies and incorporate resistance activisms of different kinds into their own political agenda. However, the "weakness" of the project also lies in its abstractness. Once the dominant power institutions like the state command more sophisticated techniques for dealing with resistance activism, participants of these activisms may become more interested in deliberating specific policies and develop their own agenda. Resultantly, the project of building civil society becomes fragmented, or performs practically no function. This is exactly what had happened in China since the late 2000s.

Ironically, as the state intensifies its control during Xi's presidency and prohibits many public discussions that used to be tolerated, the political environment in China nowadays has become suitable again for a resistance movement that unifies people from different social groups and proposes grand plans for political reform.

Nothing illustrates this point better than the political struggles during the COVID pandemic. Since the Wuhan lockdown in 2019, the Chinese government had enforced a stringent zero-COVID policy that required all people who tested positive and their close contacts to be quarantined. Because of the high contagiousness of the disease, lockdown became a frequently employed measure, which had severely violated citizens' privacy and hurt the economy. However, public debate over the issue was strictly forbidden. Even after December 2021, when the predominant variant in circulation had already become Omicron, a variant that had been proved to cause less severity, news media were still only allowed to publish commentaries that were consistent with Beijing's opinion, which suggested that the zero-COVID policy was the best option for China and the policy embodied the superiority of China's political system. Finally, in November 2022, triggered by the fire in Urumqi that killed ten people—which was believed to be associated with the lockdown policy—university students in dozens of cities and their supporters among urban residents launched protests. On most occasions, participants of the protests simply expressed strong emotions. But in some cases, the expression suddenly became politicized, involving themes like opposition to Xi Jinping's reelection, or even the one-party rule.[18] Recognizing that the protests spread quickly and were becoming uncontrollable, Beijing lifted most of its COVID policies at the beginning of December 2022.

Nonetheless, the emergence of these protest activities does not imply that the liberals and their project of building civil society will necessarily recover. After all, the social, economic, and technological environment has changed. With the rapid development of short video platforms like TikTok, intellectual elites' monopoly of public communication has further been constrained. Unlike the situation in the 1980s and 1990s, when China had just opened up to the international community, Chinese people nowadays have already been exposed to many foreign cultures and ideas. More importantly, the younger generation tends to have different feelings and intuitions toward the West. For people like me, who are often referred to in China as the generation of the '80s (*baling hou*), Western culture and institutions contain progressive values. We know there are many problems in American democracy. Yet we also believe that there are things inherent to this political institution that we can learn from. But the younger generation has grown up during the historical phase in which China has gradually become the world's second largest economy. This is also the historical phase in which political crises emerge in several major Western countries. Instead of gaining insights from an idea that has originated from the West, the younger generation is perhaps more interested in exploring an approach with "distinct Chinese characteristics."

Going Beyond the Paradox of an Ideational Movement

Then, if the idea of civil society is not good enough for promoting solidarity in a resistance movement community, is it possible that we come up with a new, better idea for achieving this goal? Many people have made attempts in this aspect. For example, in the 2000s, pointing against the neoliberal policies that had destabilized citizens' social compacts, the concept of precarity emerged as the central organizing platform for a series of social struggles that later spread across the space of Europe.[19] In the China context, a younger generation of intellectual activists expressed discontent with the fragmented and disorganized condition of resistance activism and called for the formation of new political allies.[20] Xu Xiaohong, a late Chinese sociologist and an active participant of many social movements in China and Hong Kong, coined the term sociological liberalism (*shehuixue ziyouzhuyi*) to initiate a program for building an "active society" (*xingdong shehui*) in the "global east and south" (*quanqiu dongfang nanfang shehui*). According to Xu, the idea of sociological liberalism insists on principles that have been articulated in classical liberalism, notably the freedom of speech and association. But it also goes beyond classical liberalism. A sociological liberalism is also dedicated to helping the oppressed and "politicizing" (*zhengzhihua*) these people's concerns in the public sphere.[21]

I think these efforts are inspiring. But I also think people intending to initiate a new ideational movement could learn from my story. What the project of building civil society in China reveals is that the fate of an ideational movement usually does not fully depend on the "intellectual quality" of the idea that is waiting to be disseminated and advocated; the development of an ideational movement tends to be tortuous because a movement like this by itself contains paradox. In the first place, ideas, especially those that aim to propose programs for reforming society, are often reductionist. No matter how refined they appear to be, they are an abstraction and simplification of sophisticated and unbounded realities. This implies that, when intellectual activists try to build associations between an idea and concrete social and political issues or incorporate activisms rising from very specific concerns into a presumed intellectual agenda, ignorance of details and subtleties is almost unavoidable.

My analysis of the Weiquan Movement in China shows that the problem of abstraction is that it may reproduce power inequality. This is because, when abstraction happens, it is often the concerns of socioeconomically disadvantaged groups that are bypassed and ignored. My analysis also shows that the existence of power inequality may harm the sustainability of a resistance movement. Once socioeconomically disadvantaged participants discover that their real needs and wishes are only of secondary importance to those advocates of a certain intellectual agenda, mistrust spreads and the rapport between different groups of actors within the resistance movement is endangered.

A possible "remedy" for the problem of abstraction is to keep the agenda of an ideational movement open and let more people participate in the debate about the idea. This is what had happened during the second term of the Hu-Wen regime, when labor activists and feminist activists debated with the liberals about the relevance and applicability of the idea of civil society. My study of this period shows that, by bringing more themes and more perspectives for understanding these themes back to public discussion, the contestations over the idea of civil society had largely destabilized the monopoly of the liberals and pluralized China's interstitial publics. Moreover, these contestations had even increased the vitality of civil society as an ideational movement. In a time when the state's regulation over alternative public

discussion had been intensified, leading public intellectuals had been stigmatized, and many "old" forms of civil society activism were losing critical
edge, the flourish of labor activism and feminist activism demonstrated to
the public that the project of building civil society was not parochial; rather,
it could be more widely connected.

However, any open debate runs risks. If the initiators of an ideational
movement want to keep the contestation over the idea real and sincere, they
cannot predetermine participants. This implies that participants of the contestation may include people whose concerns and ideological positions are
to different degrees divergent from those of the initiators. To some extent,
this is also what had happened to civil society as an ideational movement
in China. Among those who contested the liberals, there were labor scholars who largely identified with the idea of civil society and wanted to transform the project of building civil society from within; there were also the
new leftist intellectuals and some youth activists who believed that the project of building civil society was neoliberal and hence should be abandoned.
We cannot imagine what would happen to the project if the Chinese state
had not suppressed the public sphere and all the contestations had continued since the mid-2010s. Chances are that the liberals and social movement
activists representing subaltern interests would construct solidarity on a new
basis and advocate a civil society project that is more inclusive. But it can also
be that different groups of actors simply cannot agree with each other, and
the resistance community becomes disintegrated. From my documentation
of the different relations formed between the liberals and the three groups
of activists who claimed to represent subaltern interests, both endings are
possible. My point is that, once the debate is truly open, its consequence is
out of control.

Thus, the critical task for activists who want to initiate an ideational
movement may not just be coming up with a brilliant idea. Rather, the critical task lies in how we should face those people the movement intends to
incorporate, yet at the same time hold contrastingly different concerns and
priorities. Here I propose that we take the risks of open debate. This is not
because I like the value of open debate—though I do like it. My rationale
is that keeping the debate open is the only way to sustain the vitality of an
ideational movement. Imagining a situation in which the burden of advocating and disseminating an idea in society falls on a single group—even if the
group is sufficiently powerful—can show that their narration of the idea may
become monotonous and tedious. To maintain and periodically refresh the

connection between the idea and the common people's concrete, everyday concerns, we need to repeatedly discuss and contest in public discussions the intension, relevance, and applicability of the idea. Having such kinds of dialogues requires intellectual activists to consider the detailed mechanisms through which the enhancement of humanity is hindered in a specific context and be ready to accept the fact that, although people often face some "common enemies" like the authoritarian state, they tend to have rather distinct feelings and desires. On the surface, these discussions and contestations could slow down the organization of collective resistance. But without these efforts, we cannot form real solidarity and build an emancipatory project at a more substantive level.

NOTES

Introduction

1. To protect my informants, I conceal their names when I quote them. I use people's real names only when the quotes come from publicly available materials, such as a public lecture or an authored, published article.

2. Interview with youth activist, Guangzhou, April 24, 2013.

3. For a detailed introduction of the Jasic Incident, see Au 2018.

4. Mann 1986.

5. E.g., Habermas 1994, 1987.

6. Cohen and Arato 1992.

7. E.g., Ferguson 2007.

8. Laclau 2005; Laclau and Mouffe 1985.

9. de Leon et al. 2015, 2009.

10. For some of the examples of studies on the NGO activism as part of the public sphere, see Spires 2011; Yang, Guobin and Calhoun 2007. For studies on online discussion, see Lei and Zhou 2015; Yang, Guobin 2009. For studies on the production of critical news reports, see Lei 2016; Qian and Bandurski 2011. For studies on social movements, see Steinhardt and Wu 2016; Yang, Guobin 2010.

11. For some of the examples of studies discussing the impact of commercialization, see Liu, Qing and McCormick 2011; Qian and Bandurski 2011. For studies on the internet technology, see Sima 2011; Yang, Guobin 2010. For studies on transnational interventions, see Brownell 2012; Yang, Mayfair Mei-hui 1999. For studies on the withdrawal of state power, see Steinhardt and Wu 2016.

12. For some of the examples, see Creemers 2017; King et al. 2013; Ong 2022.

13. For some of the examples, see Eberhardt 2015; Zhou, Mujun 2017.

14. See for example, Wang, Zheng and Zhang, Ying 2010; Zhou, Mujun 2024.

15. For explanations of the idea of a relational sociology, see Diani 2015; Mische 2008.

16. For a typical discussion, see Teets 2014, 2013.

17. Cheek et al., 2018; Veg and Cheng 2021; Xu, Jilin 2004.

18. Goldman 2007, 71; Gallagher 2006; O'Brien and Li 2006, 121–26; Perry 2009.

19. Zhang, Yinxian et al., 2018.

20. For details, see Xu, Jilin 2004.

21. Veg 2019.

22. Calhoun 1993.

23. Habermas 1992, 443–44; 1987, 318–31.

24. For some of these debates, see Calhoun 1992; Fraser 1992; Habermas 1994, 1974; Rawls 1995; Somers 1993.

25. Habermas 1994, 1987.

26. For some of the discussions on the relationship between the public sphere and civil society, see Calhoun 1993; Emirbayer and Sheller 1999.

27. See for example, Baiocchi and Corrado 2010; Berman 1997.

28. Mann 1986, 30.

29. Mann 1986, 16.

30. For discussions on interstitial space as the location of the public sphere, see Emirbayer and Sheller 1999; Mische 2008; Stewart and Hartmann 2020.

31. Habermas 1991.

32. E.g., Alexander 2006; Somers 2008.

33. Clemens and Cook 1999.

34. Armstrong 2002; Fligstein and McAdam 2012; Medvetz 2012; Mische 2008; Morrill 2017; Rao et al. 2000.

35. The sociology of the state literature has long documented that the state is not a unitary entity and different state actors may have different interests. Additionally, state's intervention in society often encounters various obstacles, such as popular resistance and the domination of informal rules. For relevant discussions, see Helmke and Levitsky 2006; Migdal 2001, 1994; Rodríguez-Muñiz 2017; Scott 1998.

36. For summaries of these views, see Cohen and Arato 1992; Cox 1999; Keane 1988.

37. E.g., Arato 1981.

38. E.g., Putnam et al. 1994.

39. E.g., Fung and Wright 2001.

40. For relevant discussions, see Eliasoph 2013; Xu, Bin 2022.

41. For relevant discussions, see Howell and Pearce 2002.

42. Ferguson 2007. For more discussion on the applicability of the concept of civil society in post-colonial Africa, see Lewis 2002; Mamdani 1996. For similar discussion in the context of India, see Chatterjee 2004.

43. E.g., Calhoun 1989; Strand 1990; Sullivan 1990.

44. For those historical studies, see Rowe 1989, 1984; Wang, Di 2003.

45. Zhao, Dingxin 1998.

46. Wakeman 1993. For more discussions on whether the concept of civil society is applicable to China, see Huang, Philip C. C. 1993; Perry 1994; Unger 2008; Unger and Chan 1995.

47. Mamdani 1996.

48. Snow et al. 1986; Snow and Benford 1988.

49. Laclau 2005; Laclau and Mouffe 1985. For recent discussions, see de Leon et al. 2015, 2009.

Chapter 1

1. Kelly 1987.

2. The Gang of Four was a Maoist political faction that came to prominence during the Cultural Revolution. For discussion of the literature, see Wagner 1987.

3. For details, see Brødsgaard 1981.

4. For details, see Chen, Fong-ching and Jin, Guantao 1997; Zhao, Dingxin 2001.

5. Zhang, Zhen 2000.

6. Zhao, Suisheng 1993.

7. For details, see Goldman 2007, 161–82; Wright 2002.

8. Gu and Goldman 2004; Shirk 2011; Zhao, Dingxin 2001, 334.

9. Zhao, Dingxin 2001, 340–41.

10. For details, see Ogden 2002.

11. For an oral history of the organization of the 4th World Women Conference, see Chen, Yongling and Ma, Yanjun 2012.

12. For details, see Zhang, Li and Ong, Aihwa 2008.

13. For an interesting discussion on how the Chinese state had, consciously or unconsciously, blurred the boundary between "society" and "market" in its advocacy of "small government, big society," see Young 2001, 12.

14. Zhao, Dingxin 2001, 332–35.

15. See for example, Zhao, Yuezhi 1998.

16. Wang, Hui 2008a; Xu, Jilin and Luo, Gang 2007. Also see Liu, Qing 2007.

17. Wang, Hui 2008a; Xu, Jilin 2007.

18. Xu, Jilin 2007, 9.

19. This attitude had been well illustrated in the widely watched documentary film, *River Elegy* (He Shang). For an introduction of the production of the film, see Chen, Fong-ching and Jin Guantao 1997, 215–21. For a critical review of the film, see Zhao, Dingxin 2001, 72–74.

20. For a brief introduction of the public debate on philosophical ideas in the 1980s, see Wang, Hui 2008a, 71–75.

21. See for example, Wang, Hui 2008a; Zhao, Dingxin 2001.

22. For an elaborated introduction of the destruction of social science studies during the socialist era and its impact on the intellectual activism in the 1980s, see Zhao, Dingxin 2001, 62–66.

23. Zeng, Menglong 2017. For more details of the production of the book series, see Chen, Fong-ching and Jin, Guantao 1997, 108–27.

24. Chen, Fong-ching and Jin, Guantao 1997.

25. For details, see Jin 2003.

26. Yang, Ping 2003; Zhong, Peizhang 2003.

27. Zhu, Zhenglin 2003.

28. See for example, Wang, Hui 2000.

29. Wang, Hui 2000.

30. For a summary of these views, see Xu, Jilin 2007, 19–21.

31. Chen, Pingyuan 1991.

32. For details, see Deng, Zhenglai 2004a.

33. Chen, Fong-ching and Jin, Guantao 1997, 110–11.

34. Jin 2003.

35. My summary has drawn on discussions of Gao Like and Wu Guanjun. For details, see Gao 2007; Wu, Guanjun 2007. Also see Xu, Jilin 2004.

36. Wang, Hui 2008b.
37. Xu, Youyu 1999.
38. Qin 2001.
39. Zhu, Xueqin 2003.
40. Wang, Dingding 2000a.
41. Liu, Junning 1998a.
42. Li, Minqi 2003.
43. Wen 2007.
44. Wang, Shaoguang and Hu, Angang 1994.
45. Cui, Zhiyuan 1994; Han, Yuhai 1998.
46. Han, Yuhai 2003.
47. Kuang 2003.
48. See for example, Wang, Hui 2008a.
49. Xu, Youyu 2003.
50. Wang, Dingding 1999.
51. Gao 2007, 196–97.
52. E.g., Evans 1989.
53. For a later reflection upon the debate, see Liu, Qing 2007, 276–77.
54. A few Chinese scholars published articles on the idea of civil society in the 1980s, in which they argued that civil society was not bourgeois society. But these discussions had not drawn much attention in the '80s. For a summary of these studies, see Ma, Shu-yun 1994.
55. The Third Front Movement was a state-led industrialization project that aimed to move basic industries from coastal regions to interior regions.
56. Deng, Zhenglai 2004b.
57. For memoirs of Deng's intellectual friends, see Ye, Biao 2013.
58. Deng, Zhenglai, and Jing, Yuejin 2018, 6–28.
59. Deng, Zhenglai, and Jing, Yuejin 2018, 6–8.
60. Deng, Zhenglai, and Jing, Yuejin 2018, 8–10.
61. For details, see Liu, Jun and Li, Lin 1989.
62. Deng, Zhenglai and Jing, Yuejin 2018, 22.
63. Deng, Zhenglai and Jing, Yuejin 2018, 24–26.
64. Xia, Weizhong 1993; Xiao, Gongqin 1993.
65. Wang, Di 1996; Xu, Jilin 2003.
66. For details, see Xu, Jilin 2011.
67. Liu, Junning 1998a; Wang, Dingding 2000b; Zhang, Shuguang 1995.
68. Wang, Hui 2008a, 88–89.
69. Wang, Shaoguang 1991.
70. Cohen and Arato 1992; Habermas 1994.
71. Xu, Jilin 1998.
72. For details, see Wang, Hui and Chen, Yangu 1998.
73. Wang, Hui 2008a, 91.
74. Wang, Hui 2008b, 54.
75. Wang, Shaoguang 2014.
76. For a couple of examples, see Eliasoph 2013; McQuarrie 2013; Pacewicz 2016.

77. I hereby borrow from Jean L. Cohen's distinction between immanent critique and "unmasking" critique. For details, see Cohen 1982, 29.

78. Wang, Hui 2013.

79. Wang, Shaoguang 2014.

80. Wang, Shaoguang 2014.

81. Xu, Jilin 2011.

82. See for example, Cheng 2007; Xu, Jilin 2011.

83. Interview with NGO activist, January 12, 2013, Beijing; interview with NGO activist, January 21, 2013, Beijing; interview with NGO activist, April 17, 2013, Guangzhou; interview with NGO activist, May 20, 2013, Guangzhou.

84. See for example, Arato 1981.

85. Interview with NGO activist, July 13, 2011, Beijing; interview with NGO activist, October 16, 2012, Beijing; interview with NGO activist, January 14, 2013, Beijing.

86. The political writings of Václav Havel were translated by Cui Weiping, a professor from the Beijing Film Academy.

87. Interview with NGO activist, May 20, 2013, Guangzhou.

88. The People's Political Consultative Conference is a political advisory body, consisting of delegates from the Chinese Communist Party, the eight legally permitted political parties subservient to the Communist Party and some nominally independent members.

89. For details, see Liang 2012.

90. For details, see Long 2018.

91. Interview with NGO activist, July 16, 2011, Beijing.

92. Young 2001, 17.

93. In the 1990s, the only environmental NGO that offered legal aid to victims of environmental pollution accidents was the Helping Center for Victims of Pollution at China University of Political Science and Law. For an introduction of the organization, see Ho 2001.

94. For some examples, see Gu and Goldman 2004; Shirk 2011; Xu, Jilin 2004.

Chapter 2

1. For an excellent review of the SARS epidemic and its impact on China's politics, see Huang, Yanzhong 2004.

2. Many scholarly works have reviewed the incident. For some of these examples, see Lei 2017, 1–2; Pils 2015, 49; Zhao, Yuezhi 2008, 246–70.

3. For a review of the historical origin of the institution and its enforcement, see Zhu, Yuchao 2006.

4. Chen, Feng and Wang, Lei 2003.

5. For an English translation of the petition, see Xu, Zhiyong et al. 2013.

6. One of the law scholars who had attended the petition told me in a private conversation that he and his collaborators had no idea whether there was any necessary linkage between their petition and the government's decision to abolish the institution. Interview with law scholar, May 5, 2013, Shenzhen.

7. For a review of the historical transformation of the state's attitude toward the "custody and repatriation" law, see Liu, Weiwei 2017.

8. Li, Cheng 2003.

9. Howell and Duckett 2019.

10. Zhang, Li 2012.

11. For details, see Liu, Qing 2007, 266.

12. For relevant discussions, see Xu, Jilin 2007, 15.

13. Deng, Zhenglai 2004b, 2004c.

14. Notable examples included the Project 985 and the Project 211. In both cases, the Chinese state selected dozens of research universities and allocated great amounts of funding to help these universities improve facilities and attract world-renowned faculty. For a review of the history of these projects, see Huang, Futao 2015.

15. Some Chinese scholars, such as Xu Jilin, called this phenomenon the "feudalization of the intellectual sphere." For details, see Xu, Jilin 2007, 2.

16. For details, see Huang, Zhen 2010.

17. Wang, Shaoguang 1997.

18. In the state discourse, this kind of practice had been generalized as the "supervision by public opinion" (*yulun jiandu*). For an analysis of the power dynamics between different levels of government authorities in the "supervision by public opinion," see Jing, Yuejin 2000. For an elaborated analysis of the state discourse of supervision, see Zhao, Yuezhi 2004.

19. Zhang, Zhi'an 2008a.

20. The original intention of the state was to reduce the crowd out of newspapers at the central level. For details, see Qian and Bandurski 2011.

21. Zhao, Yuezhi 1998.

22. Zhao, Yuezhi 2008.

23. Stockmann 2013.

24. Many scholarly works have reviewed the newspaper. For some of these examples, see Lei 2016; Qian 2008; Zhang, Zhi'an 2008b; Zhao, Yuezhi 2008.

25. Qian 2008; Zhou, Zhiyi et al. 2009.

26. Zhou, Zhiyi et al., 2009.

27. Many program producers at CCTV, such as those who produced the *News Probe*, had been influenced by the CBS program in America, *60 Minutes*. For details, see Shi, Liyue 2010.

28. Zuo Fang, the founder of the *Southern Weekly*, detailed in an interview how provincial government leaders in Guangdong had protected the newspaper. For details, see Liu, Yangshuo 2014.

29. For discussion of the event, see Law Journalist Club 2008, 194.

30. For a full version of the essay on the Boxer Rebellion, see Yuan 2002.

31. E.g., Liu, Gongchang 2008; Zhang, Zhi'an 2008b.

32. For an elaborated discussion on how the "cross-regional supervision" was possible, see Zhang, Zhi'an 2008b.

33. For a brief overview of the early history of the internet in China, see Yang, Guobin 2012.

34. For details, see Qian and Bandurski 2011, 63.

35. For discussion on the role of the internet in protests in the mid-2000s, see Sullivan and Xie 2009; Yang, Guobin 2010.

36. For a detailed introduction of the event, see Steinhardt and Wu 2016.

37. Salamon and Anheier 1996.

38. For details, see Watson 2012.

39. For a comprehensive documentation of the activities of NGOs in China in the 1990s, see China Development Brief 2001.

40. For a summary of ICS's work, see Zhu, Jiangang 2018. Also see NGOCN 2020.

41. Huangpu is a dock in Guangzhou. It was where China's first modern military academy, the Huangpu Military Academy, was located. Many of its students later fought in significant military conflicts in China in the twentieth century, notably the Second Sino-Japanese war and the Chinese Civil War. In Chinese, people often use the term "Huangpu Military Academy" (*Huangpu Junxiao*) as an analogy for those education and training programs that have lasting influence in certain specialized fields. Coincidentally, the program held by the ICS was also in Guangzhou.

42. For a summary of the development of NGOs in China in the 2000s, see China Development Brief 2013.

43. Zhu, Jiangang 2004.

44. Liu, Tao 2017.

45. Spires 2011.

46. Teets 2014.

47. Because of these connections with the state, a question that early watchers of Chinese NGOs often liked to ask was whether these NGOs were autonomous. Some scholars even coined the term "government organized non-governmental organizations" (GON-GOs) to describe the nature of these organizations. For some of these discussions, see Ma, Qiusha 2002; Wu, Fengshi 2003.

48. The "mass organizations" are a component part of China's political regime. Typical "mass organizations" include the All-China Federation of Trade Unions, All-China Women's Federation, and the Communist Youth League. These are top-down organizations, with their major leaders and staff at different levels being appointed and paid by the state.

49. Howell 2003.

50. Howell 1996.

51. For an elaborated analysis of the women's NGOs in the 1990s, see Howell 2003.

52. For an introduction of environmental NGOs in China in the 1990s, see Ho 2001.

53. For details, see Sun, Yanfei and Zhao, Dingxin 2008.

54. For details of these two campaigns, see Sun, Yanfei and Zhao, Dingxin 2008; Yang, Guobin and Calhoun 2007; Zhao, Yongxin 2021.

55. For details, see Saich 2000.

56. For an elaborated discussion of the registration status of NGOs, see Hildebrandt 2011.

57. My analysis has been informed by Xu Jilin's observation. For details, see Chen, Yizhong 2011.

58. Zhang, Zhi'an 2008a; Zhou, Zhiyi et al. 2009.

59. For details, see He, Weifang 2004.

60. For a summary of these discussions, see *Southern Weekly* 2003.

61. For details, see *Southern Weekly* 2000.

62. The Anti-rightist campaign was a campaign initiated by Mao Zedong since 1957. It purged many intellectuals who favored capitalism or were against one-party rule.

63. As I have discussed above, criticism offered by journalists during this period over China's political system had been constrained. Hence, it is better to understand *Southern Weekly*'s commemoration of Chu Anping as presenting a role model, rather than depicting reality.

64. For an elaborated discussion of Chinese state's discourse of the roles of the media, see Zhao, Yuezhi 1998, 14–33. For an elaborated discussion of professionalism in journalism in China, see Lu, Ye and Pan, Zhongdang 2002.

65. For a review of the history of the magazine, see NGOCN 2020.

66. Liu, Tao 2017.

67. For a typical discussion, see Chan, Kin-man 2008.

68. For details, see Law Journalist Club 2008.

69. For details, see Wang, Yongchen and Xiong, Zhihong 2009. For activities organized by Rural Women Knowing All, see Wu, Qing 2014.

70. For details, see Li, Ying 2008; Xi, Jianrong 2012.

71. China Development Brief 2013, 2001.

72. For details, see NGOCN 2020.

73. Interview with NGO activist, April 4, 2013, Guangzhou.

74. For relevant discussions, see Oxfam Hong Kong 2014.

75. Interview with NGO activist, August 3, 2011, Guangzhou; interview with scholars studying NGOs, May 20, 2013, Guangzhou; interview with critical journalist, June 27, 2013, Shanghai.

Chapter 3

1. Gramsci 1971, 125–205.

2. For discussion on the distinction between organic intellectuals and traditional intellectuals, see Gramsci 1971, 6.

3. For an elaborated discussion of Chinese state's legal reform and its implications on the protection of human rights, see Peerenboom 2003.

4. For details, see Hooper 2000; Kang 2010.

5. Lei 2017, 35–68; Pils 2015, 47–50.

6. Perry 2009, 2008.

7. For discussion of the transformation of labor laws, see Jing, Li 2008. For discussion of the impact of the new labor laws in the Hu-Wen era, see Gallagher et al. 2015.

8. Liu, Junning 1998b; Zhang, Shuguang 1995.

9. Liu, Sida and Halliday 2011.

10. For discussions of the definition of the "rights-defending lawyers," see Fu, Hualing and Cullen 2011, 2008.

11. For a summary of these views, see Teng 2010.

12. For typical examples of liberals' discussion of the issue, see Qiu, Feng 2003; Teng 2010; Xu, Ben 2011.

13. See for example, Teng 2019.

14. Chen, Xi 2011; Jing, June 2003.

15. Lee 2007, 2002; Read 2003.

16. Chen, Guangjin 2012, 13.

17. Fan 2005; Qiu, Feng 2003; Teng 2010.

18. Deng, Zhenglai and Jing, Yuejin 2018; Liu, Junning 1998a; Wang, Dingding 2000.

19. The early translation of the term civil society was based on Marx's and Hegel's works. For relevant discussions, see He, Zengke 1994.

20. Interview with one of the editors of the Non-governmental Sphere, Guangzhou, May 20, 2013.

21. For a general discussion of the organizational basis of these contentious collective actions, see Li, Yao 2019. NGOs being established by socioeconomically disadvantaged activists, such as labor NGOs in rural migrant workers' communities, had already emerged in the early 2000s. But at this stage, these organizations' involvement in protests was still rather occasional. For relevant discussions, see Li, Chunyun 2021; Zhou, Mujun and Yan, Guowei 2020.

22. Zhu, Jiangang 2008.

23. For relevant sociological discussions, see Emirbayer and Mische 1998; Sewell 1992.

24. Kou 2013.

25. Being influenced by this rationale, many Chinese scholars studying civil society began to employ an "action-oriented approach." For relevant discussions, see Li, Youmei 2007; Shen, Yuan 2007a; Zhu, Jiangang 2008.

26. Xiao, Shu 2010a.

27. Chan, Kin-man 2009.

28. Field notes, Guangzhou, April 2, 2013.

29. Steinhardt and Wu 2016.

30. Huang, Xiuli 2009.

31. The Yuanmingyuan Park, also known as the Old Summer Palace, was an imperial garden constructed in the 18th century. The French and British troops destroyed the park during the Second Opium War. The major purpose for paving an anti-seepage membrane at the lakebed was to solve the water depletion problem in the region.

32. Zhao, Yongxin 2021.

33. For details, see Wang, Yongchen and Wang, Aijun 2012.

34. Chan, Kam Wing and Buckingham 2008.

35. Chan, Kam Wing and Zhang, Li 1999.

36. Friedman 2014; Lee 2007.

37. Cai, Fang 2011.

38. Pun and Lu 2010; Solinger 1999.

39. Han, Jun 2004; Zhang, Shuguang 2003.

40. Yu, Xiao 2005.

41. For a detailed discussion on migrant children's education problems in the 2000s, see Kwong 2004.

42. Wen 2007.

43. For an introduction to the "school of rural construction," see Hale 2013.

44. For a summary of the commentaries offered by the liberals, see Pan, Jia'en 2012, 53–60.

45. Lin, Hai 2008.

46. Read 2003.

47. Cai, Yongshun 2005; Chen, Peng 2010; Chen, Yingfang 2006.

48. Xia, Jianzhong 2003.

49. Xiao, Shu 2010b, 2010c.

50. The neighborhood party committee is the grassroots-level organization of the Communist Party. It usually works with the residents' committee, a "mass organization" in a neighborhood. These committees are partially state-funded and can be seen as state agencies. For a more detailed introduction, see Read 2000.

51. Zhou, Mujun 2014, 1850.

52. Li, Youmei 2007; Huang, Ronggui and Gui, Yong 2013.

53. Huang, Ronggui and Gui, Yong 2013.

54. Yip and Jiang 2011.

55. For details, see Zhou, Yuzhong et al. 2007.

56. For details, see Zhou, Yuzhong et al. 2007.

57. Wang, Zhengxu et al. 2013.

58. Merle 2014.

59. The election of the deputies to the people's congress in China is usually under the control of the Communist Party. In the early 2000s, many liberals believed that the people's congress could be democratized if more people participated in the election as independent candidates and more people were mobilized to vote for these independent candidates. For details, see Zhang, Jianfeng 2009.

60. Interview with activist homeowner, Beijing, October 31, 2012.

61. Interview with liberal scholar, Guangzhou, August 5, 2011.

62. Interview with "rights-defending lawyer," Beijing, December 12, 2012.

63. Cai, Rong and He, Shenjing 2022; Wong 2015.

64. Zhou, Mujun 2014.

65. Cai, Rong and He, Shenjing 2022; Wang, Ying and Clarke 2021; Wu, Fulong 2018.

66. See for example, Yip 2019.

67. Interview with "rights-defending lawyer," Beijing, December 12, 2012.

68. See for example, King et al., 2013; Li, Yao 2019.

69. For an open discussion of the "ethical dilemma," see Teng 2010.

70. Interview with NGO activist, Beijing, June 13, 2014.

71. Interview with "rights-defending lawyer," Shanghai, June 18, 2013.

72. Interview with NGO activist, Beijing, November 10, 2012.

73. Interview with activist among rural migrant workers, Guangzhou, May 4, 2013.

74. Interview with activist among rural migrant workers, Guangzhou, April 29, 2013.

75. Interview with "rights-defending lawyer," Beijing, January 29, 2013.

76. Interview with NGO activist, Beijing, July 24, 2011.

77. Lei 2017.

78. Zhao, Yuezhi 2008.

Chapter 4

1. For relevant discussions, see Kelly and Brownell 2011; Leibold 2010.

2. Brownell 2012.

3. For relevant discussions, see Xu, Bin 2013.

4. For elaborated discussions of the complex relationship between the nationalists and the Chinese state, see Johnston 2017; Zhao, Dingxin 2003.

5. Extant studies on the expression of nationalist discourses in China's public sphere highlight that those who hold nationalist opinions do not necessarily oppose many of the liberal discourses, such as the advocacy of citizenship rights and government accountability. I agree with these arguments. What I want to emphasize is that it was in the late 2000s that the divergence between the two discourses became increasingly salient in public discussions. For elaborated discussions of the relationship between the two discourses, see Zhang, Yinxian et al. 2018.

6. For details, see Lin, Fen and Zhao, Dingxin 2016.

7. For details, see Chang, Ping 2008.

8. For a summary of these voices, see Wu, Wei 2008.

9. For an analysis of people's discussions of the leaders online, see Xu, Bin 2012.

10. Zhu Xueqin's commentary on the earthquake was highly ambiguous. Even some of his intellectual friends felt confused about his intention of mentioning the term punishment. In an attempt at defending Zhu, Zhao Mu, a literary critic, suggested that the high-profile expression of national pride during a series of events happening in the first half of 2008, such as the anti-CNN activism and the Beijing Olympic torch relay, must have annoyed Zhu. In an interview conducted one year later, Zhu seemed to endorse this view. He suggested that Chinese people were too obsessed with the Olympics in 2008 and that he hoped that Chinese people would cool down and mourn for the dead. For Zhao Mu's analysis, see Zhao, Mu 2015. For the interview with Zhu, see Yangtze River Daily 2009.

11. Because of the state's quick response, the influence of the Charter 08 within China's territory had been limited. Participants of public discussions on the manifesto were mainly intellectual elites and university students who had the capacity to use VPN and read overseas internet content. For an elaborated discussion of the Charter 08 Movement and its influence, see Béja et al. 2012.

12. See for example, Guangming Daily 2013.

13. For some of Yu Keping's discussions of civil society, see Yu, Keping 2006.

14. See for example, Liu, Zhiqing 2018.

15. For relevant discussions, see Liu, Gongchang 2008.

16. Zhao, Yuezhi 2000.

17. Ye, Zicao 2013.

18. For a detailed introduction of the incident, see Guan, June 2020.

19. For details, see China Internet Museum 2023a.

20. For relevant discussions, see Li, Ke and Sparks 2018; Luo 2016; Tong, Jingrong 2019.

21. Zhang, Zhi'an and Cao, Yanhui 2017.

22. For relevant discussions, see Sparks et al. 2016.

23. This was illustrated in a slogan raised by the editorial board in 2007: It is right here that you begin to understand China (*Zai zheli dudong zhongguo*). For a detailed discussion, see Zhou, Zhiyi et al. 2009.

24. Luo 2016.

25. Wu, Jing 2015.

26. See for example, Lei 2017, chapter 5.

27. China Internet Museum 2023b.
28. Hughes and Wacker 2003.
29. Zhou, Baohua and Lü, Shuning 2011.
30. In January 2016, the word limit was increased to 2000.
31. See for example, Qiu, Jack Linchuan 2009.
32. Svensson 2014; Zhang, Pengyi 2013.
33. MacKinnon 2009.
34. For relevant discussions, see Pan, Jennifer 2017.
35. Sullivan 2012.
36. Pan, Jennifer 2017.
37. For details, see Open Constitution Initiative 2009.
38. Pils 2017.
39. Personal communication with official from civil affairs department in Guangdong, April 16, 2013.
40. For discussions of voluntary associations during the Sichuan Earthquake and their interaction with the state, see Shieh and Deng 2011, Teets 2009, Xu, Bin 2014.
41. Interview with scholar from ICS, Guangzhou, August 3, 2011.
42. Interview with NGO activist, Beijing, November 30, 2012.
43. Lu, Xuan 2019.
44. Howell 2019, 2015.
45. Howell 2008; Teets 2015.
46. Lai et al. 2015.
47. Lai and Spires 2021; Shieh 2017.
48. See for example, Deng, Guosheng 2012; Teets 2014.
49. Howell 2015.
50. For some of Chen's commentaries, see Chen, Weiguang 2012.
51. Interview with labor activist, Guangzhou, April 25, 2013; Interview with labor activist, Guangzhou, April 18, 2013; Interview with labor activist, Guangzhou, April 10, 2013.
52. Chen, Yunbo 2014.
53. Zhou, Mujun 2024.
54. For details, see Fang, Zhouzi 2005.
55. Ge and Wang 2016.
56. For discussions of the constraints facing environmental NGOs in environmental public interest litigation and the advocacy campaign for expanding litigation, see Dai and Spires 2018; Stern 2013.
57. Arantes et al. 2020; Wu, Fengshi and Martus 2021.
58. The term "fifty-cent army" had originated from a rumor that the Chinese government hired people to post online positive comments about state policies and paid fifty cents for each comment. In the beginning, it was a pejorative term, being used by those internet users who leaned toward the liberals to attack their opponents. But later it became an identity shared by many internet users who disliked the liberals. For a detailed discussion, see Han, Rongbin 2015.
59. For details, see Liu, Yu 2009.
60. For an introduction to the documentary film, see Cui, Shuqin 2017; Powers 2016.

61. Cui, Shuqin 2017.

62. See for example, Pils 2015; Tong, Jingrong 2019.

Chapter 5

1. See for example, Lin, Justin Yifu 1992.

2. Yang, Dennis Tao 1999.

3. Jahiel 1997.

4. West and Wong 1995.

5. O'Brien and Li 1995.

6. For elaborated discussions of the "three rural issues," see Li, Changping 2009; Wen 2007.

7. For detailed discussions of these organizations, see Day 2008; Hale 2013.

8. Both James Yen (also known as Yan Yangchu) and Liang Shuming were intellectual activists who had engaged in the rural construction movement in Republican China. By using their names and adopting the term "rural construction" (*xiangjian*), the movement intended to show that it was the inheritor of those predecessors who had devoted themselves to the cause of rural development. For systematic discussions of how the New Rural Reconstruction Movement established the two role models, see Wen et al. 2020. For comparative analysis on the two rural construction movements, see Yan and Chen 2013.

9. For information on the conflicts between Wen Tiejun and the associate editors at the *China Reform*, see Wen 2005.

10. For details, see Hu 2004.

11. For a comprehensive review of the state policies, see Chen, Xiwen 2009.

12. See for example, Day and Schneider 2018; Yan and Chen 2013.

13. See for example, Wen 2005.

14. Interview with activist, Beijing, January 16, 2013.

15. Interview with activist, Beijing, January 16, 2013.

16. Activists in the New Rural Reconstruction Movement summarized this transformation as "from defending rights with tear to attending rural reconstruction with joy" (*cong kuzhe weiquan dao xiaozhe xiangjian*). For details, see Bai and Lü 2011. For a discussion of how the movement discouraged peasants from attending rights-defending activism, see Dai 2021.

17. See for example, Wen 2020, 2016. For criticism of these views, see Yan et al. 2021.

18. Shi, Yan et al. 2011. For criticisms over this view, see Day and Schneider 2018; Zhou, Mujun and Xu, Yi 2020.

19. For details, see Si and Scott 2016.

20. The books in the photo are *The Last Confucian, Bibliography of James Yen, Developmental Illusions, Subaltern Studies, Women, Nation, and Feminism, Illustration of Practices in Constructing New Villages*, and *Open Veins in Latin America*.

21. See for example, Zhang, Shuguang 2007.

22. Li, Changping 2009; Wen 2007.

23. For an elaborated discussion of the movement's policy suggestion on cooperatives, see Tong, Zhihui and Wen 2009.

24. According to the government's report, eventually, 296,000 affected children were identified, among which 53,000 were hospitalized. For details, see State Council 2009.

25. Lei and Zhou 2015; Li, Haoyue C. 2019.
26. For details, see Yang, Guobin 2013.
27. Lei and Zhou 2015; Li, Haoyue C. 2019.
28. Zhou, Yan 2014.
29. Xia, Youzhi 2013. For similar views, see Li, Yuan 2012; Zhan, Jiang 2012.
30. For a summary of these views, see Xu, Huijiao et al. 2017.
31. See for example, Wen 2006.
32. Wen 2006.
33. Xu, Huijiao et al. 2017.
34. Pan, Jia'en and Du, Jie 2011.
35. For an elaborated presentation of this view, see CNTV 2011.
36. Interview with activist, Shanghai, July 2, 2011.
37. Interview with activist, Beijing, July 16, 2011.
38. Interview with activist, Hong Kong, May 30, 2017.
39. Lee 2007, 2002.
40. Lee 2007.
41. Cai, He 2010.
42. Elfstrom and Kuruvilla 2014.
43. For details, see Chan, Chris K. 2014.
44. Before that, social science scholars in China seldom studied labor issues. There were some sociological studies on rural migrant workers. But they had been carried out under the theoretical framework of social stratification or the assimilation of immigrants. For a detailed introduction to the transformation of sociological studies, see Lee and Shen 2009.
45. For details, see Shen, Yuan 2020.
46. It was those labor scholars who translated Michael Burawoy's work on public sociology into Chinese. See Shen, Yuan 2007b.
47. For details, see Chan, Chris K. 2013; Froissart 2005; Xu, Yi 2013.
48. Zhou, Mujun 2024.
49. For details, see Lee and Shen 2009.
50. For details, see Zhou, Mujun and Yan, Guowei 2020.
51. For details, see Zhou, Mujun 2022. Also see Fu, Diana 2018; Hui 2020.
52. See for example, Yang, Jibin 2010.
53. University Research Team on Foxconn 2010.
54. For details, see Pun et al. 2014.
55. For a detailed analysis of the "disappearance" of the class discourse, see Lee and Shen 2009.
56. For details, see Lü, Tu 2013.
57. For a summary of labor scholars' discussion of the "new working class," see Zheng, Guanghuai and Zhu, Jiangang 2011.
58. Pun and Lu 2010; Smith and Pun 2018.
59. See for example, Lee 2016.
60. For details, see Zhou, Mujun 2024.
61. Yilian Legal Aid Center 2014.
62. See for example, Shen, Yuan 2007c.
63. Guo, Yuhua 2010.

64. Interview with NGO practitioner, May 20, 2013, Guangzhou.

65. See for example, Social Development Commission 2010.

66. For details, see Zheng, Guanghuai and Zhu, Jiangang 2011.

67. For details, see Wang, Zheng 2005.

68. For details, see Yang, Mayfair Mei-hui 1999.

69. Gustafsson and Shi 2001.

70. Li, Hongbin et al. 2011.

71. Sun, Liping 1994; Zheng, Yefu 1994.

72. For details, see Wang, Zheng 1997.

73. Wang, Zheng 2018.

74. See for example, Wallis 2015.

75. Wu, Angela Xiao and Dong, Yige 2019.

76. For details, see Wang, Qi 2021.

77. For details, see Li, Jun and Li, Xiaoqin 2017; Han, Xiao 2018.

78. Wang, Zheng and Zhang, Ying 2010.

79. Wu, Angela Xiao and Dong, Yige 2019.

80. For a detailed discussion on how political opportunities and economic resources brought by Chinese state's AIDS prevention policies varied across gay activism and lesbian activism, see Hildebrandt and Chua 2017.

81. Wang, Zheng 2018.

82. See for example, Chen, Yongling and Ma, Yanjun 2012.

83. For a summary of these views, see Li, Sipan 2013.

84. For details, see Wang, Qi 2021.

85. Qiu, Feng 2012.

86. Li, Sipan 2013.

87. Among these activists, the most well-known one was Chen Guangcheng, a "rights-defending" lawyer who had fought the violence in the enforcement of the one-child policy in Shandong Province. For details, see Chen, Guangcheng 2015.

88. Yi 2007.

89. Li, Sipan 2012.

90. Scharping 2019.

91. For a summary of these views, see Guo, Rui 2015.

92. For a summary of these views, see Li, Sipan 2013.

93. For details, see Guo, Rui 2015.

94. See for example, Lü, Pin 2015.

95. Interview with labor activist, Guangzhou, April 25, 2013; Interview with labor activist, Shenzhen, May 15, 2013. Also see Li, Chunyun 2021.

96. Interview with labor activist, Beijing, January 8, 2014; Interview with labor activist, Beijing, July 9, 2015.

97. Interview with labor activist, Guangzhou, May 27, 2013.

Chapter 6

1. Ortmann 2015.

2. For one of the few articles appearing on Chinese media that discussed the Umbrella Movement, see Xiang 2014.

3. For relevant discussions, see Yuen 2015.

4. See for example, Chan, Kin-man 2008.

5. Chan later summarized his experience in a research article. For details, see Chan, Kin-man 2022.

6. For details, see Zhu, Jiangang 2018.

7. Zhou, Mujun 2024.

8. See for example, Liu, Mingyue et al. 2020; Wedeman 2017.

9. Yuen 2014; Zeng, Qingjie 2020.

10. For details, see Yang, Peidong and Tang, Lijun 2018.

11. The imprisonment of Liu Xiaobo was a case in point. For details, see Béja et al. 2012.

12. Tan, K. Cohen and Cheng, Shuxin 2020; Zou 2019.

13. Zhang, Zhi'an and Cao, Yanhui 2017.

14. Tan, Chris KK. et al. 2020; Zhou, Min and Liu, Shih-Diing 2022.

15. For relevant discussions, see Cunningham et al. 2019; Lin, Yao 2021.

16. For details, see Creemers 2017.

17. For details, see Hou 2020.

18. Currently there lack systematic studies on podcast programs in Chinese. For a preliminary review on podcast programs that advocate feminist discourses, see Yang, Fan 2023.

19. For relevant discussions, see Fang, Kecheng and Repnikova 2018; Liu, Hailong 2019.

20. Fang, Kecheng and Repnikova 2018.

21. Ministry of Civil Affairs 2018.

22. For details, see Spires 2020.

23. For details, see Franceschini and Nesossi 2018.

24. For discussions of donors' preference on the Tencent philanthropy platform, see Ba et al. 2020.

25. For details, see Zhou, Mujun 2024.

26. See for example, Zhicheng Legal Aid Center 2021.

27. For details, see Fu, Hualing 2018.

28. See for example, Shen, Yongdong and Yu, Jianxing 2017; Shen, Yongdong et al. 2020.

29. For a collection of Lian Yue's column articles at the *Southern Weekly*, see Lian 2003.

30. Lian 2022.

31. Liu later deleted her post on Weibo. For a repost of her article, see Liu, Yu 2018.

32. For a brief review of the article and the controversies it aroused, see Ji, Xiaocheng 2018.

33. For an overview of the issue, see Zhang, Wei 2017.

34. Xiao later deleted his article. For a critical review of his article, see Sun, Jinyu 2018.

35. For a summary of these views, see Sun, Jinyu 2018.

36. For an explanation on why some of the Chinese liberals had become conservative, see Lin, Yao 2021.

37. Interview with youth activist, Guangzhou, March 3, 2018.

38. Interview with youth activist, Shenzhen, March 7, 2018.

39. For details, see Yu, Jiangang 2023.

40. For a detailed introduction to the debate, see Chen, Zhewei 2023.

41. See for example, Day and Schneider 2018; Yan, Hairong et al. 2021; Zhou, Mujun and Xu, Yi 2020.

42. Interview with youth activist, Beijing, October 23, 2018; Interview with youth activist, Beijing, October 24, 2018.

43. For details, see Au 2018.

44. For details, see Li, Xiaotian 2019.

45. Interview with labor activist, Guangzhou, October 18, 2018.

46. For details, see Dong 2019.

47. See for example, Lei 2021; Pringle and Meng 2018.

48. For details, see Fincher 2018.

49. Wang, Qi 2021.

50. Li, Sipan 2020.

51. For details, see Angelica S 2021.

52. Interview with feminist activist, Beijing, Oct 24, 2018; Interview with feminist activist, Guangzhou, April 27, 2013; Interview with feminist activist, Guangzhou, April 10, 2013.

53. For details, see Li, Sipan 2020.

54. The Chinese characters on the left are "feminists," while those on the right are "Chinese countryside feminists."

55. The term "countryside feminist" derived from "Chinese countryside dog" (*zhonghua tianyuan quan*), implying that the feminist bloggers had not been able to understand western feminist theories that were based upon the ideas of equity and rights. The term "feminist fist" blamed the feminist bloggers for their agitational and non-cooperative attitude on gender issues. In Chinese, "fist" and "right" are homophones. For details, see Zhang, Guannan 2018.

56. For details, see Yin 2022.

57. Angelica S 2021.

58. Li, Sipan 2020.

59. For details, see Lin, Zhongxuan and Yang, Liu 2019; Yin and Sun 2021.

60. For details, see Huang, Shan and Sun, Wanning 2021; Yin and Sun 2021.

61. See for example, Angelica, S 2021.

62. For details, see Liao 2020.

Conclusion

1. See for example, Gu and Goldman 2004; Shirk 2011.

2. See for example, Lei 2017; O'Brien and Li 2006; Xia, Jianzhong 2003.

3. See for example, Qian and Bandurski 2011; Zhu, Jiangang 2008.

4. See for example, Wang, Zheng 2018; Yan et al. 2021; Zhou, Mujun 2024.

5. See for example, Deng, Yanhua and O'Brien 2013; Mattingly 2020; Ong 2018.

6. For documentation of the Wuhan lockdown, see Yang, Guobin 2022.

7. For details, see Cao et al. 2022.

8. Zhang, Tingkang 2024.

9. Habermas 1991.

10. Habermas 1987.

11. See for example Habermas 1994.
12. Mann 1986
13. Interview with human rights lawyer, Beijing, October 16, 2012.
14. Interview with NGO activist, Guangzhou, May 20, 2013.
15. See for example, Brook and Frolic 1997.
16. See for example, Ferguson 2007.
17. Chen, Xi 2017.
18. For initial attempts at analyzing the protests, see Chan, Kin-man 2023.
19. For details, see Neilson and Rossiter 2008.
20. See for example, Xi, An 2019.
21. Xu, Xiaohong 2023.

REFERENCES

Alexander, Jeffrey C. 2006. *The Civil Sphere*. Oxford University Press.

Angelica S. 2021. "Yu Xingdongpai Duanceng, Zhongguo Tese Fan Nüquan de 'Jiduan,' 'Fenhong,' 'Xiachen'" [Being Disconnected from the "Action Art" Activists, the "Radicalization" and "Grassroots-ization" of the Pan Feminist Activism in China]. *Wai Nao* [Why Not]. March 29. https://www.wainao.me/wainao-reads/fea-Mar-06-cyberfeminism-in-china-03292021

Arantes, Virginie, Can Zou, and Yue Che. 2020. "Coping with Waste: A Government-NGO Collaborative Governance Approach in Shanghai." *Journal of Environmental Management* 259: 109653.

Arato, Andrew. 1981. "Civil Society Against the State: Poland 1980–81." *Telos* 47: 23–47.

Armstrong, Elizabeth A. 2002. "Crisis, Collective Creativity, and the Generation of New Organizational Forms: The Transformation of Lesbian/Gay Organizations in San Francisco." In *Social Structure and Organizations Revisited*, vol. 19, edited by Michael Lounsbury and Marc J. Ventresca, 361–95. Elsevier Science.

Au, Loong-Yu. 2018. "The Jasic Mobilisation: A High Tide for the Chinese Labour Movement?" *Made in China Journal* 3 (4): 12–16.

Ba, Zhichao, Yuxiang Chris Zhao, Liqin Zhou, and Shijie Song. 2020. "Exploring the Donation Allocation of Online Charitable Crowdfunding Based on Topical and Spatial Analysis: Evidence from the Tencent GongYi." *Information Processing & Management* 57 (6): 102322.

Bai, Yaping, and Chengping Lü. 2011. "Woju Shidai de 'Wutuobang': Dangdai Qingnian de Xiangjian Yundong" [A "Utopia" in a Humble Place: The Rural Construction Movement Organized by Contemporary Youth]. *Wenhua Zongheng* [Beijing Cultural Review] 3: 68–73.

Baiocchi, Gianpaolo, and Lisa Corrado. 2010. "The Politics of Habitus: Publics, Blackness, and Community Activism in Salvador, Brazil." *Qualitative Sociology* 33: 369–88.

Béja, Jean-Philippe, Fu Hualing, and Eva Pils, eds. 2012. *Liu Xiaobo, Charter 08, and the Challenges of Political Reform in China*. Hong Kong University Press.

Berman, Sheri. 1997. "Civil Society and the Collapse of the Weimar Republic." *World Politics* 49 (3): 401–29.

Brødsgaard, Kjeld Erik. 1981. "The Democracy Movement in China, 1978–1979: Opposition Movements, Wall Poster Campaigns, and Underground Journals." *Asian Survey* 21 (7): 741–74.

Brook, Timothy, and B. Michael Frolic. 1997. *Civil Society in China*. Routledge.

Brownell, Susan. 2012. "Human Rights and the Beijing Olympics: Imagined Global Community and the Transnational Public Sphere." *The British Journal of Sociology* 63 (2): 306–27.

Cai, Fang. 2011. "*Hukou* System Reform and Unification of Rural-urban Social Welfare." *China & World Economy* 19 (3): 33–48.

Cai, He. 2010. "Cong 'Dixianxing Liyi' dao 'Zengzhangxing Liyi': Nongmingong Liyi Suqiu de Zhuanbian yu Laozi Guanxi Zhixu" [From "Bottom-line Interest" to "Development Interest": The Transformation of Rural Migrant Workers' Demands and the Order of Labor-capital Relations]. *Kaifang Shidai* [Open Times] (9): 37–45.

Cai, Rong, and Shenjing He. 2022. "Governing Homeowners Associations in China's Gated Communities: The Extension of State Infrastructural Power and Its Uneven Reach." *Urban Geography* 43 (4): 523–45.

Cai, Yongshun. 2005. "China's Moderate Middle Class: The Case of Homeowners' Resistance." *Asian Survey* 45 (5): 777–99.

Calhoun, Craig. 1989. "Tiananmen, Television, and the Public Sphere: Internationalization of Culture and the Beijing Spring of 1989." *Public Culture* 2 (1): 54–71.

Calhoun, Craig. 1992. "Introduction: Habermas and the Public Sphere." In *Habermas and the Public Sphere, edited by Craig Calhoun, 1–48*. MIT Press.

Calhoun, Craig. 1993. "Civil Society and the Public Sphere." *Public Culture* 5 (2): 267–80.

Cao, Xun, Runxi Zeng, and Richard Evans. 2022. "Digital Activism and Collective Mourning by Chinese Netizens during COVID-19." *China Information* 36 (2): 159–79.

Chan, Chris K. 2013. "Community-based Organizations for Migrant Workers' Rights: The Emergence of Labour NGOs in China." *Community Development Journal* 48 (1): 6–22.

Chan, Chris K. 2014. "Constrained Labour Agency and the Changing Regulatory Regime in China." *Development and Change* 45 (4): 685–709.

Chan, Kam Wing, and Will Buckingham. 2008. "Is China Abolishing the *Hukou* System?" *The China Quarterly* 195: 582–606.

Chan, Kam Wing, and Li Zhang. 1999. "The *Hukou* System and Rural-Urban Migration in China: Processes and Changes." *The China Quarterly* 160: 818–55.

Chan, Kin-man. 2008. "Cong Gongmin Shehui Zouxiang Hexie Shehui" [From Civil Society to a Harmonious Society]. *Independent Chinese Pen Center*. December 8. Available from https://www.chinesepen.org/old-posts/?p=11204

Chan, Kin-man. 2009. "Meiyou Gongmin Shehui, Nalai Hexie Shehui" [The Construction of a Harmonious Society Is Impossible Without the Construction of Civil Society]. *Minjian* [The Non-governmental Sphere]. May 27.

Chan, Kin-man. 2022. "Democracy Movement and Alternative Knowledge in Hong Kong." In *Knowledge and Civil Society, edited by Johannes* Glückler, Heinz-Dieter Meyer, and Laura Suarsana, 235–51. Springer.

Chan, Kin-man. 2023. "Unwritten Endings: Revolutionary Potential of China's A4 Protest." *Sociologica* 17 (1): 57–66.

Chang, Ping. 2008. "Xizang: Zhenxiang yu Minzu Zhuyi Qingxu" [Tibet: Truth and Nationalist Sentiment]. *FT Zhongwen Wang* [Financial Times China]. April 3. https://web.archive.org/web/20220815154317if_/https://www.china-week.com/html/3762.htm

Chatterjee, Partha. 2004. *The Politics of the Governed: Reflections on Popular Politics in Most of the World*. Columbia University Press.

Cheek, Timothy, David Ownby, and Joshua Fogel. 2018. "Mapping the Intellectual Public Sphere in China Today." *China Information* 32 (1): 107–20.

Chen, Feng, and Lei Wang. 2003. "Bei Shourong Zhe Sun Zhigang zhi Si" [The Death of Sun Zhigang]. April 25. Available from https://news.sina.com.cn/s/2003-04-25/11111 016223.html

Chen, Fong-Ching, and Guantao Jin. 1997. *From Youthful Manuscripts to River Elegy: The Chinese Popular Cultural Movement and Political Transformation, 1979–1989*. Chinese University Press.

Chen, Guangcheng. 2015. *The Barefoot Lawyer: A Blind Man's Fight for Justice and Freedom in China*. Macmillan.

Chen, Guangjin. 2012. "Maixiang Quanmian Jiancheng Xiaokang Shehui de Xin Jieduan: 2012–2013 Nian Zhongguo Shehui Xingshi Fenxi yu Yuce" [An Analysis of the Conditions of Chinese Society, 2012–2013]. In *2013 Nian Zhongguo Shehui Xingshi Fenxi yu Yuce* [Society of China Analysis and Forecast, 2013], edited by Peilin Li, Guangjin Chen, Xinxin Xu, Xueyi Lu, Yi Zhang, and Wei Li, 1–18. Social Sciences Literature Press.

Chen, Peng. 2010. "Dangdai Zhongguo Yezhu de Faquan Kangzheng: Guanyu Yezhu Weiquan Huodong de Yige Fenxi Kuangjia" [Homeowners' Resistance in Contemporary China: An Analytical Framework for Homeowners' Weiquan Activism]. *Shehuixue Yanjiu* [Sociological Studies] 25 (1): 34–63.

Chen, Pingyuan. 1991. "Xueshushi Yanjiu Suixiang" [Random Thoughts on the Study of Intellectual History]. *Xueren* [Scholars] 1 (3).

Chen, Weiguang. 2012. *You yu Si: Sanshi Nian Gonghui Gongzuo Ganwu* [Anxiety and Reflection: Comprehension of Working in the Trade Union for Three Decades]. China Social Sciences Press.

Chen, Xi. 2011. *Social Protest and Contentious Authoritarianism in China*. Cambridge University Press.

Chen, Xi. 2017. "Elitism and Exclusion in Mass Protest: Privatization, Resistance, and State Domination in China." *Comparative Political Studies* 50 (7): 908–34.

Chen, Xiwen. 2009. "Review of China's Agricultural and Rural Development: Policy Changes and Current Issues." *China Agricultural Economic Review* 1 (2): 121–35.

Chen, Yingfang. 2006. "Xingdongli yu Zhidu Xianzhi: Dushi Yundong zhong de Zhongchan Jieceng" [Agency and Institutional Constraints: The Middle Class in Urban Movements]. *Shehuixue Yanjiu* [Sociological Studies] 21 (4): 1–20.

Chen, Yizhong. 2011. "Jueqi Zhongguo de Shizi Lukou: Xu Jilin Xiansheng Zhuanfang" [A Rising China at the Cross Road: An Interview with Xu Jilin]. In *Taiwan Shi: Jiaolü yu Zixin* [Taiwan History: Anxiety and Confidence], 235–74. Linking Books.

Chen, Yongling, and Yanjun Ma. 2012. "Tan 95 Shifuhui NGO Funü Luntan" [On the Forum of Women's NGOs at the 95 World Women Conference]. In *Zhongguo NGO Koushushi, Diyi Ji* [Oral History for NGOs in China, No. 1], edited by Ming Wang, 15–37. Social Sciences Academic Press.

Chen, Yunbo. 2014. "Laogong NGO de Weibo Fuquan Fenxi: Yi Shenzhen 'Xiaoxiaocao' Zaoyu Biqian Shijian Weili" [Labor NGOs and Weibo Empowerment: A Case Study of Shenzhen "Little Grass" Eviction Event]. *Guoji Xinwen Jie* [Chinese Journal of Journalism & Communication] 36 (11): 51–64.

Chen, Zhewei. 2023. *The Strategic Action of Principled Opportunism: An Alternative History of Beijing Farmers' Market*. Master Thesis Submitted to the Department of Sociology at Zhejiang University.

Cheng, Qing. 2007. "Guojia yu Shehui de Zai Xiangxiang: Guanyu Shimin Shehui de Zhenglun" [The Re-imagination of State and Society: The Debate on Civil Society]. In *Qimeng de Ziwo Wajie: 1990 Niandai yilai Zhongguo Sixiang Wenhua Jie Zhongda Zhenglun Yanjiu* [The Self-disintegration of an Enlightenment: An Inquiry into the Significant Debates in China's Thought Sphere since the 1990s], edited by Jilin Xu and Gang Luo, 166–93. Jilin Publishing Group.

China Development Brief. 2001. *250 Chinese NGOs: Civil Society in the Making*. A Special Report from China Development Brief.

China Development Brief. 2013. *Zhongguo Gongyi Zuzhi Minglu* [A Directory of Chinese NGOs].

China Internet Museum. 2023a. "2012: Shouji Yuesheng Wei Diyi Shangwang Zhongduan" [2012: Mobile Phones Rose to the First Terminal Equipment for Getting Online]. http://www.internet.cn/history/niandu/2012.html

China Internet Museum. 2023a. "At the end of 2012: Cellphone Became the No.1 Internet Access Terminal." http://en.internet.cn/history/niandu/2012.html

China Internet Museum. 2023b. "2008: Wangluo Meiti Quanmian Jiaru Aoyun Baodao Dazhan" [2008: The Internet Media Joined the Reportage of the Olympics]. http://www.internet.cn/history/niandu/2008.html

China Internet Museum. 2023b. "Full Participation of Online Medias for the Olympics 2008." http://en.internet.cn/history/niandu/2008.html

Clemens, Elisabeth S., and James M. Cook. 1999. "Politics and Institutionalism: Explaining Durability and Change." *Annual Review of Sociology* 25: 441–66.

CNTV. 2011. "CSA Shiyan" [An Experiment of CSA]. *Xinwen Diaocha* [News Probe]. November 26. http://news.cntv.cn/program/xinwendiaocha/20111126/107104.shtml

Cohen, Jean L. 1982. *Class and Civil Society: The Limits of Marxian Critical Theory*. University of Massachusetts Press.

Cohen, Jean L., and Andrew Arato. 1992. *Civil Society and Political Theory*. MIT Press.

Cox, Robert W. 1999. "Civil Society at the Turn of the Millenium: Prospects for an Alternative World Order." *Review of International Studies* 25 (1): 3–28.

Creemers, Rogier. 2017. "Cyber China: Upgrading Propaganda, Public Opinion Work and Social Management for the Twenty-first Century." *Journal of Contemporary China* 26 (103): 85–100.

Cui, Shuqin. 2017. "Chai Jing's *Under the Dome*: A Multimedia Documentary in the Digital Age." *Journal of Chinese Cinemas* 11 (1): 30–45.

Cui, Zhiyuan. 1994. "Zhidu Chuangxin yu Dierci Sixiang Jiefang" [Institutional Innovation and the Second Emancipation of Thought]. *Ershiyi Shiji* [The Twenty-first Century] 24: 5–16.

Cunningham, Stuart, David Craig, and Junyi Lv. 2019. "China's Livestreaming Industry: Platforms, Politics, and Precarity." *International Journal of Cultural Studies* 22 (6): 719–36.

Dai, Jingyun. 2021. "Beyond Contained Activism in Authoritarian States: The New Rural Reconstruction Movement in Post-socialist China." Paper submitted to Political Sociology Roundtable. Annual Conference of the American Sociological Association.

Dai, Jingyun, and Anthony J. Spires. 2018. "Advocacy in an Authoritarian State: How Grassroots Environmental NGOs Influence Local Governments in China." *The China Journal* 79 (1): 62–83.

Day, Alexander. 2008. "The End of the Peasant? New Rural Reconstruction in China." *Boundary 2* 35 (2): 49–73.

Day, Alexander F., and Mindi Schneider. 2018. "The End of Alternatives? Capitalist Transformation, Rural Activism, and the Politics of Possibility in China." *The Journal of Peasant Studies* 45 (7): 1221–46.

de Leon, Cedric, Manali Desai, and Cihan Tuğal. 2009. "Political Articulation: Parties and the Constitution of Cleavages in the United States, India, and Turkey." *Sociological Theory* 27 (3): 193–219.

de Leon, Cedric, Manali Desai, and Cihan Tuğal. 2015. "Political Articulation: The Structured Creativity of Parties." In *Building Blocs: How Parties Organize* Society, edited by Cedric de Leon, Manali Desai, and Cihan Tuğal, 1–36. Stanford University Press.

Deng, Guosheng. 2012. "Shehui Zuzhi Zhijie Dengji Shi Zhidu Tubo" [The Direct Registration of Social Organizations Is a Breakthrough]. *Caixin*. April 01. https://china.caixin .com/2012-04-01/100375889.html

Deng, Yanhua, and Kevin J. O'Brien. 2013. "Relational Repression in China: Using Social Ties to Demobilize Protesters." *The China Quarterly* 215: 533–52.

Deng, Zhenglai. 2004a. *Zhongguo Xueshu Guifanhua* [The Normalization of Academic Studies in China]. Law Press.

Deng, Zhenglai. 2004b. "Dui Zhishi Fenzi 'Qihe' Guanxi de Fansi yu Pipan: Guanyu Zhongguo Shehui Kexue Zizhuxing de Zai Sikao" [A Reflection and Criticism on Intellectuals' "Correspondence" with Institutions: Rethinking the Autonomy of China's Social Science]. *Tianjin Shehui Kexue* [Tianjin Social Sciences] 6: 4–11.

Deng, Zhenglai. 2004c. "Zhishi Shengchan Jiqi de Fansi yu Pipan: Maixiang Zhongguo Xueshu Guifanhua Taolun de Di'er Jieduan" [Reflections on the Machine for Producing Knowledge: Toward a Second Stage of the Normalization of Academic Studies in China]. In *Zhongguo Xueshu Guifanhua* [The Normalization of Academic Studies in China], edited by Zhenglai Deng, 1–6. Law Press.

Deng, Zhenglai, and Yuejin Jing. 2018. "Jiangou Zhongguo de Shimin Shehui" [Constructing China's Civil Society]. In *Guojia yu Shehui: Zhongguo Shimin Shehui Yanjiu* [State and Society: Studies on China's Civil Society], edited by Zhenglai Deng, 6–28. China Legal Publishing House.

Diani, Mario. 2015. *The Cement of Civil Society: Studying Networks in Localities*. Cambridge University Press.

Dong, Yige. 2019. "Does China Have a Feminist Movement from the Left?" *Made in China Journal* 4 (1): 58–63.

Eberhardt, Christopher. 2015. "Discourse on Climate Change in China: A Public Sphere without the Public." *China Information* 29 (1): 33–59.

Elfstrom, Manfred, and Sarosh Kuruvilla. 2014. "The Changing Nature of Labor Unrest in China." *ILR Review* 67(2): 453–80.

Eliasoph, Nina. 2013. *The Politics of Volunteering*. Polity Press.

Emirbayer, Mustafa, and Ann Mische. 1998. "What is Agency?" *American Journal of Sociology* 103 (4): 962–1023.

Emirbayer, Mustafa, and Mimi Sheller. 1999. "Publics in History." *Theory and Society* 27 (28): 145–97.

Evans, Peter. 1989. "Predatory, Developmental, and Other Apparatuses: A Comparative Political Economy Perspective on the Third World State." *Sociological Forum* 4 (4): 561–87.

Fan, Yafeng. 2005. "Gongmin Weiquan yu Shehui Zhenghe" [Citizens' Rights-defending Activism and the Integration of Society]. *Aisixiang* [Philosophies]. February 16. Available from http://gongfa.net.cn/html/gongfazhuanti/minquanyuweiquan/20081112/32.html

Fang, Kecheng, and Maria Repnikova. 2018. "Demystifying 'Little Pink': The Creation and Evolution of a Gendered Label for Nationalistic Activists in China." *New Media & Society* 20 (6): 2162–85.

Fang, Zhouzi. 2005. "Fang Zhouzi zai Yunnan Daxue Yanjiang: Zhiji Weihuanbao Fanba Renshi" [Fang Zhouzi's Speech at Yunnan University: Criticizing the Pseudo Environmentalists]. *People.cn* [Renmin Wang]. April 11. http://tech.sina.com.cn/d/2005-04-11/1357577996.shtml

Ferguson, James. 2007. "Power Topographies." In *A Companion to the Anthropology of Politics*, edited by David Nugent and Joan Vincent, 383–99. Blackwell Publishing.

Fincher, Leta Hong. 2018. *Betraying Big Brother: The Feminist Awakening in China*. Verso.

Fligstein, Neil, and Doug McAdam. 2012. *A Theory of Fields*. Oxford University Press.

Franceschini, Ivan, and Elisa Nesossi. 2018. "State Repression of Labor NGOs: A Chilling Effect?" *The China Journal* (80): 111–29.

Fraser, Nancy. 1992. "Rethinking the Public Sphere: A Contribution to the Critique of Actually Existing Democracy." In *Habermas and the Public Sphere*, edited by Craig Calhoun, 109–42. MIT Press.

Friedman, Eli. 2014. *Insurgency Trap: Labor Politics in Postsocialist China*. ILR Press.

Froissart, Chloé. 2005. "The Rise of Social Movements among Migrant Workers: Uncertain Strivings for Autonomy." *China Perspectives* (61): 30–40.

Fu, Diana. 2018. *Mobilizing without the Masses: Control and Contention in China*. Cambridge University Press.

Fu, Hualing. 2018. "The July 9th (709) Crackdown on Human Rights Lawyers: Legal Advocacy in an Authoritarian State." *Journal of Contemporary China* 27 (112): 554–68.

Fu, Hualing, and Richard Cullen. 2008. "*Weiquan* (Rights Protection) Lawyering in an Authoritarian State: Building a Culture of Public-Interest Lawyering." *The China Journal* 59: 111–27.

Fu, Hualing, and Richard Cullen. 2011. "Climbing the '*Weiquan*' Ladder: A Radicalizing Process for Rights-Protection Lawyers." *The China Quarterly* 205: 40–59.

Fung, Archon, and Erik Olin Wright. 2001. "Deepening Democracy: Innovations in Empowered Participatory Governance." *Politics & Society* 29 (1): 5–41.

Gallagher, Mary E. 2006. "Mobilizing the Law in China: 'Informed Disenchantment' and the Development of Legal Consciousness." *Law & Society Review* 40 (4): 783–816.

Gallagher, Mary E., John Giles, Albert Park, and Meiyan Wang. 2015. "China's 2008 Labor Contract Law: Implementation and Implications for China's Workers." *Human Relations* 68 (2): 197–235.

Gao, Like. 2007. "Ruhe Renshi Zhuanxing Zhongguo: Guanyu Ziyou Zhuyi yu Xin Zuopai de Lunzheng" [How to Understand China in Transition? On the Debate between the Liberals and the New Left]. In *Qimeng de Ziwo Wajie: 1990 Niandai yilai Zhongguo Sixiang Wenhua Jie Zhongda Zhenglun Yanjiu* [The Self-disintegration of an Enlightenment: An Inquiry into the Significant Debates in China's Thought Sphere since the 1990s], *edited by Jilin* Xu and Gang Luo, 194–250. Jilin Publishing Group.

Ge, Mengchao, and Caizhen Wang. 2016. "Qinghuayuan lide Kexue Chuanbozhe" [The Propagator of Science at Tsinghua]. *Qinghua Xinwen* [Tsinghua News]. June 12. https://www.tsinghua.edu.cn/info/1177/23953.htm

Goldman, Merle. 2007. *From Comrade to Citizen: The Struggle for Political Rights in China.* Harvard University Press.

Gramsci, Antonio. 1971. *Selections from the Prison Notebooks.* International Publishers.

Gu, Edward, and Merle Goldman. 2004. "Introduction: The Transformation of the Relationship between Chinese Intellectuals and the State." In *Chinese Intellectuals between State and Market*, edited by Edward Gu and Merle Goldman, 1–17. Routledge.

Guan, Jun. 2020. *Silencing Chinese Media: The* Southern Weekly *Protests and the Fate of Civil Society in Xi Jinping's China.* Translated by Kevin Carrico. Rowman & Littlefield.

Guangming Daily. 2013. "Jielu: Meiguo shi Alabo zhi Chun Beihou de Tuishou" [Revelation: The United States of America Is the Promoter of the Arab Spring behind the Scenes]. Jan 10. http://theory.people.com.cn/n/2013/0110/c136457-20154891.html

Guo, Rui. 2015. "Nüquan Huodongjia Lü Ping: Renwei Kaifang Erhai Nüren Jiuhui Sheng Shi Yixiang Qingyuan" [Feminist Activist Lü Ping: It Is Just a Wishful Thinking that Women Would Be Willing to Have More Children after the Relaxation of the One Child Policy]. *Fenghuang Wang* [Ifeng News]. October 30. https://news.ifeng.com/a/20151030/46058531_0.shtml

Guo, Yuhua. 2010. "Zhimian Maodun, Chongjian Shehui" [Let's Face Conflicts and Reconstruct Society]. *Aisixiang* [Philosophies]. November 23. https://www.aisixiang.com/data/37413.html

Gustafsson, Björn, and Li Shi. 2001. "The Anatomy of Rising Earnings Inequality in Urban China." *Journal of Comparative Economics* 29 (1): 118–35.

Habermas, Jürgen. 1974. "The Public Sphere: The Encyclopedia Article." *New German Critique* 3: 49–55.

Habermas, Jürgen. 1987. *The Theory of Communicative Action: (Vol. 2) Lifeworld and System: A Critique of Functionalist Reason.* Beacon Press.

Habermas, Jürgen. 1991. *The Structural Transformation of the Public Sphere: An Inquiry into a Category of Bourgeois Society.* MIT Press.

Habermas, Jürgen. 1994. *Between Facts and Norms: Contributions to a Discourse Theory of Law and Democracy.* MIT Press.

Hale, Matthew A. 2013. "Tilling Sand: Contradictions of 'Social Economy' in a Chinese Movement for Alternative Rural Development." *Dialectical Anthropology* 37: 51–82.

Han, Jun. 2004. "Cong Nongmin dao Shimin de Bilei" [The Barricade Between Peasants and Citizens]. *Nanfang Zhoumo* [Southern Weekly]. June 17.

Han, Rongbin. 2015. "Defending the Authoritarian Regime Online: China's 'Voluntary Fifty-cent Army'." *The China Quarterly* 224: 1006–25.

Han, Xiao. 2018. "Searching for an Online Space for Feminism? The Chinese Feminist Group Gender Watch Women's Voice and Its Changing Approaches to Online Misogyny." *Feminist Media Studies* 18 (4): 734–49.

Han, Yuhai. 1998. "Zai 'Ziyou Zhuyi' Zitai de Beihou" [Behind the Stance of the Liberals]. *Tianya* [Skyline] 5: 12–18.

Han, Yuhai. 2003. "Manchang de Geming: Mao Zedong de Shehui Zhuyi" [A Long Revolution: Mao Zedong's Socialism]. In *Sichao: Zhongguo "Xin Zuopai" jiqi Yingxiang* [Surge of Thoughts: The New Left in China and Its Influence], edited by Gongyang, 157–72. Social Sciences Press.

He, Weifang. 2004. "Xianzheng Shiyexia de Renda Zhidu Gaige" [The Reform of People's Congress from the Perspective of Constitutionalism]. *Independent Chinese Pen Center*. Sep 24. Available from https://www.chinesepen.org/blog/archives/179381

He, Zengke. 1994. "Shimin Shehui Gainian de Lishi Yanbian" [The Historical Evolution of the Concept of Civil Society]. *Zhongguo Shehui Kexue* [Chinese Social Sciences] 5: 67–81.

Helmke, Gretchen, and Steven Levitsky. 2006. *Informal Institutions and Democracy: Lessons from Latin America*. Johns Hopkins University Press.

Hildebrandt, Timothy. 2011. "The Political Economy of Social Organization Registration in China." *The China Quarterly* 208: 970–89.

Hildebrandt, Timothy, and Lynette J. Chua. 2017. "Negotiating In/Visibility: The Political Economy of Lesbian Activism and Rights Advocacy." *Development and Change* 48 (4): 639–62.

Ho, Peter. 2001. "Greening without Conflict? Environmentalism, NGOs and Civil Society in China." *Development and Change* 32 (5): 893–921.

Hooper, Beverley. 2000. "Consumer Voices: Asserting Rights in Post-Mao China." *China Information* 14 (2): 92–128.

Hou, Rui. 2020. "The Commercialisation of Internet-opinion Management: How the Market Is Engaged in State Control in China." *New Media & Society* 22 (12): 2238–56.

Howell, Jude. 1996. "The Struggle for Survival: Prospects for the Women's Federation in Post-Mao China." *World Development* 24 (1): 129–43.

Howell, Jude. 2003. "Women's Organizations and Civil Society in China Making a Difference." *International Feminist Journal of Politics* 5 (2): 191–215.

Howell, Jude. 2008. "Civil Society and Migrants in China." In *Labour Migration and Social Development in Contemporary China*, edited by Rachel Murphy, 185–208. Routledge.

Howell, Jude. 2015. "Shall We Dance? Welfarist Incorporation and the Politics of State-labour NGO Relations." *The China Quarterly* 223: 702–23.

Howell, Jude. 2019. "NGOs and Civil Society: The Politics of Crafting a Civic Welfare Infrastructure in the Hu-Wen Period." *The China Quarterly* 237: 58–81.

Howell, Jude, and Jane Duckett. 2019. "Reassessing the Hu-Wen Era: A Golden Age or Lost Decade for Social Policy in China?" *The China Quarterly* 237: 1–14.

Howell, Jude, and Jenny Pearce. 2002. *Civil Society and Development: A Critical Exploration*. Lynne Rienner Publishers.

Hu, Yifan. 2004. "Zhongyang Yihao Wenjian Qiujie 'Sannong' Kunjing" [Document No. 1 of the Central Government Seeks to Solve the "Three Rural Issues"]. *Caijing* [Finance]. February 20. https://finance.sina.com.cn/g/20040220/1415640973.shtml

Huang, Futao. 2015. "Building the World-class Universities: A Case Study of China." *Higher Education* 70: 203–15.

Huang, Philip C. C. 1993. "'Public Sphere'/ 'Civil Society' in China? The Third Realm between State and Society." *Modern China* 19 (2): 216–40.

Huang, Ronggui, and Yong Gui. 2013. "Weishenme Kuaxiaoqu de Yezhu Zuzhi Lianmeng Cunzai Chayi: Yixiang Jiyu Zhili Jiegou yu Zhengzhi Jihui (Weixie) de Chengshi Bijiao Fenxi" [Why Does Homeowners' Cross-Neighborhood Organizational Coalition in Shanghai Differ from That in Guangzhou? A City-level Comparative Analysis of the Governance Structures and Political Opportunities "Threats"]. *Shehui* [The Chinese Journal of Sociology] 3(5): 88–117.

Huang, Shan, and Wanning Sun. 2021. "#MeToo in China: Transnational Feminist Politics in the Chinese Context." *Feminist Media Studies* 21 (4): 677–81.

Huang, Xiuli. 2009. "Yu Deng Yujiao An Xiangguan: Badong 37 Tian" [On the Deng Yujiao Case: The 37 Days in Badong]. *Nanfang Zhoumo* [Southern Weekly]. June 17. Available from http://www.infzm.com/contents/30225

Huang, Yanzhong. 2004. "The SARS Epidemic and Its Aftermath in China: A Political Perspective." In *Learning from SARS: Preparing for the Next Disease Outbreak: Workshop Summary*. National Academies Press. Available from https://www.ncbi.nlm.nih.gov/books/NBK92479/

Huang, Zhen. 2010. "Shuangchong Shenfen de Shidai Chong'er: 20 Shiji 80 Niandai Baogao Wenxuere de Huigu yu Sikao" [The Idol of the Day: A Review of the Reportage Literature in the 80s]. In *Qianru Shenhai: Shendu Baodao 30 Nian Muhou Guiji* [Delving into the Sea: The Trajectory of the Development of In-depth Reporting in the Past 30 Years], edited by Zhi'an Zhang, 94–107. Nanfang Daily Press.

Hughes, Christopher R., and Gudrun Wacker. 2003. *China and the Internet: Politics of the Digital Leap Forward*. Routledge.

Hui, Elaine S. 2020. "Labor-related Civil Society Actors in China: A Gramscian Analysis." *Theory and Society* (49): 49–74.

Jahiel, Abigail R. 1997. "The Contradictory Impact of Reform on Environmental Protection in China." *The China Quarterly* 149: 81–103.

Ji, Xiaocheng. 2018. "Zhongguo MeToo Da Bianlun: Bingfei Liu Yu Daozhi Silie, Liehen Yizhi Jiuzai Nali" [The Great Debate in China's MeToo Movement: It Is Not Liu Yu Who Has Created Fissures; The Fissures Have Always Been There]. *Duan Meiti* [The Initium]. August 1. https://theinitium.com/article/20180801-opinion-jixiaocheng-metoodebate/

Jin, Dacheng. 2003. *Shengji: Xinshiqi Zhuming Renwen Qikan Sumiao* [Vitality: A Description of Significant Humanity Journals in a New Era]. China Federation of Literary and Art Publishing House.

Jing, Jun. 2003. "Environmental Protests in Rural China." In *Chinese Society: Change, Conflict and Resistance*, edited by Elizabeth J. Perry and Mark Selden, 197–214. Routledge.

Jing, Li. 2008. "China's New Labor Contract Law and Protection of Workers." *Fordham International Law Journal* 32 (3): 1083–131.

Jing, Yuejin. 2000. "Ruhe Kuoda Yulun Jiandu de Kongjian: 'Jiaodian Fangtan' de Shijian yu Xinwen Gaige de Sikao" [How to Expand the Space for Supervision: The Practice of the "Focus Report" and the Reflection upon the Reform of Journalism]. *Kaifang Shidai* [Open Times] 5: 59–68.

Johnston, Alastair Iain. 2017. "Is Chinese Nationalism Rising? Evidence from Beijing." *International Security* 41 (3): 7–43.

Kang, Kai. 2010. "Jiti Xingdongshi de Yulun Jiandu: 'Zhongguo Zhiliang Wanlixing' Huodong Huigu" [A Collective Supervision by the Media: "China's Long March for Quality" in Retrospect]. In *Qianru Shenhai: Shendu Baodao 30 Nian Muhou Guiji* [Delving into the Sea: The Trajectory of the Development of In-depth Reporting in the Past 30 Years], edited by Zhi'an Zhang, 119–27. Nanfang Daily Press.

Keane, John. 1988. *Civil Society and the State: New European Perspectives.* Verso.

Kelly, David A. 1987. "The Emergence of Humanism: Wang Ruoshui and the Critique of Socialist Alienation." In *China's Intellectuals and the State: In Search of a New Relationship, edited by* Merle Goldman, Timothy Cheek, and Carol Lee Hamrin, 159–82. Harvard University Press.

Kelly, William W., and Susan Brownell. 2011. "The Olympics in East Asia: Nationalism, Regionalism, and Globalism on the Center Stage of World Sports." *Yale CEAS Occasional Publication Series.* Book 3.

King, Gary, Jennifer Pan, and Margaret E. Roberts. 2013. "How Censorship in China Allows Government Criticism but Silences Collective Expression." *American Political Science Review* 107 (2): 326–43.

Kou, Yanding. 2013. *Xingdong Gaibian Shengcun: Gaibian Women Shenghuo de Minjian Liliang* [Actions Change Survival: The Social Forces that Have Changed Our Life]. Zhejiang University Press.

Kuang, Xinnian. 2003. "Feng yu Qi: 90 Niandai de Yuedu" [Wind and Flag: Readings in the 90s]. In *Sichao: Zhongguo "Xin Zuopai" jiqi Yingxiang* [Surge of Thoughts: The New Left in China and Its Influence], edited by Gongyang, 129–41. Social Sciences Press.

Kwong, Julia. 2004. "Educating Migrant Children: Negotiations between the State and Civil Society." *The China Quarterly* 180: 1073–88.

Laclau, Ernesto. 2005. *On Populist Reason.* Verso.

Laclau, Ernesto, and Chantal Mouffe. 1985. *Hegemony and Socialist Strategy: Towards a Radical Democratic Politics.* Verso.

Lai, Weijun, and Anthony J. Spires. 2021. "Marketization and Its Discontents: Unveiling the Impacts of Foundation-led Venture Philanthropy on Grassroots NGOs in China." *The China Quarterly* 245: 72–93.

Lai, Weijun, Jiangang Zhu, Lin Tao, and Anthony J. Spires. 2015. "Bounded by the State: Government Priorities and the Development of Private Philanthropic Foundations in China." *The China Quarterly* 224: 1083–92.

Law Journalist Club. 2008. *Wei Gongzheng er Baodao* [Report for Justice]. Falü Jizhe Shalong [Law Journalist Club], Vol 1. Beijing.

Lee, Ching-Kwan. 2002. "From the Specter of Mao to the Spirit of the Law: Labor Insurgency in China." *Theory and Society* 31 (2): 189–228.

Lee, Ching-Kwan. 2007. *Against the Law: Labor Protests in China's Rustbelt and Sunbelt.* University of California Press.

Lee, Ching-Kwan. 2016. "Precarization or Empowerment? Reflections on Recent Labor Unrest in China." *The Journal of Asian Studies* 75 (2): 317–33.

Lee, Ching-Kwan, and Yuan Shen. 2009. "China: The Paradox and Possibility of a Public Sociology of Labor." *Work and Occupations* 36 (2): 110–25.

Lei, Ya-Wen. 2016. "Freeing the Press: How Field Environment Explains Critical News Reporting in China." *American Journal of Sociology* 122 (1): 1–48.

Lei, Ya-Wen. 2017. *The Contentious Public Sphere: Law, Media, and Authoritarian Rule in China.* Princeton University Press.

Lei, Ya-Wen. 2021. "Delivering Solidarity: Platform Architecture and Collective Contention in China's Platform Economy." *American Sociological Review* 86 (2): 279–309.

Lei, Ya-wen, and Daniel Xiaodan Zhou. 2015. "Contesting Legality in Authoritarian Contexts: Food Safety, Rule of Law and China's Networked Public Sphere." *Law & Society Review* 49 (3): 557–93.

Leibold, James. 2010. "The Beijing Olympics and China's Conflicted National Form." *The China Journal* 63: 1–24.

Lewis, David. 2002. "Civil Society in African Contexts: Reflections on the Usefulness of a Concept." *Development and Change* 33 (4): 569–86.

Li, Changping. 2009. *Wo Xiang Zongli Shuo Shihua* [I Tell the Truth to the Premier]. People's Publishing House, 2009.

Li, Cheng. 2003. "The 'New Deal': Politics and Policies of the Hu Administration." *Journal of Asian and African Studies* 38 (4–5): 329–46.

Li, Chunyun. 2021. "From Insurgency to Movement: An Embryonic Labor Movement Undermining Hegemony in South China." *ILR Review* 74 (4): 843–74.

Li, Haoyue C. 2019. "The Alternative Public Sphere in China: A Cultural Sociology of the 2008 Tainted Baby Milk Scandal." *Qualitative Sociology* 42 (2): 299–319.

Li, Hongbin, Junjian Yi, and Junsen Zhang. 2011. "Estimating the Effect of the One-child Policy on the Sex Ratio Imbalance in China: Identification Based on the Difference-in-differences." *Demography* 48 (4): 1535–57.

Li, Jun, and Xiaoqin Li. 2017. "Media as a Core Political Resource: The Young Feminist Movements in China." *Chinese Journal of Communication* 10 (1): 54–71.

Li, Ke, and Colin Sparks. 2018. "Chinese Newspapers and Investigative Reporting in the New Media Age." *Journalism Studies* 19 (3): 415–31.

Li, Minqi. 2003. "Du Wolesitan Ziben Zhuyi Shijie Jingji" [On Wallerstein's Capitalist World-Economy]. In *Sichao: Zhongguo "Xin Zuopai" jiqi Yingxiang* [Surge of Thoughts: The New Left in China and Its Influence], edited by Gongyang, 89–109. Social Sciences Press.

Li, Sipan. 2020. "Weibo Nüquan de Qianshi Jinsheng: Cong 'Zhengzhi Zhengque' dao 'Shangye Zhengque'" [The History of Feminist Activism on Weibo: From "Political Correctness" to "Commercial Correctness"]. *Pengpai* [The Paper]. June 16. https://www.thepaper.cn/newsDetail_forward_7854160

Li, Sipan. 2012. "Wo Weishenme Yaozai 'Daguo Kongchao' Zuozhe Yi Fuxian Xiansheng de Zhongda Jiangzuo shang Jiaoju?" [Why Did I Spoil the Lecture of Mr. Yi Fuxian, the Author of 'Big Country with Empty Nest', at the Sun Yat-sen University?] *Nüquan Youjianzu* [Email Group of Women's Rights]. June 7. https://groups.google.com/g/xmtnx/c/G086XaligcU

Li, Sipan. 2013. "Zhongguo Dalu Ziyou Zhuyi Zhe Weihe Bu Zhichi Nüquan Zhuyi?" [Why Don't the Liberals in Mainland China Support Feminism?] *Sixiang* [Reflection] 23: 175–96.

Li, Xiaotian. 2019. "The 996.ICU Movement in China: Changing Employment Relations and Labour Agency in the Tech Industry." *Made in China Journal* 4 (2): 54–59.

Li, Yao. 2019. *Playing by the Informal Rules: Why the Chinese Regime Remains Stable Despite Rising Protests*. Cambridge University Press.

Li, Ying. 2008. "Mengxiang, Jiqing, Xingdong: Beijing Daxue Faxueyuan Funü Falü Yanjiu yu Fuwu Zhongxin de Funü Quanyi Falü Yuanzhu zhi Lu" [Dream, Passion, and Action: Legal Aid at Women Law Research and Service Center at Peking University]. In *2006–2007 Nian: Zhongguo Xingbie Pingdeng yu Funü Fazhan Baogao* [2006–2007: A Report on Gender Equity and the Development of Women in China], edited by Yongping Jiang, Lin Tan, and Xiuhua Jiang, 325–28. Social Sciences Academic Press.

Li, Youmei. 2007. "Shequ Zhili: Gongmin Shehui de Weiguan Jichu" [Community Governance: The Micro-base of Civil Society]. *Shehui* [Chinese Journal of Sociology] 27 (2): 159–69.

Li, Yuan. 2012. "Yueshu Gongquanli Caineng Zouchu Shipin Beiju Shidai" [Constraining the Public Power is the Only Way to Get Out of the Tragedy of Food Safety Issues]. *Aisixiang* [Philosophies]. June 18. https://www.aisixiang.com/data/54470.html

Lian, Yue. 2003. *Lai Qu Ziyou* [Free to Come and Go]. Sichuan People's Press.

Lian, Yue. 2022. "Rensheng yu Aiguo" [Life and Patriotism]. May 4. https://posts.careeren gine.us/p/6275b61c695edf28c407b942

Liang, Congjie. 2012. "Tan Ziran zhi You" [On the Friends of Nature]. In *Zhongguo NGO Koushushi, Diyi Ji* [Oral History for NGOs in China, No. 1], edited by Ming Wang, 1–14. Social Sciences Academic Press.

Liao, Sara. 2020. "Feminism without Guarantees: Reflections on Teaching and Researching Feminist Activism in China." *Asian Journal of Women's Studies* 26 (2): 259–67.

Lin, Fen, and Dingxin Zhao. 2016. "Social Movements as a Dialogic Process: Framing, Background Expectancies, and the Dynamics of the Anti-CNN Movement." *Chinese Sociological Review* 48 (3): 185–208.

Lin, Hai. 2008. "Gailiang Zhuyi Zhe Baiju" [The Defeat of a Reformist]. *Nanfang Renwu Zhoukan* [Southern Figures Weekly]. January 22. Available from http://news.sohu.com /20080122/n254819918.shtml

Lin, Justin Yifu. 1992. "Rural Reforms and Agricultural Growth in China." *American Economic Review* 82 (1): 34–51.

Lin, Yao. 2021. "Beaconism and the Trumpian Metamorphosis of Chinese Liberal Intellectuals." *Journal of Contemporary China* 30 (127): 85–101.

Lin, Zhongxuan, and Liu Yang. 2019. "Individual and Collective Empowerment: Women's Voices in the #MeToo Movement in China." *Asian Journal of Women's Studies* 25 (1): 117–31.

Liu, Gongchang. 2008. "Nanfang Zhoumo de Qianshi Jinsheng" [The History of the Southern Weekly]. *Ershiyi Shiji, Wangluoban* [The Twenty-first Century, the Internet Version]. Available from https://www.cuhk.edu.hk/ics/21c/media/online/0810068.pdf

Liu, Hailong. 2019. *From Cyber-nationalism to Fandom Nationalism: The Case of Diba Expedition in China*. Routledge.

Liu, Jun, and Lin Li. 1989. *Xin Quanwei Zhuyi: Dui Gaige Lilun Gangling de Zhenglun* [New Authoritarianism: A Debate on the Theoretical Programs of Reform]. Beijing School of Economics Publishing House.

Liu, Junning. 1998a. "Feng Neng Jin, Yu Neng Jin, Guowang Buneng Jin" [The Storm May Enter, The Rain May Enter, But the King Cannot Enter]. In *Gonghe, Minzhu, Xianzheng* [Republics, Democracy, and Constitutionality], edited by Junning Liu, 138–62. SDX Joint Publishing Company.

Liu, Junning. 1998b. "Zhijie Minzhu yu Jianjie Minzhu: Jinyi, haishi Fanyi?" [Direct Democracy and Indirect Democracy: Synonyms or Antonyms?] In *Zhijie Minzhu yu Jianjie Minzhu* [Direct Democracy and Indirect Democracy], edited by Junning Liu. SDX Joint Publishing Company.

Liu, Mingyue, Xiaolong Feng, Sangui Wang, and Huanghuang Qiu. 2020. "China's Poverty Alleviation over the Last 40 Years: Successes and Challenges." *Australian Journal of Agricultural and Resource Economics* 64 (1): 209–28.

Liu, Qing. 2007. "Dangdai Zhongguo Zhishi Changyu yu Gonggong Lunzheng de Xingtai Tezheng" [The Knowledge Field in Contemporary China and the Characters of Public Debate]. In *Qimeng de Ziwo Wajie: 1990 Niandai yilai Zhongguo Sixiang Wenhua Jie Zhongda Zhenglun Yanjiu* [The Self-disintegration of an Enlightenment: An Inquiry into the Significant Debates in China's Thought Sphere since the 1990s], edited by Jilin Xu and Gang Luo, 251–79. Jilin Publishing Group.

Liu, Qing, and Barrett McCormick. 2011. "The Media and the Public Sphere in Contemporary China." *Boundary 2* 38 (1): 101–34.

Liu, Sida, and Terrence C. Halliday. 2011. "Political Liberalism and Political Embeddedness: Understanding Politics in the Work of Chinese Criminal Defense Lawyers." *Law & Society Review* 45 (4): 831–65.

Liu, Tao. 2017. "Cong 'Canyushi Fazhan' dao 'Gongyi Shichanghua': Zhongguo NGO Changyu de Fanshi Zhuanxing" [From "Participatory Development" to "Commercialization of Philanthropy": The Transformation of the Paradigms in China's NGO Sphere]. *Fazhan Guancha* [Development Observer]. October 17. Available from https://mp.weixin.qq.com/s/CiQeN481zy_31ztVce40pQ

Liu, Weiwei. 2017. *Zhengce Zhongjie de Duoyuanliu Fenxi: Jiyu Shourong Qiansong Zhidu de Jingyan Yanjiu* [Multiple Streams Analysis of Policy Termination: Empirical Study of the Custody and Repatriation System]. Law Press.

Liu, Yangshuo. 2014. "Zaijian Baoer: Zuofang he Tade Nanfang Zhoumo Shidai" [Goodbye Paul: Zuofang and His Time at the *Southern Weekly*], August 17. Available from https://news.qq.com/rain/a/20240926A018DX00

Liu, Yu. 2009. *Minzhu de Xijie: Meiguo Dangdai Zhengzhi Guancha Suibi* [The Details of Democracy: Essays on Contemporary American Democracy]. SDX Joint Publishing Company.

Liu, Yu. 2018. "Guanyu MeToo" [On MeToo]. July 27. https://2newcenturynet.blogspot.com/2018/07/metoo.html

Liu, Zhiming. 2018. "Kuoqing Xifang Gongmin Shehui Lilun Miwu" [A Clarification of the Western Concept of Civil Society]. *Guangming Daily* [Guangming Ribao]. Jan 29. Available from https://epaper.gmw.cn/gmrb/html/2018-01/29/nw.D110000gmrb_201 80129_3-11.htm

Long, Yan. 2018. "The Contradictory Impact of Transnational AIDS Institutions on State Repression in China, 1989–2013." *American Journal of Sociology* 124 (2): 309–66.

Lü, Pin. 2015. "Xingbie Geming Buhuishi Tanhua Yixian" [Gender Revolution Will Last Long]. *Nüquan zhi Sheng* [Feminist Voices]. January 19. https://www.163.com/lady/ar ticle/AGB7BJK100264NDR.html

Lü, Tu. 2013. *Zhongguo Xin Gongren* [New Workers in China]. The Law Press.

Lu, Xuan. 2019. "Shehui Zuzhi Zhijie Dengji Zhengce de Qianshi Jinsheng." [The History of the Policies That Allow Social Organizations to Directly Register]. *Pengpai* [The Paper]. March 20. https://www.sohu.com/a/302665406_260616

Lu, Ye, and Zhongdang Pan. 2002. "Chengming de Xiangxiang: Zhongguo Shehui Zhuanxing Guochengzhong Xinwen Congyezhe de Zhuanye Zhuyi Huayu Jiangou" [Imagining Professional Fame: Constructing Journalistic Professionalism in China's Social Transformation]. *Xinwenxue Yanjiu* [Mass Communication Research] 71: 17–59.

Luo, Shihong. 2016. "'Huangjin Shidai' de Zhongjie: Zhongguo Dalu Chuantong Shichanghua Meiti Xingshuai yu Xinwen Lixiang Shijian de Lingpi Xijing" [The End of a "Golden Era": The Rise and Fall of the Marketized Press and Possible Way-outs of Investigative Journalism in China]. *Nanhua Shehui Kexue Luncong* [Nanhua Journal of Social Sciences] 2: 3–27.

Ma, Qiusha. 2002. "The Governance of NGOs in China since 1978: How Much Autonomy?" *Nonprofit and Voluntary Sector Quarterly* 31 (3): 305–28.

Ma, Shu-yun. 1994. "The Chinese Discourse on Civil Society." *The China Quarterly* 137: 180–93.

MacKinnon, Rebecca. 2009. "China's Censorship 2.0: How Companies Censor Bloggers" *First Monday* 14 (2).

Mamdani, Mahmood. 1996. *Citizen and Subject: Contemporary Africa and the Legacy of Late Colonialism*. Princeton University Press.

Mann, Michael. 1986. *The Sources of Social Power: Volume 1, A History of Power from the Beginning to AD 1760*. Cambridge University Press.

Mattingly, Daniel C. 2020. *The Art of Political Control in China*. Cambridge University Press.

McQuarrie, Michael. 2013. "Community Organizations in the Foreclosure Crisis: The Failure of Neoliberal Civil Society." *Politics & Society* 41 (1): 73–101.

Medvetz, Thomas. 2012. *Think Tanks in America*. University of Chicago Press.

Merle, Aurore. 2014. "Homeowners of Beijing, Unite! The Construction of a Collective Mobilisation." *China Perspectives* 118 (6): 7–15.

Migdal, Joel S. 1994. "The State in Society: An Approach to Struggles for Domination." In *State Power and Social Forces, edited by Joel S*. Migdal, Atul Kohli, and Vivienne Shue, 7–34. Cambridge University Press.

Migdal, Joel S. 2001. *State-in-society: Studying How States and Societies Transform and Constitute One Another*. Cambridge University Press.

Ministry of Civil Affairs. 2018. "Shehui Zuzhi Xinyong Xinxi Guanli Banfa" [The Regulation on Managing the Credit Information of Social Organizations]. The Ministry of Civil Affairs of People's Republic of China.

Mische, Ann. 2008. *Partisan Publics: Communication and Contention across Brazilian Youth Activist Networks*. Princeton University Press.

Morrill, Calvin. 2017. "Institutional Change through Interstitial Emergence: The Growth of Alternative Dispute Resolution in U.S. law, 1970–2000." *Brazilian Journal of Empirical Legal Studies* 4 (1): 10–36.

Neilson, Brett, and Ned Rossiter. 2008. "Precarity as a Political Concept, or, Fordism as Exception." *Theory, Culture & Society* 25 (7–8): 51–72.

NGOCN. 2020. "Lixiang Zhuyi Shiwu Nian" [The Fifteen Years for Idealism]. Available from https://tsb2blog.com/what-is-ngocn

O'Brien, Kevin J., and Lianjiang Li. 1995. "The Politics of Lodging Complaints in Rural China." *The China Quarterly* 143: 756–83.

O'Brien, Kevin J., and Lianjiang Li. 2006. Rightful Resistance in Rural China. Cambridge University Press.

Ogden, Suzanne. 2002. *Inklings of Democracy in China*. Harvard University Press.

Ong, Lynette H. 2018. "Thugs and Outsourcing of State Repression in China." *The China Journal* 80: 94–110.

Ong, Lynette H. 2022. *Outsourcing Repression: Everyday State Power in Contemporary China*. Oxford University Press.

Open Constitution Initiative. 2009. "Zangqu 3.14 Shijian Sehui Jingji Chengyin Diaocha Baogao" [An Investigative Report on the Social and Economic Causes of the 3.14 Incident in Tibet]. *Independent Chinese PEN Center*. March 14. Available from https://www.chinesepen.org/blog/archives/98398

Ortmann, Stephan. 2015. "The Umbrella Movement and Hong Kong's Protracted Democratization Process." *Asian Affairs* 46 (1): 32–50.

Oxfam Hong Kong. 2014. *Qinian Tansuolu: Leshihui Zhongguo Xiangmu Jingyan Zongjie, 2006–2013* [Seven Years of Exploration: A Summary of Oxfam Hong Kong's China Projects, 2006–2013]. Beijing.

Pacewicz, Josh. 2016. *Partisans and Partners: The Politics of the Post-Keynesian Society*. University of Chicago Press.

Pan, Jennifer. 2017. "How Market Dynamics of Domestic and Foreign Social Media Firms Shape Strategies of Internet Censorship." *Problems of Post-Communism* 64 (3–4): 167–88.

Pan, Jia'en. 2012. *Ziwo Baohu yu Linglei Shijian: Shuangxiang Yundong Shiyexia de Zhongguo Xiangcun Jianshe*. [Self-protection and Alternative Practices: The Double Movement and China's Rural Construction]. Dissertation submitted to the Department of Cultural Studies, Lingnan University.

Pan, Jia'en, and Jie Du. 2011. "Xiandai Meng de Bieyang Huisheng: Xiangcun Jianshe de Ziyuan yu Maodun" [An Alternative Response to the Dream of Modernity: The Resources for Rural Construction and the Movement's Contradiction]. *Kaifang Shidai* [Open Times] 3: 70–83.

Peerenboom, Randall. 2003. "A Government of Laws: Democracy, Rule of Law and Administrative Law Reform in the PRC." *Journal of Contemporary China* 12 (34): 45–67.

Perry, Elizabeth J. 1994. "Trends in the Study of Chinese Politics: State-Society Relations." *The China Quarterly* 139: 704–13.

Perry, Elizabeth J. 2008. "Chinese Conceptions of 'Rights': From Mencius to Mao—and Now." *Perspectives on Politics* 6 (1): 37–50.

Perry, Elizabeth J. 2009. "China since Tiananmen: A New Rights Consciousness?" *Journal of Democracy* 20 (3): 17–24.

Pils, Eva. 2017. "From Independent Lawyer Groups to Civic Opposition: The Case of China's New Citizen Movement." *APLPJ* 19: 110.

Pils, Eva. 2015. *China's Human Rights Lawyers: Advocacy and Resistance*. Routledge.

Powers, Diana S. 2016. "'Under the Dome' on Chinese Air Pollution, a Documentary by Chai Jing." *Journal of Public Health Policy* 37 (1): 98–106.

Pringle, Tim, and Quan Meng. 2018. "Taming Labor: Workers' Struggles, Workplace Unionism, and Collective Bargaining on a Chinese Waterfront." *ILR Review* 71 (5): 1053–77.

Pun, Ngai, and Huilin Lu. 2010. "Unfinished Proletarianization: Self, Anger, and Class Action among the Second Generation of Peasant-Workers in Present-day China." *Modern China* 36 (5): 493–519.

Pun, Ngai, Yuan Shen, Yuhua Guo, Huilin Lu, Jenny Chan, and Mark Selden. 2014. "Worker-intellectual Unity: Trans-border Sociological Intervention in Foxconn." *Current Sociology* 62 (2): 209–22.

Putnam, Robert D., Robert Leonardi, and Raffaella Y. Nanetti. 1994. *Making Democracy Work: Civic Traditions in Modern Italy*. Princeton University Press.

Qian, Gang. 2008. *Zhongguo Chuanmei yu Zhengzhi Gaige* [The Chinese Media and the Political Reform]. Cosmos Books.

Qian, Gang, and David Bandurski. 2011. "China's Emerging Public Sphere: The Impact of Media Commercialization, Professionalism, and the Internet in an Era of Transition." In *Changing Media, Changing China*, edited by Susan L. Shirk, 38–76. Oxford University Press.

Qin, Hui. 2001. "Zhuangui Jingjixue zhong de Gongzheng Wenti" [On the Issue of Justice in the Economics of Transition]. *Zhanlüe yu Guanli* [Strategy and Management] 2: 47–53.

Qiu, Feng. 2003. "Xin Minquan Xingdong Nian" [A Year of New Civil Rights Movement]. *Xinwen Zhoukan* [News Week]. December 18. Available from http://news.sina.com.cn/c/2003-12-18/15172408126.html

Qiu, Feng. 2012. "Lisu Youxian yu Quanli" [Etiquette Goes before Right]. *Nanfang Dushi Bao* [Southern Metropolis Daily]. June 27. https://www.aisixiang.com/data/54877.html

Qiu, Jack Linchuan. 2009. *Working-Class Network Society: Communication Technology and the Information Have-less in Urban China*. MIT Press.

Rao, Hayagreeva, Calvin Morrill, and Mayer N. Zald. 2000. "Power Plays: How Social Movements and Collective Action Create New Organizational Forms." *Research in Organizational Behavior* 22: 237–81.

Rawls, John. 1995. "Political Liberalism: Reply to Habermas." *The Journal of Philosophy* 92 (3): 132–80.

Read, Benjamin. 2000. "Revitalizing the State's Urban 'Nerve Tips.'" *The China Quarterly* 163: 806–20.

Read, Benjamin. 2003. "Democratizing the Neighbourhood? New Private Housing and Home-Owner Self-Organization in Urban China." *The China Journal* 49: 31–59.

Rodríguez-Muñiz, Michael. 2017. "Cultivating Consent: Nonstate Leaders and the Orchestration of State Legibility." *American Journal of Sociology* 123 (2): 385–425.

Rowe, William T. 1989. *Hankow: Conflict and Community in a Chinese City, 1796–1895.* Vol. 2. Stanford University Press.

Rowe, William T. 1984. *Hankow: Commerce and Society in a Chinese City, 1796–1889.* Vol. 1. Stanford University Press.

Saich, Tony. 2000. "Negotiating the State: The Development of Social Organizations in China." *The China Quarterly* 161, 124–41.

Salamon, Lester M., and Helmut K. Anheier. 1996. *The Emerging Nonprofit Sector: An Overview.* Manchester University Press.

Scharping, Thomas. 2019. "Abolishing the One-child Policy: Stages, Issues and the Political Process." *Journal of Contemporary China* 28 (117): 327–47.

Scott, James C. 1998. *Seeing Like a State.* Yale University Press.

Sewell, William H., Jr. 1992. "A Theory of Structure: Duality, Agency, and Transformation." *American Journal of Sociology* 98 (1): 1–29.

Shen, Yongdong, and Jianxing Yu. 2017. "Local Government and NGOs in China: Performance-based Collaboration." *China: An International Journal* 15 (2): 177–91.

Shen, Yongdong, Jianxing Yu, and Jun Zhou. 2020. "The Administration's Retreat and the Party's Advance in the New Era of Xi Jinping: The Politics of the Ruling Party, the Government, and Associations in China." *Journal of Chinese Political Science* 25: 71–88.

Shen, Yuan. 2007a. "Shehui de Shengchan" [Producing Society]. *Shehui* [Chinese Journal of Sociology] 27 (2): 170–91.

Shen, Yuan. 2007b. *Gonggong Shehuixue* [Public Sociology]. Social Sciences Academic Press.

Shen, Yuan. 2007c. *Shichang, Jieji yu Shehui: Zhuanxing Shehuixue de Guanjian Yiti* [Market, Class and Society: Critical Issues in the Sociology of Transition]. Social Sciences Academic Press.

Shen, Yuan. 2020. "Laogong Shehuixue Sanshi Nian" [The Development of China's Labor Sociology in the Past 30 Years]. *Shehuixue Pinglun* [Sociological Review of China] 8 (5): 3–17.

Shi, Liyue. 2010. "Xinwen Diaocha: Zhuiwen yu Ziwen" [News Probe: A Reflexive Review]. In *Qianru Shenhai: Shendu Baodao 30 Nian Muhou Guiji* [Delving into the Sea: The Trajectory of the Development of In-depth Reporting in the Past 30 Years], edited by Zhi'an Zhang, 181–94. Nanfang Daily Press.

Shi, Yan, Cunwang Cheng, Peng Lei, Tiejun Wen, and Caroline Merrifield. 2011. "Safe Food, Green Food, Good Food: Chinese Community Supported Agriculture and the Rising Middle Class." *International Journal of Agricultural Sustainability* 9 (4): 551–58.

Shieh, Shawn. 2017. "Same Bed, Different Dreams? The Divergent Pathways of Foundations and Grassroots NGOs in China." *VOLUNTAS: International Journal of Voluntary and Nonprofit Organizations* 28: 1785–1811.

Shieh, Shawn, and Guosheng Deng. 2011. "An Emerging Civil Society: The Impact of the 2008 Sichuan Earthquake on Grass-roots Associations in China." *The China Journal* 65: 181–94.

Shirk, Susan L. 2011. "Changing Media, Changing China." In *Changing Media, Changing China*, edited by Susan L. Shirk, 1–37. Oxford University Press.

Si, Zhenzhong, and Steffanie Scott. 2016. "The Convergence of Alternative Food Networks within 'Rural Development' Initiatives: The Case of the New Rural Reconstruction Movement in China." *Local Environment* 21 (9): 1082–99.

Sima, Yangzi. 2011. "Grassroots Environmental Activism and the Internet: Constructing a Green Public Sphere in China." *Asian Studies Review* 35 (4): 477–97.

Smith, Chris, and Ngai Pun. 2018. "Class and Precarity: An Unhappy Coupling in China's Working Class Formation." *Work, Employment and Society* 32 (3): 599–615.

Snow, David A., and Robert D. Benford. 1988. "Ideology, Frame Resonance, and Participant Mobilization." *International Social Movement Research* 1 (1): 197–217.

Snow, David A., E. Burke Rochford Jr., Steven K. Worden, and Robert D. Benford. 1986. "Frame Alignment Processes, Micromobilization, and Movement Participation." *American Sociological Review* 51: 464–81.

Social Development Commission. 2010. "Zenme Chongjian Shehui" [How to Reconstruct Society]. Department of Sociology, Tsinghua University. *Nanfang Zhoumo* [Southern Weekly]. September 16.

Solinger, Dorothy J. 1999. *Contesting Citizenship in Urban China: Peasant Migrants, the State, and the Logic of the Market*. University of California Press.

Somers, Margaret R. 1993. "Citizenship and the Place of the Public Sphere: Law, Community, and Political Culture in the Transition to Democracy." *American Sociological Review* 58 (5): 587–620.

Somers, Margaret R. 2008. *Genealogies of Citizenship: Markets, Statelessness, and the Right to Have Rights*. Cambridge University Press.

Southern Weekly. 2000. "Yinwei Women Shi Jizhe" [Because We Are Journalists]. November 9.

Southern Weekly. 2003. "Zhongguo Meiti: Zeren yu Fangxiang" [Chinese Media: Responsibility and Direction]. February 28.

Sparks, Colin, Haiyan Wang, Yu Huang, Yanhua Zhao, Nan Lü, and Dan Wang. 2016. "The Impact of Digital Media on Newspapers: Comparing Responses in China and the United States." *Global Media and China* 1 (3): 186–207.

Spires, Anthony J. 2011. "Contingent Symbiosis and Civil Society in an Authoritarian State: Understanding the Survival of China's Grassroots NGOs." *American Journal of Sociology* 117 (1): 1–45.

Spires, Anthony J. 2020. "Regulation as Political Control: China's First Charity Law and Its Implications for Civil Society." *Nonprofit and Voluntary Sector Quarterly* 49 (3): 571–88.

State Council. 2009. Weishengbu Lixing Xinwen Fabuhui [The Routine Press Conference of the Department of Health]. January 13. http://www.scio.gov.cn/xwfbh/gbwxwfbh/fbh/Document/311421/311421.htm

Steinhardt, H. Christoph, and Fengshi Wu. 2016. "In the Name of the Public: Environmental Protest and the Changing Landscape of Popular Contention in China." *The China Journal* 75: 61–82.

Stern, Rachel E. 2013. *Environmental Litigation in China: A Study in Political Ambivalence*. Cambridge University Press.

Stewart, Evan, and Douglas Hartmann. 2020. "The New Structural Transformation of the Public Sphere." *Sociological Theory* 38 (2): 170–91.

Stockmann, Daniela. 2013. *Media Commercialization and Authoritarian Rule in China.* Cambridge University Press.

Strand, David. 1990. "Protest in Beijing: Civil Society and Public Sphere in China." *Problems of Communism* 39: 1–19.

Sullivan, Jonathan. 2012. "A Tale of Two Microblogs in China." *Media, Culture & Society* 34 (6): 773–83.

Sullivan, Jonathan, and Lei Xie. 2009. "Environmental Activism, Social Networks and the Internet." *The China Quarterly* 198: 422–32.

Sullivan, Lawrence R. 1990. "The Emergence of Civil Society in China, Spring 1989." In *The Chinese People's Movement: Perspectives on Spring 1989,* edited by Tony Saich, 126–44. M. E. Sharpe.

Sun, Jinyu. 2018. "Zhengzhi Zhengque 'Shasi' Yanlun Ziyou: Zhenshi Youlü haishi Huashu Xianjing?" [Political Correctness "Kills" the Freedom of Speech: A Real Concern or a Discourse Trap?] *Sixiang* [Thoughts] 35: 115–32.

Sun, Liping. 1994. "Chongjian Xingbie Juese Guanxi" [Reconstructing Gender Roles]. *Shehuixue Yanjiu* [Sociological Studies] 6: 65–68.

Sun, Yanfei, and Dingxin Zhao. 2008. "Environmental Campaigns." In *Popular Protest in China, edited by* Kevin J. O'Brien, 144–62. Harvard University Press.

Svensson, Marina. 2014. "Voice, Power and Connectivity in China's Microblogosphere: Digital Divides on SinaWeibo." *China Information* 28 (2): 168–88.

Tan, Chris KK, Jie Wang, Shengyuan Wangzhu, Jinjing Xu, and Chunxuan Zhu. 2020. "The Real Digital Housewives of China's *Kuaishou* Video-sharing and Live-Streaming App." *Media, Culture & Society* 42 (7–8): 1243–59.

Tan, K. Cohen, and Shuxin Cheng. 2020. "*Sang* Subculture in Post-reform China." *Global Media and China* 5 (1): 86–99.

Teets, Jessica C. 2015. "The Evolution of Civil Society in Yunnan Province: Contending Models of Civil Society Management in China." *Journal of Contemporary China* 24 (91): 158–75.

Teets, Jessica C. 2009. "Post-earthquake Relief and Reconstruction Efforts: The Emergence of Civil Society in China?" *The China Quarterly* 198: 330–47.

Teets, Jessica C. 2013. "Let Many Civil Societies Bloom: The Rise of Consultative Authoritarianism in China." *The China Quarterly* 213: 19–38.

Teets, Jessica C. 2014. *Civil Society under Authoritarianism: The China Model.* Cambridge University Press.

Teng, Biao. 2010. "Gongmin Weiquan yu Shehui Zhuanxing" [Rights-defending Actions and Social Transition]. *Zhongguo Renquan Shuangzhoukan* [China Human Rights Biweekly]. Available from https://tengbiao.wordpress.com/2020/08/30/%E5%85%AC %E6%B0%91%E7%BB%B4%E6%9D%83%E4%B8%8E%E7%A4%BE%E4%BC%9A%E8 %BD%AC%E5%9E%8B-%E5%9C%A8%E5%8C%97%E4%BA%AC%E4%BC%A0%E7 %9F%A5%E8%A1%8C%E7%A4%BE%E4%BC%9A%E7%BB%8F%E6%B5%8E%E7%A0 %94/

Teng, Biao. 2019. "Zhongguo Weiquan Yundong de Qiqi Luoluo" [The Rise and Fall of the Rights-defending Movement in China]. Radio Free Asia. April 22. Available from https://www.rfa.org/mandarin/duomeiti/guandian/gd-04222019111314.html

Tong, Jingrong. 2019. "The Taming of Critical Journalism in China: A Combination of Political, Economic and Technological Forces." *Journalism Studies* 20 (1): 79–96.

Tong, Zhihui, and Tiejun Wen. 2009. "Ziben he Bumen Xiaxiang yu Xiaononghu Jingji de Zuzhihua Daolu—Jiandui Zhuanyehua Hezuo Daolu Tichu Zhiyi" [Transference of Capital and Departments to Rural Areas and the Organizational Path of Small Farming Household Economy—Concurrently Questioning the Path of Specialized Cooperatives]. *Kaifang Shidai* [Open Times] 4: 5–26.

Unger, Jonathan. 2008. *Associations and the Chinese State: Contested Spaces*. M. E. Sharpe.

Unger, Jonathan, and Anita Chan. 1995. "China, Corporatism, and the East Asian Model." *The Australian Journal of Chinese Affairs* 33: 29–53.

University Research Team on Foxconn. 2010. *"Liang'an Sandi" Gaoxiao Fushikang Diaoyan Zongbaogao* [A Research Report on Foxconn Conducted by University Students from China, Hong Kong, and Taiwan]. October 9. https://tech.sina.cn/it/2010-10-09/detail -ichmifpy4588808.d.html?from=wap

Veg, Sebastian. 2019. *Minjian: The Rise of China's Grassroots Intellectuals*. Columbia University Press.

Veg, Sebastian, and Edmund W. Cheng. 2021. "Alternative Publications, Spaces and Publics: Revisiting the Public Sphere in 20th- and 21st-Century China." *The China Quarterly* 246: 317–30.

Wagner, Rudolf G. 1987. "The Chinese Writer in His Own Mirror: Writer, State, and Society—The Literary Evidence." In *China's Intellectuals and the State: In Search of a New Relationship*, edited by Merle Goldman, Timothy Cheek, and Carol Lee Hamrin, 183–248. Harvard University Press.

Wakeman, Frederic, Jr. 1993. "The Civil Society and Public Sphere Debate: Western Reflections on Chinese Political Culture." *Modern China* 19 (2): 108–38.

Wallis, Cara. 2015. "Gender and China's Online Censorship Protest Culture." *Feminist Media Studies* 15 (2): 223–38.

Wang, Di. 1996. "Wanqing Changjiang Shangyou Diqu Gonggong Lingyu de Fazhan" [The Development of the Public Sphere at the Upper Reaches of the Yangtze River in Late Qing Dynasty]. *Lishi Yanjiu* [Historical Studies] 1: 5–16.

Wang, Di. 2003. *Street Culture in Chengdu: Public Space, Urban Commoners, and Local Politics, 1870–1930*. Stanford University Press.

Wang, Dingding. 1999. "Qimeng Sile, Qimeng Wansui! Ping Wanghui guanyu 'Zhongguo Wenti' de Xushuo" [The Enlightenment is Dead. Long Live the Enlightenment! On Wang Hui's Analysis of "China Problems"]. *Zhanlüe yu Guanli* [Strategy and Management] 1: 68–83.

Wang, Dingding. 2000a. "Guanyu Fubai de Jingjixue Fenxi" [An Economic Analysis on Corruption]. *Zhanlüe yu Guanli* [Strategy and Management] 6: 112–15.

Wang, Dingding. 2000b. "Lun Gongmin Shehui yu 'Ziben Zhuyi' Shizhi" [On Civil Society and the Essence of "Capitalism"]. In *90 Niandai Sixiang Wenxuan, Di Er Juan* [Selected Readings of Thoughts in the 90s, Vol. 2], edited by Gang Luo and Wenjian Ni, 101–24. Guangxi People's Publishing House.

Wang, Hui. 2000. "Xiaoxiao Shinian: Ershiyi Shiji yu Xueren" [A Short Decade: The Twenty-first Century and the Scholars]. *Ershiyi Shiji* [Twenty-first Century] 61: 142–47.

Wang, Hui. 2008a. "Dangdai Zhongguo de Sixiang Zhuangkuang yu Xiandaixing Wenti" [The Condition of Thought and the Question of Modernity in Contemporary China]. In *Qu Zhengzhihua de Zhengzhi: Duan 20 Shiji de Zhongjie yu 90 Niandai* [The Depoliticized Politics: The End of the Short 20th Century and the 90s], 58–97. SDX Joint Publishing Company.

Wang, Hui. 2008b. "Qu Zhengzhihua de Zhengzhi, Baquan de Duochong Goucheng yu 60 Niandai de Xiaoshi" [Depoliticized Politics, the Multiple Structure of Hegemony, and the Waning of the 60s]. In *Qu Zhengzhihua de Zhengzhi: Duan 20 Shiji de Zhongjie yu 90 Niandai* [The Depoliticized Politics: The End of the Short 20th Century and the 90s], 1–57. SDX Joint Publishing Company.

Wang, Hui. 2013. "Daoyan" [Preface]. In *Zhongguo Xingongren: Mishi yu Jueqi* [Chinese New Working Class: Getting Lost and Rise], edited by Tu Lü, 1–12. Law Press.

Wang, Hui, and Yangu Chen. 1998. *Wenhua yu Gonggongxing* [Culture and Publicity]. SDX Joint Publishing Company.

Wang, Qi. 2021. "From 'Non-governmental Organizing' to 'Outer-system'—Feminism and Feminist Resistance in Post-2000 China." In *Gender and Generation in China Today, edited by Harriet Bjerrum* Nielsen, 5–22. Routledge.

Wang, Shaoguang. 1991. "Guanyu 'Shimin Shehui' de Jidian Sikao" [Some Thoughts on "Civil Society"]. *Ershiyi Shiji* [Twenty-first Century] 8: 102–14.

Wang, Shaoguang. 1997. "China's 1994 Fiscal Reform: An Initial Assessment." *Asian Survey* 37 (9): 810–17.

Wang, Shaoguang. 2014. "Shehui Jianshe de Fangxiang: 'Gongmin Shehui' haishi Renmin Shehui" ["Civil Society" or People's Society]. *Kaifang Shidai* [Open Times] 6: 26–48.

Wang, Shaoguang, and Angang Hu. 1994. "Zhongguo Zhengfu Jiqu Nengli de Xiajiang jiqi Houguo" [The Decline of China's State Capacity and Its Consequence]. *Ershiyi Shiji* [The Twenty-first Century] 21: 5–14.

Wang, Ying, and Nick Clarke. 2021. "Four Modes of Neighbourhood Governance: The View from Nanjing, China." *International Journal of Urban and Regional Research* 45 (3): 535–54.

Wang, Yongchen, and Aijun Wang. 2012. *Shouwang: Zhongguo Huanbao NGO Meiti Diaocha* [A Media Research on Environmental NGOs in China]. China Environmental Science Press.

Wang, Yongchen, and Zhihong Xiong. 2009. *Guanzhu: Huanjing Jizhe Shalong* [Attention: Environmental Journalists' Salon]. SDX Joint Publishing Company.

Wang, Zheng. 1997. "Maoism, Feminism, and the UN Conference on Women: Women's Studies Research in Contemporary China." *Journal of Women's History* 8 (4): 126–52.

Wang, Zheng. 2005. "'State Feminism'? Gender and Socialist State Formation in Maoist China." *Feminist Studies* 31 (3): 519–51.

Wang, Zheng. 2018. "Feminist Struggles in a Changing China." In *Women's Movements in the Global Era: The Power of Local Feminisms, edited by Amrita* Basu, 155–81. Routledge.

Wang, Zheng, and Ying Zhang. 2010. "Global Concepts, Local Practices: Chinese Feminism since the Fourth UN Conference on Women." *Feminist Studies* 36 (1): 40–70.

Wang, Zhengxu, Long Sun, Liuqing Xu, and Dragan Pavlićević. 2013. "Leadership in China's Urban Middle Class Protest: The Movement to Protect Homeowners' Rights in Beijing." *The China Quarterly* 214: 411–31.

Watson, Andrew. 2012. "Tan Fute Jijinhui" [On the Ford Foundation]. In *Zhongguo NGO Koushushi, Diyi Ji* [Oral History for NGOs in China, No. 1], 123–38. Social Sciences Academic Press.

Wedeman, Andrew. 2017. "Xi Jinping's Tiger Hunt: Anti-corruption Campaign or Factional Purge?" *Modern China Studies* 24 (2): 35–94.

Wen, Tiejun. 2005. "Nongcun Ban Ji" [In Memory of the Rural Edition]. *Aisixiang* [Philosophy]. Jan 2. https://www.aisixiang.com/data/5186.html

Wen, Tiejun. 2006. "Shipin Anquan Wenti Beihou de Wuran Wenti" [The Pollution Issue behind the Food Safety Issue]. *Wenhui Bao* [Wenhui Daily]. December 1. http://news.sohu.com/20061201/n246728523.shtml

Wen, Tiejun. 2007. *Sannong Wenti yu Shiji Fansi* [The Three Rural Problems and the Centenary Reflection]. SDX Joint Publishing Company.

Wen, Tiejun. 2016. "*Gaobie Bainian Jijin: Wen Tiejun Yanjianglu*" [Farewell to the Radicalness in the Past Century: Volume of Wen Tiejun's Speeches]. Orient Press.

Wen, Tiejun. 2020. "*Quanqiuhua yu Guojia Jingzheng: Xinxing Qiguo Bijiao Yanjiu* [Globalization and International Competitions: A Comparative Study on Seven Newly Developed Countries]. Orient Press.

Wen, Tiejun, Shaoxiong Liang, and Liang Liu. 2020. *Xiangjian Biji: Xin Qingnian yu Xiangcun de Shengming Duihua* [Rural Construction Notebook: Living Dialogues between New Youths and Villages]. Orient Press.

West, Loraine A., and Christine P. W. Wong. 1995. "Fiscal Decentralization and Growing Regional Disparities in Rural China: Some Evidence in the Provision of Social Services." *Oxford Review of Economic Policy* 11 (4): 70–84.

Wong, Siu Wai. 2015. "Urbanization as a Process of State Building: Local Governance Reforms in China." *International Journal of Urban and Regional Research* 39 (5): 912–26.

Wright, Teresa. 2002. "The China Democracy Party and the Politics of Protest in the 1980s–1990s." *The China Quarterly* 172: 906–26.

Wu, Angela Xiao, and Yige Dong. 2019. "What Is Made-in-China Feminism(s)? Gender Discontent and Class Friction in Post-socialist China." *Critical Asian Studies* 51 (4): 471–92.

Wu, Fengshi. 2003. "Environmental GONGO Autonomy: Unintended Consequences of State Strategies in China." *The Good Society* 12 (1): 35–45.

Wu, Fengshi, and Ellie Martus. 2021. "Contested Environmentalism: The Politics of Waste in China and Russia." *Environmental Politics* 30 (4): 493–512.

Wu, Fulong. 2018. "Housing Privatization and the Return of the State: Changing Governance in China." *Urban Geography* 39 (8): 1177–94.

Wu, Guanjun. 2007. "Dangdai Zhongguo Sixiang Zhuangkuang de Huayu Fenxi: Yi 'Ziyou Zhuyi' yu 'Xin Zuopai' de Zhuzhong Fuhao Douzheng Weili" [A Discourse Analysis of the Condition of Thought Sphere in Contemporary China: Symbolic Struggles between the Liberals and the New Left]. In *Qimeng de Ziwo Wajie: 1990 Niandai yilai Zhongguo Sixiang Wenhua Jie Zhongda Zhenglun Yanjiu* [The Self-disintegration of an Enlightenment: An Inquiry into the Significant Debates in China's Thought Sphere since the 1990s], edited by Jilin Xu and Gang Luo, 280–324. Jilin Publishing Group.

Wu, Jing. 2015. "Ci'er de Shengyin Bujian le? Zhongguo Diaocha Baodao de Dongtian" [The Disappearance of Harsh Sound? The Winter of Investigative Journalism in China]. *Duan Meiti* [Initium Media]. August 14. https://theinitium.com/article/20150814 -china-investigative-reporting-two/

Wu, Qing. 2014. "Tan 'Nongjianü' ji Renshengshi" [On Rural Women Knowing All and My Life Story]. In *Zhongguo NGO Koushushi, Di'er Ji* [Oral History for NGOs in China, No. 2], edited by Ming Wang, 148–80. Social Sciences Academic Press.

Wu, Wei. 2008. "Xizang Wenti: Women Xuyao de Shi Lixing de Sikao" [Tibetan Problems: What We Need is Rational Thinking]. *Aisixiang* [Philosophies]. October 29. https:// www.aisixiang.com/data/21754.html

Xi, An. 2019. "Hou Lengzhan Niandai de Bajiu Liusi" [The June 4th in the Post Cold War Years]. *Wanyou Yinli zhi Chong* [Gravity's Warm]. May 27. https://theinitium.com/zh -Hans/article/20190527-opinion-june4-postcoldwar-new-theory

Xi, Jianrong. 2012. "Huanjing Fazhi de Jianshou he Chengnuo: Zhongguo Zhengfa Daxue Wuran Shouhaizhe Falü Bangzhu Zhongxin Diaocha" [Commitment on Environmental Protection and Rule of Law: A Study on the Helping Center for Victims of Pollution at China University of Political Science and Law]. In *Shouwang: Zhongguo Huanbao NGO Meiti Diaocha* [A Media Research on Environmental NGOs in China], edited by Yongchen Wang and Aijun Wang, 151–70. China Environmental Science Press.

Xia, Jianzhong. 2003. "Zhongguo Gongmin Shehui de Xiansheng: Yi Yezhu Weiyuanhui Weili" [The Pioneer of China's Civil Society: A Case Study of Homeowners' Associations]. *Wen Shi Zhe* [Literature, History, and Philosophy] 3: 115–21.

Xia, Weizhong. 1993. "Shimin Shehui: Zhongguo Jinqi Nanyuan de Meng" [Civil Society: A Dream That Cannot Be Realized in China in the Near Future]. *Zhongguo Shehui Kexue Jikan* [China Social Sciences Quarterly] 5: 176–82.

Xia, Youzhi. 2013. "Shipin Anquan cong Xianzhi Zhengfu Quanli Zuoqi" [Defending Food Safety Should Start from Constraining Government Power]. *Nanfang Zhoumo* [Southern Weekly]. June 28. http://news.sina.com.cn/pl/2013-06-28/103327522549.shtml

Xiang, Biao. 2014. "Fansi Xianggang: Dazhong Yundong zhong de Minzhu Suqiu yu Zhengdang Zhengzhi" [Reflecting Hong Kong: Demand for Democracy in a Popular Movement and Party Politics]. *Wenhua Zongheng* [Beijing Cultural Review] 6: 38–45.

Xiao, Gongqin. 1993. "Shimin Shehui yu Zhongguo Xiandaihua de Sanchong Zhang'ai" [Civil Society and the Three Obstacles in China's Modernization]. *Zhongguo Shehui Kexue Jikan* [China Social Sciences Quarterly] 5: 183–88.

Xiao, Shu. 2010a. "Guanzhu Jiushi Liliang, Weiguan Gaibian Zhongguo" [Watching Is Power. China Could Be Changed by Onlookers]. Jan 13. *Nanfang Zhoumo* [Southern Weekly]. Available from https://www.infzm.com/contents/40097

Xiao, Shu. 2010b. "Tanxun Gaige Lujing, Gongmin Shehui Xianxing" [Civil Society Should Be the Antecedent in the Exploration of the Approach for Reform]. *Zhongguo Qingnian Bao* [China Youth Daily]. September 7. Available from http://zqb.cyol.com/conte nt/2010-09/07/content_3407901.htm

Xiao, Shu. 2010c. "Shequ Zizhi Keneng Bi Zhenggai Geng Zhongyao" [The Self-organization in Community Can Be More Important Than the Political Reform]. *Nanfang Zhoumo* [Southern Weekly]. September 7.

Xu, Ben. 2011. "Chuanmei Gongzhong he Gonggong Shijian Canyu" [The Public Media and the Public Participation]. In *Shenme Shi Haode Gonggong Shenghuo* [Cultivating the Common Good: Essays on Civic Life and Citizenship]. Jilin Publishing Group.

Xu, Bin. 2012. "Grandpa Wen: Scene and Political Performance." *Sociological Theory* 30 (2): 114–29.

Xu, Bin. 2013. "For Whom the Bell Tolls: State-society Relations and the Sichuan Earthquake Mourning in China." *Theory and Society* 42: 509–42.

Xu, Bin. 2014. "Consensus Crisis and Civil Society: The Sichuan Earthquake Response and State-Society Relations." *The China Journal* 71: 91–108.

Xu, Bin. 2022. *The Culture of Democracy: A Sociological Approach to Civil Society*. Polity Press.

Xu, Huijiao, Congzhi He, and Jingzhong Ye. 2017. "'Qu Xiaononghua' yu 'Zai Xiaononghua?'—Chongsi Shipin Anquan Wenti" ["Peasants Decreasing" and "Peasants Re-increasing"?—Rethinking Food Safety Issue]. *Nongye Jingji Wenti* [Issues in Agricultural Economy] 38 (8): 66–75.

Xu, Jilin. 1998. "Cong Fanxing de Queli Zhuanxiang Fanli de Lunzheng" [From Norms to Facts]. In *Guojia yu Shehui* [State and Society], edited by Jing Zhang, 303–7. Zhejiang People's Publishing House.

Xu, Jilin. 2003. "Jindai Zhongguo de Gonggong Lingyu: Xingtai, Gongneng, yu Ziwo Lijie" [The Public Sphere in Modern China: The Structure, Function, and Self-interpretation]. *Shilin* [Collection of Historical Studies] 2: 77–89.

Xu, Jilin. 2007. "Zonglun" (Introduction). In *Qimeng de Ziwo Wajie: 1990 Niandai yilai Zhongguo Sixiang Wenhua Jie Zhongda Zhenglun Yanjiu* [The Self-disintegration of an Enlightenment: An Inquiry into the Significant Debates in China's Thought Sphere since the 1990s], edited by Jilin Xu and Gang Luo, 1–42. Jilin Publishing Group.

Xu, Jilin. 2011. "Jinru 21 Shiji yilai de Guojia Zhuyi Sichao" [The Rise of Statism in the 21st Century]. In *Dangdai Zhongguo de Qimeng yu Fan Qimeng* [Enlightenment and Anti-enlightenment of Contemporary China], edited by Jilin Xu, 236–75. Social Sciences Academic Press.

Xu, Jilin, and Gang Luo. 2007. *Qimeng de Ziwo Wajie: 1990 Niandai yilai Zhongguo Sixiang Wenhua Jie Zhongda Zhenglun Yanjiu* [The Self-disintegration of an Enlightenment: An Inquiry into the Significant Debates in China's Thought Sphere since the 1990s]. Jilin Publishing Company.

Xu, Jilin, Geremie R. Barmé, and Gloria Davies. 2004. "The Fate of an Enlightenment: Twenty Years in the Chinese Intellectual Sphere." In *Chinese Intellectuals between State and Market, edited by* Edward Gu and Merle Goldman, 183–203. Routledge.

Xu, Xiaohong. 2023. "Lun Shehuixue Ziyouzhuyi: Cong Quanqiu Nanfang/Dongfang Chufa Chonggou Shehuixue Jingdian [For a Sociological Liberalism: Reconstructing the Sociological Classics from the Perspective of Global South/East]. *Qinghua Shehuixue Pinglun* [Tsinghua Sociological Review] 2: 16–20.

Xu, Yi. 2013. "Labor Non-governmental Organizations in China: Mobilizing Rural Migrant Workers." *Journal of Industrial Relations* 55 (2): 243–59.

Xu, Youyu. 1999. "Ziyou Zhuyi yu Dangdai Zhongguo" [Liberalism and Contemporary China] *Kaifang Shidai* [Open Times] 3: 42–51.

Xu, Youyu. 2003. "Erping 90 Niandai 'Xin Zuopai': Zhongguo de Xiandaixing yu Pipan" [A Second Comment on the New Left in the 90s: China's Modernity and Its Critique]. In *Sichao: Zhongguo "Xin Zuopai" jiqi Yingxiang* [Surge of Thoughts: The New Left in China and Its Influence], edited by Gongyang, 271–77. Social Sciences Press.

Xu, Zhiyong, Biao Teng, and Jiang Yu. 2013. "Proposal for Examining the Measures for the Custody and Repatriation of Urban Vagrants and Beggars." *Chinese Law & Government* 46 (5–6): 21–23.

Yan, Hairong, Ku Hok Bun, and Siyuan Xu. 2021. "Rural Revitalization, Scholars, and the Dynamics of the Collective Future in China." *The Journal of Peasant Studies* 48 (4): 853–74.

Yan, Hairong, and Yiyuan Chen. 2013. "Debating the Rural Cooperative Movement in China, the Past and the Present." *Journal of Peasant Studies* 40 (6): 955–81.

Yang, Dennis Tao. 1999. "Urban-biased Policies and Rising Income Inequality in China." *American Economic Review* 89 (2): 306–10.

Yang, Fan. 2023. "Feminist Podcasting: A New Discursive Intervention on Gender in Mainland China." *Feminist Media Studies* 23 (7): 3308–23.

Yang, Guobin. 2009. *The Power of the Internet in China: Citizen Activism Online*. Columbia University Press.

Yang, Guobin. 2010. "Brokering Environment and Health in China: Issue Entrepreneurs of the Public Sphere." *Journal of Contemporary China* 19 (63): 101–18.

Yang, Guobin. 2012. "A Chinese Internet? History, Practice, and Globalization." *Chinese Journal of Communication* 5 (1): 49–54.

Yang, Guobin. 2013. "Contesting Food Safety in the Chinese Media: Between Hegemony and Counter-Hegemony." *The China Quarterly* 214: 337–55.

Yang, Guobin. 2022. *The Wuhan Lockdown*. Columbia University Press.

Yang, Guobin, and Craig Calhoun. 2007. "Media, Civil Society, and the Rise of a Green Public Sphere in China." *China Information* 21 (2): 211–36.

Yang, Jibin. 2010. "Pojie Fushikang Yuangong de Zisha 'Mozhou'" [Breaking the "Myth" of Foxconn Employees' Suicide]. *Nanfang Zhoumo* [Southern Weekly]. May 12. https://www.infzm.com/contents/44883

Yang, Mayfair Mei-hui. 1999. "From Gender Erasure to Gender Difference: State Feminism, Consumer Sexuality, and Women's Public Sphere in China." In *Spaces of Their Own: Women's Public Sphere in Transnational China*, edited by Mayfair Mei-hui Yang, 35–67. University of Minnesota Press.

Yang, Peidong, and Lijun Tang. 2018. "'Positive Energy': Hegemonic Intervention and Online Media Discourse in China's Xi Jinping Era." *China: An International Journal* 16 (1): 1–22.

Yang, Ping. 2003. "Sixiang de Meilu: Zhanlüe yu Guanli Ruogan Zhenglun de Huigu" [The Charm of Thoughts: A Review of the Debates at Strategy and Management]. In *Sheng-ji: Xinshiqi Zhuming Renwen Qikan Sumiao* [Vitality: A Description of Significant Humanity Journals in a New Era], edited by Dacheng Jin, 484–503. China Federation of Literary and Art Publishing House.

Yangtze River Daily. 2009. "Zhu Xueqin Huiying Dizhen 'Tianqian Lun'" [Zhu Xueqin's Review of the Commentary on "Punishment"]. March 7. https://news.ifeng.com/society/2/200903/0307_344_1049173.shtml

Ye, Biao. 2013. "Deng Zhenglai he Tade Jianghu" [Deng Zhenglai and His Rivers and Lakes]. *Nanfang Zhoumo* [Southern Weekly]. Feb 21. Available from https://www.infzm.com /contents/88244

Ye, Zicao. 2013. "Zhengzai Shoujin de Zhongguo Xinwen Shencha Zhidu" [An Increasingly Stringent Censorship Institution in China]. *Niuyue Shibao Zhongwen Wang* [New York Times China]. January 23. https://cn.nytimes.com/china/20130123/cc23media/

Yi, Fuxian. 2007. *Daguo Kongchao* [Big Country with an Empty Nest]. Strong Wind.

Yilian Legal Aid Center. 2014. "Gongshang Baoxian Xianxing Zhifu Shishi San Zhounian Diaoyan Baogao" [A Research Report on the Enforcement of 'Pay in Advance' in Industrial Injury Accidents]. *Yilian Laodongfa Yuanzhu Zhongxin* [Yilian Labor]. July 1. http://www.yilianlabor.cn/yanjiu/2014/1505.html

Yin, Siyuan. 2022. "Re-articulating Feminisms: A Theoretical Critique of Feminist Struggles and Discourse in Historical and Contemporary China." *Cultural Studies* 36 (6): 981–1004.

Yin, Siyuan, and Yu Sun. 2021. "Intersectional Digital Feminism: Assessing the Participation Politics and Impact of the MeToo Movement in China." *Feminist Media Studies* 21 (7): 1176–92.

Yip, Ngai-ming. 2019. "Housing Activism in Urban China: The Quest for Autonomy in Neighbourhood Governance." *Housing Studies* 34 (10): 1635–53.

Yip, Ngai-ming, and Yihong Jiang. 2011. "Homeowners United: The Attempt to Create Lateral Networks of Homeowners' Associations in Urban China." *Journal of Contemporary China* 20 (72): 735–50.

Young, Nick. 2001. "Introduction: Searching for Civil Society." In Development Brief, *Civil Society in the Making: 250 Chinese NGOs*, 9–19.

Yu, Jiangang. 2023. "Fanxiang Shi'er Zai, Tudi You Shenling" [Twelve Years in Rural Area: God Is On the Land]. *Shi Tong She* [Food Think]. January 19. https://mp.weixin.qq .com/s/vMjDOrOFYzpnaXKAC6xsaQ

Yu, Keping. 2006. "Zhongguo Gongmin Shehui: Gainian, Fenlei yu Zhidu Huanjing" [Chinese Civil Society: Concept, Classification and Institutional Environment]. *Zhongguo Shehui Kexue* [Social Sciences in China] 1: 109–22.

Yu, Xiao. 2005. "Yiwu Jiaoyu Burong Xingzheng Longduan" [State's Monopoly Should Not Be Allowed in Compulsory Education]. *Nanfang Zhoumo* [Southern Weekly]. December 8.

Yuan, Weishi. 2002. "Xiandaihua yu Zhongguo de Lishi Jiaokeshu Wenti" [Modernization and the Problems in China's History Textbook]. *Aisixiang*. December 9. Available from http://star.news.sohu.com/20100517/n272166982.shtml

Yuen, Samson. 2014. "Disciplining the Party: Xi Jinping's Anti-corruption Campaign and Its Limits." *China Perspectives* 3 (3): 41–47.

Yuen, Samson. 2015. "Hong Kong after the Umbrella Movement: An Uncertain Future for 'One Country Two Systems.'" *China Perspectives* 1: 49–53.

Zeng, Menglong. 2017. Zuowei Qimeng de Zouxiang Weilai Congshu he Xiandai Zhongguo de Weilai [The Toward the Future Book Series as an Enlightenment and the Future of Modern China]. *Haoqixin Ribao* [The Curiosity Daily]. July 20. Available from https://www.chinesepen.org/blog/archives/127090

Zeng, Qingjie. 2020. "Managed Campaign and Bureaucratic Institutions in China: Evidence from the Targeted Poverty Alleviation Program." *Journal of Contemporary China* 29 (123): 400–415.

Zhan, Jiang. 2012. "Cong Meiti Jielu dao Gongmin Xingdong" [From Muckraking Reports to Citizens' Actions]. *Aisixiang* [Philosophies]. June 27. https://www.aisixiang.com/data/54857.html

Zhang, Guannan. 2018. "Zhonghua Tianyuan Nüquan Ciyi Kao: Wangluo Huanjing Chuanbo zhong Nüxing Quanli de Wuminghua" [Genealogies of the Chinese Countryside Feminism: The Stigmatization of Women's Rights on the Cyberspace]. *Xinmeiti Yanjiu* [New Media Research] 4 (5): 99–101.

Zhang, Jianfeng. 2009. "Duli Renda Daibiao Shinian Chenfu" [The Rise and Fall of the Independent Deputies to the People's Congress]. *Nanfengchuang* [South Reviewers]. August 4. Available from http://news.sina.com.cn/c/sd/2009-08-04/131918362058.shtml

Zhang, Li. 2012. *In Search of Paradise: Middle-Class Living in a Chinese Metropolis*. Cornell University Press.

Zhang, Li, and Aihwa Ong, eds. 2008. *Privatizing China: Socialism from Afar*. Cornell University Press.

Zhang, Pengyi. 2013. "Social Inclusion or Exclusion? When Weibo (Microblogging) Meets the 'New Generation' of Rural Migrant Workers." *Library Trends* 62 (1): 63–80.

Zhang, Shuguang. 1995. "Geren Quanli he Guojia Quanli" [Individual Rights and State Power]. In *Shichang Luoji yu Guojia Guannian* [The Market Logic and the View of the State], edited by Junning Liu, 1–5. SDX Joint Publishing Company.

Zhang, Shuguang. 2003. "Zhongguo Jingji de Sange Badian" [The Three Targets of China's Economy]. *Nanfang Zhoumo* [Southern Weekly]. May 22.

Zhang, Shuguang. 2007. "Chengshihua Beijing xia Tudi Chanquan de Shishi he Baohu" [The Protection of Land Rights in Urbanization]. *Aisixiang* [Philosophies]. August 26. https://m.aisixiang.com/data/15742.html

Zhang, Tingkang. 2024. *Visualization and Emotionalization of Increasing Control: Uncontrolled Online Activism in the Death of Dr. Li Wenliang during Pandemic*. Bachelor Thesis Submitted to the Department of Sociology at Zhejiang University.

Zhang, Wei. 2017. "Feng Gang: Nüquan de 'Diren'" [Feng Gang: The "Enemy" of Women's Rights]. *Xinjing Bao* [The Beijing News]. November 2. http://k.sina.com.cn/article_6367828994_17b8d5c02019004jxd.html?from=auto&subch=bauto

Zhang, Yinxian, Jiajun Liu, and Ji-Rong Wen. 2018. "Nationalism on Weibo: Towards a Multifaceted Understanding of Chinese Nationalism." *The China Quarterly* 235: 758–83.

Zhang, Zhen. 2000. "Mediating Time: The 'Rice Bowl of Youth' in Fin de Siècle Urban China." *Public Culture* 12 (1): 93–113.

Zhang, Zhi'an. 2008a. "30 Nian Shendu Baodao Guiji de Huiwang yu Fansi" [A Review of the In-depth Reporting in the Past 30 Years]. *Xinwen Jizhe* [Shanghai Journalism Review] 10: 22–24.

Zhang, Zhi'an. 2008b. "Xinwen Shengchan yu Shehui Kongzhi de Zhangli Chengxian: Dui Nanfang Dushi Bao Shendu Baodao de Ge'an Fenxi" [The Tension between the Production of News and Social Control: An Analysis of the In-depth Reporting at the

Southern Metropolis Daily]. *Xinwen yu Chuanbo Pinglun* [News and Communication Review] 1: 165–73.

Zhang, Zhi'an, and Yanhui Cao. 2017. "Xinmeiti Huanjing xia Zhongguo Diaocha Jizhe Hangye Shengtai Bianhua Baogao [A Report on the Transformation of Investigative Reporters in the Age of New Media]. *Xiandai Chuanbo* [Contemporary Communications] 11: 27–33.

Zhao, Dingxin. 1998. "Ecologies of Social Movements: Student Mobilization during the 1989 Prodemocracy Movement in Beijing." *American Journal of Sociology* 103 (6): 1493–529.

Zhao, Dingxin. 2001. *The Power of Tiananmen: State-Society Relations and the 1989 Beijing Student Movement.* University of Chicago Press.

Zhao, Dingxin. 2003. "Nationalism and Authoritarianism: Student-Government Conflicts during the 1999 Beijing Student Protests." *Asian Perspective* 27 (1): 5–34.

Zhao, Mu. 2015. "Zhu Xueqin: Hechu 'Tianqian' zhi Yu?" [Why Did Zhu Xueqin Talk about the "Punishment?"] In *Jiyi de Liliang* [The Power of Memory]. Jinan University Press.

Zhao, Suisheng. 1993. Deng Xiaoping's Southern Tour: Elite Politics in Post-Tiananmen China. *Asian Survey.* 33 (8): 739–56.

Zhao, Yongxin. 2021. *Yuanmingyuan Fangshen zhi Zheng* [The Debate on the Anti Seepage Project at Yuanmingyuan]. Dongfang Publishing House.

Zhao, Yuezhi. 1998. *Media, Market, and Democracy in China: Between the Party Line and the Bottom Line.* University of Illinois Press.

Zhao, Yuezhi. 2000. "From Commercialization to Conglomeration: The Transformation of the Chinese Press within the Orbit of the Party State." *Journal of Communication* 50 (2): 3–26.

Zhao, Yuezhi. 2004. "Underdogs, Lapdogs and Watchdogs: Journalists and the Public Sphere Problematic in China." In *Chinese Intellectuals between State and Market*, edited by Edward Gu and Merle Goldman, 43–89. Routledge.

Zhao, Yuezhi. 2008. *Communication in China: Political Economy, Power, and Conflict.* Rowman & Littlefield Publishers.

Zheng, Guanghuai, and Jiangang Zhu. 2011. *Gonggong Shenghuo Pinglun Di'er Ji Xingongren Jieji: Guanxi, Zuzhi yu Jiti Xingdong* [Public Life Review No. 2 New Working Class: Relationship, Organization and Collective Actions]. Chinese Social Science Press.

Zheng, Yefu. 1994. "Nannü Pingdeng de Shehuixue Sikao" [Some Thoughts on Gender Equality]. *Shehuixue Yanjiu* [Sociological Studies] 2: 108–13.

Zhicheng Legal Aid Center for Rural Migrant Workers. 2021. Waimai Pingtai Yonggong Moshi Falü Yanjiu Baogao [A Legal Research Report on the Employment Mode on Food Delivery Platforms]. https://zgnmg.org/wp-content/uploads/2021/09/zhicheng -report-on-food-delivery-workers.pdf

Zhong, Peizhang. 2003. "Dongfang Sannian" [The Three Years at the Orient]. In *Shengji: Xinshiqi Zhuming Renwen Qikan Sumiao* [Vitality: A Description of Significant Humanity Journals in a New Era], edited by Dacheng Jin, 210–31. China Federation of Literary and Art Publishing House.

Zhou, Baohua, and Shuning Lü. 2011. "Shanghaishi Xinshengdai Nongmingong Xinmeiti

Shiyong yu Pingjia de Shizheng Yanjiu" [An Empirical Study of Rural Migrant Worker Youths' Use of New Media in Shanghai]. *Xinwen Daxue* [Journalism Quarterly] 108 (2): 145–50.

Zhou, Min, and Shih-Diing Liu. 2022. "Be My Boss: Migrant Youth and the Contradiction of Hope Labour on *Kuaishou*." *New Media & Society* 26 (10): 5858–76. https://doi.org 14614448221141828

Zhou, Mujun. 2014. "Debating the State in Private Housing Neighborhoods: The Governance of Homeowners' Associations in Urban Shanghai." *International Journal of Urban and Regional Research* 38 (5): 1849–66.

Zhou, Mujun. 2017. "The Void in Public Discourse and the Limitations of the Equal Education Campaign in Beijing." *China Information* 31 (2): 176–94.

Zhou, Mujun. 2022. "Contesting Counterpublics: The Transformation of the Articulation of Rural Migrant Workers' Rights in China's Public Sphere, 1992–2014." *Politics & Society* 50 (3): 351–83.

Zhou, Mujun. 2024. "The Interstitial Emergence of Labor NGO Activism in China and Its Contradicting Institutionalization, 1996–2020." *Social Science History* 48 (1): 121–44.

Zhou, Mujun, and Guowei Yan. 2020. "Advocating Workers' Collective Rights: The Prospects and Constraints Facing 'Collective Bargaining' NGOs in the Pearl River Delta, 2011–2015." *Development and Change* 51 (4): 1044–66.

Zhou, Mujun, and Yi Xu. 2020. "Kechixu Nongye Chixu le Shenme? Zhongguo Linglei Shiwu Wangluo de Shijian Tujing he Kunjing" [What Does Sustainable Agriculture Sustain? The Prospects and Constraints Facing Alternative Food Networks in China]. *Shehui Fazhan Yanjiu* [Journal of Social Development] 24: 67–94.

Zhou, Yan. 2014. "Pochu Shipin Anquan zhong Zhengfu Jianguan de Mixin" [Breaking the Myth of Government Supervision in Food Safety Issues]. *Nanfang Dushi Bao* [Southern Metropolis Daily]. November 23. https://sog.sysu.edu.cn/article/872

Zhou, Yuzhong, Jianfeng Jing, and Weili Sun. 2007. *Yezhu Meng, Yezhu Hun: Goufang Weiquan yu Yezhu Zizhi* [The Dream of Homeowners: Homeowners' Weiquan Activism and Self-organization]. Guangdong Economics Press.

Zhou, Zhiyi, Yiqiu Huang, and Bo Peng. 2009. "Lixiang Zhaoyao Zhongguo: Nanfang Zhoumo Ershiwu Nian Chengzhangshi" [The Development of the Southern Weekly in the Past Twenty-five Years]. *Chuanmei* (Media) 8: 40–47.

Zhu, Jiangang. 2004. "Caogen NGO yu Zhongguo Gongmin Shehui de Chengzhang" [Grassroots NGOs and the Growth of Civil Society in China]. *Kaifang Shidai* [Open Times] 6: 36–48.

Zhu, Jiangang. 2008. *Xingdong de Liliang: Minjian Zhiyuan Zuzhi Shijian Luoji Yanjiu* [The Power of Action: A Study on the Practical Logic of Voluntary Associations]. The Commercial Press.

Zhu, Jiangang. 2018. "Jianshe Bentu Gongmin Shehui: Yi ICS Wei Ge'an" [Building a Localized Civil Society: A Case Study of ICS]. Available from http://www.riccimac.org/doc /ccc/6.4/ch/2A.pdf

Zhu, Xueqin. 2003. "'Xin Zuopai' yu Ziyou Zhuyi zhi Zheng" [The Debate between the New Left and the Liberals]. In *Sichao: Zhongguo "Xin Zuopai" jiqi Yingxiang* [Surge of Thoughts: The New Left in China and Its Influence], edited by Gongyang, 261–63. Social Sciences Press.

Zhu, Yuchao. 2006. "Proclamation, Implementation, and Abolishment of China's Custody & Repatriation Law—An Institutionalist Analysis." *American Journal of Chinese Studies* 13 (2): 187–208.

Zhu, Zhenglin. 2003. "Dongfang: Wo Xianzai Keyi Shuo de Yixie Shiqing" [Orient: Something I Can Tell]. In *Shengji: Xinshiqi Zhuming Renwen Qikan Sumiao* [Vitality: A Description of Significant Humanity Journals in a New Era], edited by Dacheng Jin, 232–41. China Federation of Literary and Art Publishing House.

Zou, Sheng. 2019. "When Nationalism Meets Hip-hop: Aestheticized Politics of Ideotainment in China." *Communication and Critical/Cultural Studies* 16 (3): 178–95.

INDEX

abortion, sex-selective, 153, 158

abstraction in public sphere, 8–9, 35, 197–98

academia: academic journals, 32, 37–39, 43, 58; centers for feminist studies, 154; gender discrimination, 175; and new liberal camp, 74–75; professionalization of, 38, 57–58; and rise of NGO sphere, 65–66; sexual harassment in, 184–85

Academy of Social Science, 147

ACFTU (All-China Federation of Trade Unions), 125, 126, 209n48

action art activities, 155, 181–82, 185

action networks, 86

ACWF (All-China Women's Federation), 10, 67, 125, 153, 154

agriculture: agricultural taxes, 56, 140; community-supported (CSAs), 141, 144, 145, 177; and food safety and scandals, 143, 144, 177; and New Rural Reconstruction Movement, 94, 140–45

AIDS activism, 4, 84, 156

Aizhi Action Project, 50

All-China Federation of Trade Unions (ACFTU), 125, 126, 209n48

All-China Women's Federation (ACWF), 10, 67, 125, 153, 154

Anti Domestic Violence Network, 181–82

Anti-CNN, 112

Anti-Domestic Violence Law, 67

anti-PX protests, 64, 128–29, 174

Anti-rightist Campaign, 72

Apple, 149

Applicant Committee for Homeowners' Society, 95–96

Arab Spring, 25, 109, 114, 140

Arato, Andrew, 46

BBSes (Bulletin Board Systems), 63, 119, 169–70

Beijing: and homeowners' protests, 94, 95–96; as liberal center, 75–76; and NGOs, 124, 147; and Olympics, 109, 110, 111, 213n10

Beijing News, 63

Bill & Melinda Gates Foundation, 65, 124

blogs: decline of, 120–21; and feminist activism, 182–83, 185; institutionalization of, 131–32; rise of, 64, 70, 119. See also Weibo

bourgeois public sphere, 10, 46

Boxer Rebellion, 62–63

"boxing" *(daquan)*, 184

Bulldog (blog), 64

Bulletin Board Systems (BBSes), 63, 119, 169–70

Burawoy, Michael, 147

Caijing Magazine, 63

CCTV (Central China Television), 60, 61–62, 156, 171, 185

censorship: and discrepancies in state sectors, 63; in fragmentation stage (2014-2019), 25, 181–82; institutionalization of, 168–69; in internal contestation stage (2008-2013), 24, 115–17, 118; internet